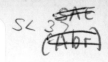

MORALITY & THE LAW

By the same author

MORALITY
&
THE LAW

GERALD ABRAHAMS, M.A. (Oxon.)
(*Barrister-at-Law*)

LONDON
CALDER & BOYARS

First published in Great Britain 1971
by Calder and Boyars Ltd
18 Brewer Street London W1

© *Gerald Abrahams 1971*

ISBN 0 7145 0662 1 Cloth edition
ISBN 0 7145 0663 X Paper edition

R. Waterfield 25025 £5.40. 6. 84

Printed in Great Britain by
Western Printing Services Ltd, Bristol

CONTENTS

CONTENTS

I

Introduction

'Permissive society'. The phrase is much in present day use as an umbrella covering the social-political organisations which are Britain, some nations of western Europe, the United States of America, and cognate transmarine powers. That this social ordering is desirable is clear to anyone who knows about 'prohibitive society', a system which is not in demand over here, not even on the part of those who are in revolt, however revolting.

What the social rebel seeks is, for himself at least, not fewer permissions but more permissions: perhaps not realising that excess of permission, excessively accepted, can render him, to use a legal phrase, 'a danger to himself and to others'. This policy, of course, is selfishness. Against the demands of the selfish speaks the critic (this does *not* mean the opponent) of the permissive society, who says as follows: that the demand for self-expression and self-fulfilment is in a good tradition, and congenial to the spirit of those urbane institutions which tend (as ours do) to promote an equal degree of freedom for each and every citizen. Then, having so pronounced, the critic appeals to the claimant, clean shaven or pogoniferous, that he should think philosophically as to the nature of the self which he seeks to indulge. This self is not an atom bombinating in the void (or a voice crying in Hyde Park). The self is constituted, to a great extent, by the society in which it flourishes, and can best flourish in social, not anti-social, conditions. 'No man is an island'. Secondly, it may be pointed out, the notion of permission carries with it the notion of control. Authority for the one is authority for the other. Between the extremes of permissive and prohibitive societies the critic, therefore, intra-polates the notion of a 'controlled society'; and that term, admittedly a variable, is surely a useful description of what western people mean, nowadays, by civilisation.

Control, be it understood, does not signify oppression. Necessarily some elements in control must be external to the self; but some must be internal. The acceptance of the external social demand is, if it is valuable, an internal commitment; and those that are thought to be internal resolutions are, for the most part, socially derived, socially inspired.

In an oppressive society the distribution is different. Nevertheless, it was said that 'the controlled society' is a variable function. Not all civilised societies achieve the same result in the shape of citizenship.

Thus the legal arguments read in the Supreme Court of the United States (a court with different functions from any British court) have, until recently, been concerned with the preservation of the constitutional privacy of the individual from interferences, however socially justified. This in the spirit of an individualism which dominated the English courts of the eighteenth century. The statutes of Britain, which no court can control, have moved our laws on to a different (that is not to say a better) plane. And other lands, other laws. In various political systems the legal and the moral controls are differently stated, differently related. In reading this book the reader is concerned mainly with the British system. In our conventions the external controls are described as legal; the internal as moral and/or religious. This, be it quickly said, is an oversimplification; but it is useful because it helps in the analysis of some present discontent.

The demand is currently expressed that, over a larger field of conduct than at present, the state should discontinue the external control, leaving behaviour in that field to the control of the moral consciousness. It is believed that this is a socially unscientific claim; and, withal, a disingenuous one. The plea is for abandonment of control to those who will, in turn, abandon control. Whatever benefits ensue, the beneficiary will not be morality, and will not be religion. The beneficiaries of such an abdication would be the sheer materialists, including the hedonist who says to his betters: 'Think not, because you are Puritan, that we shall have no more cakes and ale'.

Any request to British authority to cease to think of itself as moral is an impudent one; especially when made by those who, when in trouble, rely on state morality. Certainly, the history of Britain does not call for national sanctification. But we know that in this century Britain has sacrificed an empire in two wars for what the people conceived (and rightly) to be moral causes. Some historians, whose ethical amaurosis renders them ill-equipped to do justice to their topics, are denying this, and describing other causalities. But it is within memory of living persons who use such words, that Britain fought twice against brute force and bad faith, and that only the ever-present awareness of that truth enabled our population to refrain from compromise, and to turn many defeats into ultimate victory.

Since the last armistice some twenty-five years have passed, and present day observers of Britain have become sceptical as to the national ethos. Standards of life are said to have fallen, even while averages have risen. Phrases like social irresponsibility are hurled about. It is said that life is made easy for criminals. The suggestion is made that industry is geared to the lay-about and the social services to the malingerer. It is not for the writer of a law book, or even a book on ethics (for this is both), to enter into transient appraisements. What can usefully be done is to exhibit our institutions such as they are; to show the structure of authority; to demonstrate (where it takes place) the interplay of legal and moral acts and judgments; and some results immanent in our lives.

The task entails some inquiry into the nature of law as such, of morals as such. But the emphasis will be more on the contents than on the formal characteristics of these two orders; because, as here described, these are not closed systems.

Finally, let it be said that since, in the author's view, the realm of sexual conduct is only one part of the scope of moral conduct, there will be found insufficient material in this book to make it a desirable addition to any library of erotica. This is said to prevent any putative buyer from suffering a disappointment comparable to that of the small boy lepidopterist who bought a book of 'Advice to Young Mothers'.

STANDARDS OF THE FORUM

'This court is not a court of morals'. That proposition has been stated from many benches. But let the reader be warned that compendious pronouncements of this type invariably mean less than they seem to say. Some judge or magistrate has uttered a principle that has governed his deliberations in a specific case. He has described an ethical tolerance that was, no doubt, appropriate in that case and similar cases. But he has not exhausted the relevant jurisprudence. When the statement that 'this court is not a court of morals' is properly understood, it will be found not inconsistent with the equally tenable, equally arguable, proposition that the English courts are moral courts. (That has been the standard since Year Book days, ancient corruptions notwithstanding.)

To say that a court is ethically tolerant does not mean that the court is ethically neutral. Tolerance is a humane concession by those whose standards are high to those whose practices are low. Relying on legal tolerance the prisoner accused of burglary can face his trial with equanimity, knowing that the judge will not reject his alibi merely because it shows him to have been 'living in sin'.[1]

On occasion the apparent moral amnesia of the court is not tolerance, but is a policy forced on the court by the limitations of the law; as when the pious wishes of a testator are ignored by the beneficiaries, who refuse 'to be kind to Nelly', because the testator's language does not express the certainty and definition that are required to constitute a trust. The informality of Nelly's status is (in these days at least) irrelevant. Indeed if she can submit a claim based on her material contributions to the welfare of the deceased, she will not be out of court.[2]

In that narrow sphere of morality which is governed by the

[1] An inept phrase. It may be the case that the man's only sin is a tendency to burgle.

[2] Interesting is Diwell v Farnes [1959] All Eng. R. 379 a case under the Married Women's Property Act in which the mistress of an intestate failed to retain the house she had shared with the deceased for twenty years, but not (as the court made clear) on 'moral' grounds. On the other hand the mistress's moral claim was only defeated by the widow's statutory right. More serious from an ethical standpoint is the

conventional sexual code, the court shows tolerance when it allows the prosecutor in blackmail to conceal his identity. Even so, he enjoys no monopoly of the tolerance. Thus when a discarded mistress demanded, with threats, money for her maintenance, it was argued on her behalf that she was pressing 'a claim of right made in good faith'. A stern lower court said: 'no, this is a claim of wrong, not of right'; but the Court of Criminal Appeal held the defence of a sincere, albeit erroneous, claim to be a good one in the circumstances.[3] Nevertheless, a claim directed by a female plaintiff against a male defendant, and arising from a contract of carnality, would be rejected by the court on the principle *ex turpi causa non oritur actio*.[4] That principle prevents tolerance from changing into acquiescence.

But morals in the sexual context are only one segment of the domain of ethics. A wider field is covered when one investigates the belief that the English courts are characterised by an immanent morality. One aspect of this is the impartiality of tribunals. The court of today is required to be moral, in a sense that includes justice as a moral practice. When two able men are arguing as unfairly as possible against each other, the court sits back and judges impartially. 'Impartially' is the most important adverb in 'adverb law'. Also the substantive law is a 'corpus' containing evidence of conscience. Frequently the court can find itself faced with legal issues that involve moral issues, and the court can, in a proper case, base a determination of legal rights on such concepts as 'the duty of the conscientious man'. That phrase sounds in many instances.

fact that an 'unmarried wife' has no such status in a claim for damages on the death of a breadwinner as a legal widow has.

[3] R. v Bernhard [1938] All Eng. R. 140. Not immaterial may be the circumstance that the accused was a foreigner. The legal position in France is of interest. France inherits the Roman theory that (as Cicero puts it) 'we have wives for progeny, concubines for comfort, harlots for pleasure'.

In recent case law (the claim of Mme Gaudras) at least one court has held that a concubinage 'which does not present an adulterous character', is a legal relationship, and that the mistress is, accordingly, entitled to damages if her protecter is tortiously killed. The question is currently being argued.

[4] From a 'base' cause arises no action.

Admittedly the legal problems that beset the courts are frequently matters of ethical irrelevance, for all their importance. Thus one of the most important recent problems in the law of tort was whether or not, when a sum is awarded as compensation for loss of future earnings, a notional income tax should be deducted from it. The arguments in this context are speculations as to economic probabilities: What if income tax (*per improbabilitatem*) be reduced in the future? What if the man invests his money and procures an income which is taxable? Considering these, and arguments against (what has he actually lost?) the Law Lords deducted tax.[5] In case that decision be suspect as a show of favour to a state-owned corporation, there are examples to show that the courts will not give an unfair advantage to the financial interests of the state. Thus, when the Burmah Oil litigation came to the Law Lords a quite ethical issue, as to the continued obligation of a nation to fulfil promises made in days preceding defeat, was implicit in the argument.[6] The Law Lords found for the plaintiffs; and retrospective legislation, which many (including John Locke) have declared to be in its nature immoral, was introduced to undo the effect of the opinions.

This introduces the legislature. Whatever ethical scope the courts have, the legislature has infinitely more, because Parliament can create new laws out of nothing. We shall see that, in fact, there has been a high coefficient of the morally positive in many

[5] B.T.C. v Gourley [1955] 3 All Eng. R. 796. The interesting obverse of this is Taylor v O'Connor [1970] 1 All Eng. R. 365, in which the court allowed an award to include the probable tax that the plaintiff widow would have to pay on an annuity. In some other arguments on measure of damages ethics can be relevant. For example, is the court entitled to assume that a young widow will remarry? Here we encounter one of the 'inequalities' that are regarded by many as unfair. This should be considered alongside the principle that damages are assessed without reference to insurances and similar compensations, whether of plaintiff or defendant (Gower v Hales [1928] 1 K.B. 191). On a similar principle, in Torquay Hotel Co. Ltd. v Cousins and others [1969] All Eng. R. 522 the court refused to allow the defendant trade unionist to interfere with contracts even though the contracts contained strike clauses. These cases suggest a doctrine that the courts will not penalise prudence. The relevance of the widow's charms is unsettled.

[6] Burmah Oil Companies v Lord Advocate [1964] 2 All Eng. R. 348.

of the laws of this century and earlier. Parliament can make laws which meet with ethical approval, and probably more modern enactments satisfy ethical demands (when relevant) than dissatisfy them.

With regard to many of the laws that are made by Parliament, or found by judges, there will necessarily be divergence of opinion as to whether the enactment or the finding is ethically acceptable in the circumstances. In days of distributive justice, not every-one agrees with the adopted principles of distribution. But as to the ethical relevance of many laws there is likely to be agreement between protagonist and antagonist. 'Bad'; 'good'; but un-doubtedly in the ethical field.

In these days the state is much concerned with welfare; has, indeed, removed the burden of charity from private persons to itself. Moreover, in much collectivist legislation some purpose is discernible, which, short of the eleemosynary, is yet socially benevolent. That social purposes protective of the public are good purposes is now generally accepted doctrine. It is observable, even in the United States, whose constitution and amendments are suffused by the ethics of individualism, that, since the days of the second Roosevelt, socially beneficial action is being accepted by the courts in derogation of individual rights; and moral overtones sound in the pronouncements.[7]

Whether any particular law of today be regarded as bad or good, there is undoubtedly a great moral 'content' in modern English law. That fact (which is being studied here) renders a trifle abstract much of the investigation that concerns itself with the differences between legal obligation as such and moral obli-

[7] In point is Breithaupt v Abram (1957) 352 U.S. 445 wherein the Supreme Court held that evidence based on blood taken, by the police, from an unconscious man (*scilicet,* unwilling) was acceptable, for the purposes of the 14th Amendment, because of the paramount social importance of road safety. It is to be observed that in England and the U.S.A. alike, the common law will not compel a person to submit to 'operations' on the body. But our Road Safety Act 1967 does seem to make a blood (or urine) test compulsory. In D.P.P. v Carey [1969] 3 All Eng. R. 1662, the Law Lords refuted 'technical' defences that had prevailed in this context. In the divorce and bastardy jurisdictions there is a discretion in the court as to the taking of blood samples from infants (see B. v B. and E. [1969] 3 All Eng. R. 1106).

gation as such. The latter questions are, of course, important, and not untopical; and in this century much good jurisprudence and philosophy has been devoted to them since (in 1905) a great Dean of Harvard (Professor Roscoe Pound) wrote his classic *Law and Morals*.

That work embodies the older learning; and later learning has been admirably collated in the writings of Professor Hart in Britain and by Professor Fuller in the United States. Notwithstanding the almost plethora of good literature on some aspects of the topic, recent controversies seem to call for a survey and analysis of the particular moral problems that present themselves to the law, and for some discussion on the degree to which English law expresses and has expressed morality. These disputations, and the further fact that the whole content of morality is, in our day, under attack, not only by 'sinners' but by heretics who pronounce a *quo warranto* against all valuations, encourage the author to believe that a survey should be of interest and, perhaps, value to many readers, lawyers and laymen alike.

For the rest, no apology should be required today from anyone who thinks about morality.

This is an age in which chaos threatens to come again. Perhaps the misdeeds, the crimes and the wars, are too overwhelming in themselves for theory to be more than mere spectating. On the other hand, some of the violences may be symptoms of misguided thinking and unguided feeling. Trends of thought as different as anarchism and totalitarianism have this in common – that they belittle any principle of obedience which is not reflex or otherwise mechanical. The hand of power has once again become more dominant than the voice of authority. Even in democracies there occur, to change the metaphor, short-circuits in the ordered currents of political life. The first casualty in the breakdown of ordered authority is the sense of responsibility. Of this fact there is great temporary awareness. Unhappily this awareness is accompanied, not by indignation, but by scepticism. From this scepticism the legislators of England are not immune. Yet we in England enjoy a legal system which is a bastion against many contemporary doubts. For that reason, if for no other, the elements of morality in the English law deserve study and recognition.

2

The Relationship Between Morality and the Law

A VERBAL SURVEY

The legal world is a world of words. Nevertheless the lawyer does not follow the method recommended by semantics, working out exact definitions before expounding his topic. Rather he follows the example of the Oxford logician who 'plunged *in medias res* and so reached the heart of the subject'. Definitions, in any event, seem to be less important when applied to the framework of a topic than they are inside the topic. It is more important to define a 'colloid', for example, than to define chemistry. The 'definitions clause' should, therefore, be temporarily postponed (as it usually is in statutes); if not totally, as when the draftsmen of the Theft Act 1968 forbore to define dishonesty. It may be added that if writers on law and morals required pedantic satisfaction in advance as to the nature of their subjects, then of the writing of many books there would be no beginning.

Accordingly an author's policy should be to immerse the reader and himself into the instances and quillets of the law, in the hope that both will emerge with a better understanding of two important words, and of our legal system.

Let us start by using ordinary words heuristically, trying them out on 'the man in the Clapham omnibus', who is a fairly sophisticated fellow these days. Thus, if a duty is said to be moral only, the man in the omnibus will understand that its performance is uncompelled by any external authority (whatever that expression means); whereas if a duty is said to be legal, then he will under-

15

stand that, directly or indirectly, its performance can be compelled by some external authority.

For survey purposes it is less important to define the notion of compulsion than to consider what is compelled or not compelled. By way of illustration let it be taken, as a piece of general knowledge, that to tell lies is morally wrong in a majority of instances. Yet lies are told with impunity. There are only special instances in which the law operates to prevent or penalise a lie. The leading instance of such legal operation is the criminality of perjury. By section (1) of the consolidating statute (the Perjury Act of 1911) it is enacted that: 'If any person lawfully sworn as a witness or as an interpreter in a judicial proceeding wilfully makes a statement, material in that proceeding, which he knows to be false or does not know to be true, he shall be guilty of perjury': and so qualify for imprisonment. Allowing for plenty of argument, on what constitutes a 'person lawfully sworn' (must he be 'competent'?), on what constitutes a tribunal, and on what is 'material', the proposition emerges that, whereas, in general, one *ought not to* tell a lie, 'on oath' one *must not* tell a lie.[1]

These words 'ought not', 'must not' are not (in the legal phrase) 'terms of art', but are used here on the Humpty Dumpty principle. There are writers who use the words MUST and MUST NOT in the ethical context. Also we find the word OUGHT used in the law, as when it is pleaded that 'he knew or ought to have known' [e.g. that his brakes were defective]. In the latter case it may be said that a 'principle' of law (or evidence) is being used, analogous to, though less elevated than, moral principle.[2] And here we encounter jurists who would describe laws as 'rules', moral pronouncements as 'principles'. This distinction, in turn, would be unacceptable at once to the sterner moralist whose

---

[1] 'On oath' is not limited to 'in the witness-box'. The petitioner or respondent who swears a petition or answer in divorce; the solicitor or client who makes an affidavit that he believes the defendant to have no defence; these are exposing themselves to guilt of perjury if they are less than careful in their allegations. Similar observations apply to those who are now permitted to tender written statements, instead of depositions, in criminal causes. (Unsworn lies may be frauds.)

[2] The moral factor is that our law, like the Roman, religiously influenced, law, usually relates liability to fault, however venial.

imperative is a categorical 'rule', and to the lawyer who finds
himself investigating principles which have more elasticity than
rules; in, for example, some such conflict as that between the
principle of the sanctity of contract and some principle of public
policy that would justify a repudiation.[3]

These difficulties of verbal classification, which we must accept
as part of the data, do suggest the explanation that in the English
life and language of modern times, moral and legal notions have
run in double harness, and continue to do so. The intimacy,
which is concealed from those who seek classifications by external
container-words, and who would formalise the orders of obedience, becomes clear when one looks at the content of the two
aggregates of rules and/or principles which common usage
roughly but usefully recognises as laws and morals.

This intimacy is clear whenever legislation corrects (or worsens)
a moral average in the citizenry. In point are some recent
changes.

It was argued in the nineteenth century, in Carlill's case,[4] that
an undertaking to pay a reward to the demonstrator of a defect
in the product advertised was not binding because it amounted
only to an advertiser's 'puff'. The plaintiff succeeded, because the
court held the promise to be specific; but the learning of the
period was consistent with the belief that the exaggerations of
salesmen were of no legal significance, not being classifiable as
warranties, deceits, or misrepresentations. So the exaggerations of
advertisements have rivalled those of epitaphs (which are
posthumous advertisements). That practice and theory has per-

[3] See e.g. the arguments in Beresford v Royal Assurance Co. [1938]
2 All Eng. R. 602, in which it was held that suicide by the self-insured
person defeats a policy of life assurance notwithstanding the claims of
dependants and creditors. The wide (ethical) principle, that a person
must not benefit from his own wrong, is well illustrated by recent case,
Burns v Edman [1970] 1 All Eng. R. 886, in which the widow of a
criminal killed in an accident was not granted compensation against the
defendants because the court held that her maintenance had, in the
past, been the wages of crime. The estate of the deceased was granted
a small sum for 'loss of expectation of an unhappy life'. Interesting
also are in the estate of Crippen 1911 P. 108 and Cleaver v Mutual
Assurance [1892] 1 Q.B. 147. (The last arose from the famous Maybrick
case.)   [4] Carlill v Carbolic Smoke Ball Co. [1893] 1 Q.B. 256.

vaded the atmosphere of commerce. Accordingly, the honesty of
a salesman (when it was not evidently the best policy) was determined by a concept of the respectability of 'the accepted thing'.

By way of correction, a law enacted in 1968 (Trade Descriptions
Act 1968) prohibits many of these advertisers' exaggerations, and
makes their utterance punishable by the state.[5] There are
civil as well as criminal consequences. So an OUGHT NOT is reinforced by a MUST NOT.[6]

Let it be noticed that the word 'reinforced' is used in preference
to the word 'replaced'. If law were one set of rules, changed only
by legislation, and morals were another, completely disparate, set
of rules, then the change might be thought of as a replacement.
But the reformer who advocates legislative changes in order to
bring about the establishment of a higher standard (or average)
of conduct is not contemplating that the moral obligation shall
cease, or lose importance. Rather he hopes for the creation of a
sort of 'feed-back' mechanism which will serve to heighten public
awareness of moral standards; and he is also expressing a moral
demand that the law ought to embody moral values. That, indeed,
is the tradition of English law, which is not an abstract isolated
system, rigid until mechanically changed, but is a self-conscious,
maturing, changing system, in which Parliamentary legislation is
not the only important principle of growth.

The result of the inquiry so far seems to be that though law
and morals are difficult to define, yet they are not difficult to
recognise. There are imperatives, there are permissions, which the
man in the omnibus knows to be laws. They control his action,
not describe it. In a perfect world, conceivably, the utterances of

[5] The language of the statute seems to confine most of the responsibilities to traders ('persons who in the course of a trade or business' . . .)
A private person can be guilty of an offence if he makes a false statement about previous prices, but not, it seems, if he falsely praises.

It is also of interest that statutory corporations and other authorities
can be prosecuted for offences under this and other statutes (N.W. Gas
Board v Apsden). The government has no privileges.

[6] Also relevant is the Misrepresentation Act 1967, which (in effect)
makes possible a claim for damages for a misrepresentation which is
not fraudulent but is negligent. This, too, constitutes a raising of standards of conduct. The common law of fraud is discussed later.

authority would be in the indicative rather than the imperative, as if they were the descriptions that scientists call laws. But society is not perfect, and the imperative is not the indicative. Also the man in the omnibus knows of moral imperatives, and these, if not more imperative, are even less indicative.[7]

The importance of these distinctions is made clear in every situation of conflict; when moral judgments are pronounced against existing laws or against impending laws, or when disputes are in process in the courts, whether criminal or civil, and it appears that moral and legal values differ.

To mention a few instances: is it ethically right that a person be bound by a contract made on the basis of an error which the other party did not share? Is it ethically right that a person be defeated by a technicality? Is it ethically right that legal rigidity should impose penalties which kindlier persons regard as too severe?

Always a distinction should be drawn between morality and sentimentality. Yet what is called, or mis-called, sentimentality sometimes expresses feelings that eventually penetrate and suffuse later moral judgments. We see its effect in rising damage awards; also in falling sentences. Thus it is unthinkable now that a person should be imprisoned, as was Lord Russell, seventy years ago, for marrying after obtaining an American divorce. Sentimentality can become sentiment.[8] Sentiment easily becomes accepted value – ethical value – and so an influence on the law. The contemporaries of Dickens would laugh if they could witness our care of children and servants, our protection of animals. Certainly no Dickensian would believe that a man was punished (this, in a recent unreported case) for bringing tears to the eyes of a crocodile. Values change, and the law does not claim to be 'the

[7] Some social scientists speak of morals as a descriptive science, not a normative system. For someone who is not obliged to obey our set of laws, our law can be treated as a descriptive science. From the standpoint of the obeyer, both law and ethics are normative systems; and only so are they practically significant.

[8] Relevant are recent cases (in which sentimentality failed, or sentiment was inadequate) concerned with squatters and gypsy caravans (e.g. Manchester Corporation v Connolly [1970], 1 All Eng. R. 961, in which the gypsies failed, but were left undisturbed over Christmas.

embodiment of everything that's excellent'. In no case does the
law claim to be the sole repository of morals. Nor, however, should
it ever be regarded as a moral vacuum. Indeed the first impression
could well be one of prevailing harmony, not of difference between the orders.

In legislation it is clear (and few would dispute) that moral
considerations, sometimes the quintessence of public opinion,
determine some content of the law. But the fact that the law and
morality run, as was said above, in double harness, is evidenced
not only in legislation. It is evidenced in litigation: that is to say
in the daily practice of the law as it stands, for the time being
unaltered. A law already cited is of illustrative value. We have
seen that there are penal sanctions for perjury. Now the taking of
the oath (or the making of a solemn affirmation) is an event
which is to be observed in every legal proceeding, criminal or
civil, whenever a witness is called to give evidence. Do these witnesses tell the truth in fear of the possible consequences of lying?
There are those who think that the oath, or affirmation, is an
outmoded relic of religions which, though still believed, are little
practised. The average witness tells the truth, it is argued, because
he knows that the lie he has in mind can be exposed in cross-
examination, with resulting embarrassment or ridicule. They
draw the conclusion that a person will *always* tell the truth only
if he is honest, and for no other reason.

This is a good example of a conclusion which is true, but not
because it follows from the premises. In practice, judges and
juries are, in different ways or aspects, good assessors of credi-
bility; and their assessment is usually, not of the witness's fears,
but of his integrity.

From some witnesses, prisoners on serious charges, or persons
involved in proceedings arising from sexual or marital conduct,
unstated allowances are made for the psychological necessity of
concealing the socially unspeakable. From the witness in less
desperate cases truth is, in large measure, forthcoming, for the
simple reason that very many witnesses are honest. Some would
criticise this assessment of witnesses' honesty. But even if honesty
were only evident in limited, few, and particular cases, those cases
would show a person, in one and the same act, being moral and

being law-abiding. The OUGHT coincides here with the MUST, and makes it possible for English law to be what, in a degree, it is – a moral process.

When the moral element in the law is clear, it will be found to correspond to a moral element in the accepted thought of the people. To take another example of the legal and moral estimations of truth, this time from the substantive law, we have the concept of defamation. The right-minded person may or may not speak or write badly of another, but if he does so, it will be with a belief in the truth of what he utters. Defamation takes place (if a definition may be offered which is not orthodox, but which covers the cases) when one person makes about another a statement which, in the circumstances, a reasonable man would, in his own case, reasonably resent – and which is not true. With that reasonable resentment the law agrees and awards damages in compensation for the untruth. In turn, truth is regarded as a justification, and is so called.

Between the public and the law in this field there is no complete coincidence of thinking. Nor between lawyers. Thus the courts of Australia have held the words R.D. (Refer to Drawer) on a cheque to warrant a legally expressible resentment. The English courts have not done so. In relation to defamation, the public goes further than the law, and most people believe that even true statements can, in certain circumstances, be wrongful. That is the view of the legislatures of some American States, but not of the English civil courts.

From such differences it is clear that valuations differ: also that the law does not fully express all that morality maintains. But, by and large, in this type of litigation there is an awareness of right and wrong (including the moral duty which gives privilege). Such awareness, actualised in law, makes the law moral.

To say that English law is a moral process is not to say that all our laws are moral pronouncements, or morally praiseworthy, nor that all moral laws are incorporated in our legal system. Yet the proposition is an important one; and the importance of the assertion that our law is a moral process is enhanced because there are many people who hold that the law (by reason of its penalties) is the only valid principle of obedience, and others who, not committing themselves so far, would separate the spheres of law and morality to the detriment of one if not both. What man has joined they would put asunder. That way, it is thought, lies anarchy.

VARIETIES OF AUTHORITY

History knows a hand, which is the hand of power, and a voice which is the voice of authority. In that antithesis we are presented with a distinction between a function of immediate coercion, physical compulsion, inevitable, and (in contrast) a function of obedience; an acceptance mediated by the personality of the obeyer; acts and decisions clearly different from any automatic, inevitable set of responses. A psychologist may say that there is no human reaction, even to physical force, which is not mediated by some process in the personality; some fear, some acquired auto-mation (conditioned reflex), some habit-system, some easily stimu-lated instinct of fear, of gregarious mustering, of nutrition-need. Merely to be pushed or pulled is not to obey.[9]

But without over-refinement one can distinguish two degrees of voluntary responsiveness. One recognises the effects of fear. One also recognises an obedience by clear consent, very different from fear, and we call some instances of it morality, for want of a better word.[10] Here the responder is not overwhelmed. The obeyer is listening to a still small voice, persuasive, not coercive; conceiv-ably he is imitating a pattern, or aspiring to a standard, awesome rather than awful. Certainly he is not cowering before the hand that hurls the lightning, or the menace in the declaration and the thunder.

In the distinction between authority and power[11] there may be found a seminal notion enabling us to characterise a feature

[9] In our law the involuntary act, the 'automatism', is not an 'act in law' (Bratty v Att. Gen. for N. Ireland [1961] 3 All Eng. R. 523).

[10] The word morality is derived from the Latin *mores*, meaning customs. No certainty exists as to how 'moral' were *mores*. The French *moeurs* connotes a high standard of conduct. Significantly the German *Sitten* includes in its compass etiquette and politeness.

[11] Made difficult by usages in which 'power' seems to mean 'authority' and vice versa.

which is present in legal systems and apparently absent from moral systems: a certain type of necessitation. That notion would be more valuable than it is if legal and moral systems were isolable; or if it could be established that at any stage in the history of authority the order of threats could be disentangled from the order of persuasions.

But the data of authority at various periods include requests, demands, commands, orders, etc., so related amid differences, that we lack a useful terminology for their classification; and basic words, like norm, rule, law, etc., cannot be defined without reference to a defined authority – which means that they cannot be defined or described without circularity.[12] Scholars have long since abandoned, as guides, any theories of primeval tyranny, or primeval solidarity. (According to anthropology 'social contracts' never took place.) What can be said is that in various phases of history, including the movements of modern times, there have been changes in the form and content of those norms, etc., which we call laws; including change from specific commands, as of a leader in battle, to general rules, as of guidance in a peaceful, friendly group.

Such a movement is discernible in phases of religious systems, and in phases of the nation-state. Since the state is a habit system for human beings, there is to be expected, and there seems to take place, a recapitulation in social conduct of development from levels of fear to levels of acceptance, even of devotion.

But evolution is not rectilinear. Rather is it spiral, with the lower levels always discernible from above. [The Greeks, who had no concept of evolution, knew of the 'reversion to primitive type'.]

We cannot completely ignore the elements of terror, and the function of physical – or psycho-physical – coercion that survives in our modern life, because we have seen many and quick reversions from the sophistications of the bourgeoisie in the Hanging Gardens to the terrorism of the age of Nimrod. Nevertheless

---

[12] Circularity does not spoil a definition, though it sets limits to speculative synthesis. From apparent tautologies we learn things that are new to us. In point is the clarification achieved by the Law Lord who said: income tax, if I may say so, is a tax on income. [From this flows law about capital increases etc.]

laws, among those who stay civilised, are generally so stated (in universals rather than particulars) that obedience seems to be the following of a rule in a game rather than quick response to military command.[13]

In the laws – however advanced – there are sanctions; and some sanctions are proximate; where, e.g., police powers are great. A simple example of differences in the 'proximity' of the sanction, is afforded by the difference between criminal law and civil law.[14] In the criminal law the important statement is precisely the statement of a punishment that can follow disobedience and be directly administered in personam. The criminal process is moved by the state and, once instituted, cannot easily be stayed.[15] The authority, here, is mediated by a fear, not only of physical discomfort, or pecuniary loss, but of a certain 'shame' that attaches to the notion of punishment. (This factor is absent from some large classes of punishable 'offences' which are part of the organisation of public health, traffic control, clear air, etc., etc., where the penalties are small fines, summarily inflicted (by magistrates). That class, however, creates difficulties which are verbal only.) Psychologically the notion of crime and punishment is a clear one, and a clear example of proximate sanction. But, for the law-abiding, serious sanctions are remote; they seem to lie in a world of other people, or in the historical background. What physical power enforces a conveyancing act, or a statute of interpretations, or the construction of wills? or, in crime, the judge's rules? Many writers use some such questioning, in conjunction with theories about ancient legal systems, in order to try and eliminate the notion of sanction from law. That thinking, it is here submitted, is erroneous (not only because powers exist).

Certainly no sword hangs over the head of the Chancery draftsman. But it does hang over the head of the peculator from the

[13] In a very sophisticated system, military commands could be generalised as a special set of game-rules.

[14] A distinction not fully achieved in ancient codes. The Romans knew crime before they knew tort. (Criminal process was an appeal to the legislature.) The Bible lies on an old stratum of tort. The Bible does, however, treat some conduct (including bestialities) as being publicly punishable. The class penalty, it seems, is capital. (Lev. xix-xx.)

[15] See p. 84 *et seq.*

company of which the lawyer drew the articles. Nor is the threat entirely irrelevant to the affairs of those directors who so mis-manage the company that they become civilly liable for misfeas-ance, and find that civil liability to be directly or indirectly enforceable by the state. Similarly, although it is not punishable crime to draw a testament otherwise than in accordance with the Wills Act, yet civil rights depend on these forms, and the ultimate effect is that a court will not enforce claims based on the informal documents, and will enforce rights which the document fails to alter. (In crime, by analogy, statements wrongly obtained are inadmissible in evidence.)

The notion of sanction, be it interpolated, is in bad odour these days. Yet law cannot be adequately described without reference to it. That the whole of law is a set of commands by a sovereign authority, sword in hand, is, of course unrealistic; and remains unrealistic if swordsman be replaced by gunman.

Tyranny of that type we call lawless. Typical of it is the Czarist ukase, an *in personam*, arbitrary, command, the frequent use of which in Russia caused that great idealist analyst T. H. Green to banish the state of the Czar from among the republics. Succeeding Czardoms (such as we see now) are open to the same commination on the part of idealists. Such analysis, however, may be too facile. In fact no state could flourish, not those tyrannies that prevail over large populations, and certainly not modern democracies, if every legal pronouncement made direct reference to punishments. That way anarchy lies. But, unless it be conceded that legal systems contain sanctions, derive support from them, even without direct logical dependence (when law is argued), there would be no way of distinguishing (from laws) those rules, whatever they are, which find no place in legal systems.[16]

The result of the historical study of legal systems supports this analysis, if only because there is revealed, in the history of

---

[16] Sanction, pedantically, fails even here as a criterion. If a person departs from the rules of chess, the sanction exists that people will not play with him unless he adheres to the rules. This applies to football, freemasonry and other social cooperations.

Indeed it may be argued that the order of morals cannot be described

religions and nation states alike, some period, at least, in which (even among elaborate untyrannic customs) the threat of force was highly relevant: and from no system have the vestiges disappeared. What our own system owes to despots, and to rebels against despots, is too well known to require elaboration. Indeed the function of coercion remains important.

But the reference to despotism tells us (to whom, happily, despotism is only history) something of how our laws have evolved. Processes of history, including many revolutions and the growth of populations too numerous and strong to be easily controlled, too prosperous not to be favoured, have changed the content of laws, and the direction of authority. Democracy is one stage – perhaps the culmination, though this is not clear – of a process translating the objects of laws into the subjects of the legal system.[17]

Consequently the modern law tends to be an aggregate of descriptions of the relations that do, or should, or must, obtain between persons. The law tells us about the socially important conduct of individuals *inter se*; between individuals and groups, between individuals (or groups) and that person or group which is the State. To us who live in communities which do not frequently hear the voice of Nimrod, no weapons overshadow this

as sanctionless. Even the Kantian 'unconditional obeyer' suffers loss of pride or self-respect if he disobeys or misbehaves.

The proper distinction seems to be that law includes sanctions describable in material terms; having effect on person and property; and that other sanctions (of rules which are not called laws) are, in the material sense, weaker.

It hardly needs saying that 'law', as used here, does not include scientific laws, which are descriptions of patterns and uniformities in the universe of things. The term 'law' used there owes its use to theology – the notion of laws given, by God, to the planets etc.

There is, however, a sense in which, even here, an idea of sanction could be relevant. If an engineer misunderstood the laws of physics, and worked, as it were, against them, he would incur the sanction of failure in his constructions. 'Obedience' to the laws of physics enables men to visit the moon.

[17] Marxism, with its theory of inevitable processes from the status of worker to the status of owner of the instruments of production, may well amount to nothing more than a misstatement, or incomplete statement, of this fairly evident truth.

law. The law *contains* sanctions. That fact is part of the definition or description of law – not the whole of it. The technique of the enforcement of law is, to lawyers and laity alike, a *sine qua non*, a background feature, and not helpful in the understanding of the workings of the system. The normal legal situation for the bulk of the citizenry is an affair, not of dictates but of valuations: valuations expressed in words like rightness and fairness and utility. Centuries of development have caused the major valuations made by human beings to be absorbed into legal systems, and the legal system, in turn, crystallises, preserves, and develops, those nascent valuations for the society which is their matrix.

In the axiological gamut some values seem to stand on different levels of importance from others. Thus, though the German word *Sitten* is translatable as morals or as etiquette, the Anglo-Saxons recognise a considerable difference between the two orders. We recognise, also, the difference between social utilities, economic and social proprieties (that is to say 'what is proper'); and between these, in turn, and the major necessities of civilised life, such as the duties of respect for life and person and the domain of the individual.[18]

TRANSVALUATIONS

It is precisely the complexity of our value system which makes the analysis of the relation between morals and law at once difficult and fascinating. Some simplification can be achieved in the following way. Let us regard laws as the valuations which have become integrated into the workings of the state.[19] Immediately it is clear that many valuations are not included, because the state (even the totalitarian state) has never succeeded in absorbing the whole of society.[20]

Of what is included, some laws express moral valuations, whereas other laws express the lower levels. Nor is it always easy

[18] These distinctions exist inside and outside the law.

[19] Some restatement would be necessary for religious–legal systems; but the principle holds.

[20] This is consistent with the historical fact that states can restrict the freedom, the articulation, of society.

to distinguish what the purposes of the law really are. This question is always to be asked when any change of law is mooted. (It is in the changes of law that the values of the people tend to express themselves.) The purpose, or the effect, of change can appear moral, even when it is the articulation of purposes below that level. As to value, it must not be forgotten in the course of theorising, that a system of law which governs a modern nation-state, especially a collectivist state, is concerned with a myriad of matters which are expressive of human values, yet are not moral issues. Reforms, in fact, have taken place which have moral value, but which were not enacted as moral reforms. In point is a modern instance in the British law of road transport. Before 1930 it could reasonably be said that the owner of a motor vehicle, unless possessed of very great wealth, was morally bound to insure his vehicle so as to make certain of the payment of compensation to persons injured by his vehicle. In 1930 it was enacted in the Road Traffic Act that it was thenceforth a punishable offence to use, or cause or permit to be used, a motor vehicle on the road unless there was in force, in relation to that vehicle, a valid Insurance Policy covering third party risks.[21]

So an ought may be said to have become a must. But the purpose of the legislature was not, primarily, the absorption of a moral duty into the law. The state was concerned with the protection of persons and families made physically and economically vulnerable by the increase of road traffic. It was no longer practical (as it was forty years previously) to expect men with red flags to walk in front of self-propelled vehicles, giving warning of the

[21] This law falls far short, protectively, of the law of the Irish Free State, by which the government compensates the injured irrespectively of fault on the part of drivers. In England the 'cover' is usually consequential on the fault of the driver. If the driver is not 'liable' there is nothing insured. Also in England the notion of a third party is a restricted one. Passengers, for example, need not be insured except in classes of passenger vehicles. Moreover, if the policy of insurance proves to be invalid because the insured person has misled his insurance company in one of the infinite ways in which those gullible institutions can be misled, then the insured person is punishable, but the injured third person is left to sue 'a man of straw'. It is only by grace of the Tariff Companies that compensation is paid when insurers prove insolvent.

approach of danger. The alternative was to minimise the damage that the dangerous vehicles might do to the public.

In the reverse direction, where MUST NOT becomes MAY, the legislature is not necessarily expressing a moral or religious judgment. When the restrictions of the Lord's Day Act are relaxed, so as to allow of Sunday entertainment, the purpose is to cater for the social needs of persons whose employment and economic circumstances have restricted their leisure to that one day.[22] On a different level an act permissive of abortion can be regarded as public health legislation – not as an ethical approval.

The moral-legal dialogue proper is heard when some fundamental human right is being considered, as when Lord Mansfield pronounced the status of slavery to be incompatible with English law.[23] This was followed by the statutory prohibition of the slave trade. A materialist may object that the motive was an economic one, protective of paid labour, and may point to the fact that child labour, which concerned English capitalists, was not rendered illegal until long after. But there is enough morality in the English law to justify mitigation of that criticism. In support of that mitigation, we have, from half a century later, a demonstration of moral tradition when John Bright persuaded many cotton workers, against their economic interest, to oppose the cause of their customers, the slave owners of the southern states. Moral issues are raised, not always with moral effect, in cases under extradition treaties, and under the Fugitive Offenders Acts, where the court has to consider whether it is being asked to return to another jurisdiction a person charged with a crime which we also regard as a crime, or whether the process is being used in order to

[22] The Lord's Day Act (Sunday Observance Act, 1677) is not a 'dead letter'. Recently, in Rolloswin Investments Ltd. v Chromolit Portugal S.A.R.L. ([1970] IWL. R. 912), it was argued that a contract signed on a Sunday was not binding. Mocatta J. ingeniously found that the Act does not apply to companies, which cannot go to church! This finding coheres with the nineteenth-century dictum that a company is a thing without a body to be kicked or a soul to be damned.

[23] R. v Sommersett (20 State Trials 1). This doctrine was followed in 1949 in the case of Eisler, a refugee from a communist ship, whom the English court refused to extradite. A recent problem is set by the Visiting Forces Act, which causes our government to surrender deserting Americans, some of whom are determined by conscience.

enable a dictator to acquire custody of a political opponent.
Clearly it was awareness of this that caused the Law Lords in the
case of the Ghanaian Armah (*ex parte* Armah [1966] 3 All Eng. R.
177) to declare that the standard of proof in cases of this type
(that come before the Bow Street Magistrate) is higher than the
proof required when a magistrate is asked to commit someone for
trial in a British court. 'A strong and probable presumption of
guilt' (the statutory words) means more than a 'prima facie case'.
This may well be regarded as an instance of the changes in the
law effected by judges.

Frequently we find the expression of moral purpose more
explicit in judicial findings, in the now established realm of
judicial legislation, than in the enactments of Parliament. Similar
is the juristic experience of the U.S.A., as when, in the 1950's, an
activist Supreme Court, faced with difficulties in the application
of desegregation law, adopted an attitude to the laws and the
constitution which the great Marshall had manifested a century
earlier; an emphasis on human rights, but differently conceived.
In the case of a coloured girl, coincidentally named Brown, they
had to decide whether 'equality' in the field of education was
provided in schools equally equipped with pedagogy, but 'segre-
gated'. This they held not to be equality.[24]

Britain is rarely a forum for such spectacular issues, but some
important controversies provide half-heard melodies in our technically reported litigation. So a theme was stated when Sir William
Erle held in 1853 (Lumley v Gye 2 E. & B. 216) that interference
with the contract of a singer was wrong in law as well as in ethics.
That departure from doctrines of free competition was destined,
paradoxically, to make life difficult, half a century later, for those
creatures of collectivism which are the trade unions. Those cases,
which would have pleased Sir William – a great critic of collective
bargaining – are less exciting now, because a legislative reaction –
the Trade Disputes Act of 1906 – changed them from drama into
history.[25]

[24] Brown v Board of Education (1954) 345 U.S. 972.
[25] But see p. 41 for a musical echo.

3
Trends and Developments

The moral coefficient of the law is likely to be at its most evident when laws change. All systems of law change – there is none immutable.

We know from the Book of Esther that the laws of the Medes and Persians 'which could not be altered' were in fact altered – and that, by as arbitrary a determination as has ever characterised the ukases of Czars, or the dictates of those who express, at any moment of time, a 'party line'.

In the Pentateuch, which embodies a righteous code, we read that 'it must not be added to or diminished'. Yet in those pages we learn that after one aspect of the law had crystallised (the law of inheritance) a change was made, in order to solve the problem presented to Moses by the daughters of Zelophehad. The subsequent history of Jewish theocratic law, an elaborate and mature system, and of the Canon law, reveals a legal growth from the Pentateuch, which, though it is mediated by doctrines held to be implicit in the Bible text, constitutes great change, calculated to meet the needs of developing society and a changing world.

'The law', said the scriptor, 'is not in Heaven.' That is one way of saying that it has to be applied to the problems of human beings living on earth. Laws, which are compendiously stated, require to be elaborated. Frequently elaboration reveals that the situation before the judges is not precisely covered by the law: therefore the judges must do their best to solve the problem in the spirit of the laws of which they are the ministers. Then they

31

express what to them is the principle (not necessarily a moral principle) latent in the law; 'they find it in their bosoms': and some principle of justice, however that word be defined, is required even where the problem is one where no great moral issue is at stake – as where economic claims come to be decided, with ethical 'merits' on both sides.

In the English system, where judicial activity is at its maximum, since our rule is by accumulation of precedent rather than by deduction from the language of code, there is a constant presentation to the courts of issue 'of first impression'. In a sense every case before English judges is 'of first impression', in that the judge is engaged in evaluating a situation before he tries mentally to classify it among the generalities. To paraphrase an ancient jurist, both parties appear as persons suspect, and both leave the court faultless.

But 'first impression' describes also the situation where precedent is not clear. Here, often, the decision is an attribution of responsibilities, and liabilities, so that if loss is to fall it shall fall where it should (in a moral sense) be borne. In point is such a situation as that of the solicitor whose managing clerk had converted money belonging to the client, where the only apparent neglect on the part of the solicitor was the appointment of a person who later proved to be dishonest. Here[1] the Law Lords, in finding the solicitor liable, pronounced a principle of absolute liability, which is against the normal doctrine that liability depends on personal fault. In this, and in the cases in the law of master and servant generally, English judges have developed a principle of vicarious liability of master for servant, which is an absolute liability: and this is, in normal economic circumstances, a humane doctrine, because it throws liability on to a class more likely to be able to bear (and insure against) loss.

This may be described as a case where equity is not equality. But equality is a hard word. The principle of absolute liability of master for servant is typical of a class of cases which have moral relevance, but in which it cannot be said that the rule laid down

[1] Lloyd v Grace Smith [1912] A.C. 716. (The wrong was not for the employers benefit, but was within the ostensible scope of employment.)

is moral as against an immoral opposite, or more moral than its opposite. Rather let it be said that here is a principle of distribution which has merits and has defects.[2]

In this way, it may be said, the judges legislate. In a sense judicial legislation is an undesirable thing because, as John Locke expresses it, persons should be governed by established laws and not by extempore pronouncements. But, in the way that Locke feared, English judges do not govern by extempore pronouncement. The logic of the process is that all systems of law are incomplete. Laws require elaboration. Judges come to 'fulfil'. Even codes, however well drafted, require interpretation, and choices of possible interpretation. (This is evident in the French code and in the American Constitution.) In that way systems of law grow. The English system is the one that reveals its growth most clearly. There is, of course, case law even in the lands which rely on codes: and, although there is less reliance there on precedent, yet precedents are valuable. Thus the French code places duties of care on the concierges of apartment houses and on their employers. But the code does not explain what respite the worker has: e.g. is he negligent if he takes time off in order to eat, or to sleep? These questions have been debated and decided, and precedent followed.

On the other hand, precedent, as in England, can achieve something of the rigidity of a code: and the codification of precedents is seen in many statutes. For the rigidity of the system good examples are afforded by rules against which judges have unsuccessfully struggled. One such rule is that no binding agreement can be made to accept less than the debtor owes by way of

[2] An interesting feature of the rule of absolute liability of master for servant is that the authorities do not make it clear whether the servant (who is a wrong-doer) is liable to indemnify the master who has paid damages. The question was academic until (a) joint tortfeasors became suable *inter se,* and until (b) insurance companies transmuted men of straw into men of substance. The best opinion seems to be that the servant is liable to the master. See Romford Ice Co. Ltd. v Lister [1955] 3 All Eng. R. 460. In the U.S.S.R. employers do sue servants for damages in order to keep the books straight. If the employer is the state, then the suit is a prosecution.

settlement. To take, for example, a smaller sum than the sum due, 'in full settlement' is a legally ineffective gesture, because something has been given for no consideration.[3]

If that rule were altered the moral difference in the law would be imperceptible, but the change would facilitate practical adjustments which are so frequently desirable in commerce.

Let it not be supposed that every judicial finding (of old or new) is a moral one in the sense of contributive to a morally better order of things: and let it not be assumed that every judicial finding is a moral one, in the sense of a good one. The findings, let it rather be said, can be ethically relevant. They can, indeed, be ethically bad, or prove, in the long run, to be unfair precedents.

If bad law is wanted for illustration, what could be worse than the pronouncement of that great jurist Coke, who held that infidels are without rights because they are *perpetui inimici* . . . like the devils whose servants they are.[4] It is only fair to add that this teaching, a relic, in Protestant times, of Inquisition doctrines, was recognised for what it was and strongly disapproved by preceding and immediately following jurists, headed by Littleton, the great expositor.

Of doctrines less malevolent, there are, at lower levels, plenty; deriving from shortsighted, unimaginative, or perverse applications of legal learning and logic. Thus when judges pronounced that a servant cannot claim compensation from his master if his injury were the result of the negligence of a fellow servant, they were applying, or misapplying, the doctrine *volenti non fit injuria*[5] to a class of persons as unlikely to be able to guide their lives in the light of it as they were unlikely to understand the Latin. That doctrine was mitigated by statutes and by an ingenious plea

[3] An ingenious by-passing of this rule is to be found in Central London Properties Ltd. v High Trees Houses Ltd., [1956] 1 All Eng. R. 256. The great lawyer whose efforts are expressed in that case has also made interesting attack on another – cramping – rule, that a third person who benefits from a contract cannot, himself, enforce it.

[4] Calvin's Case (1608) 7 Co. Rep. 1(a).

[5] A person who willingly takes a risk does not suffer a (legally remediable) injury.

of 'bad system', but its mischief (as bar to a common law claim) was eventually legislated away in a Law Reform Act of 1948.

Of judicial elaborations more will be said in later chapters. Here suffice it to say that laws do not only require elaborations; they require alteration, amendment even unto abrogation. The law, notwithstanding the dogmas, must be added to. In political legal systems, this is the normal. We legislate; and legislation may, or may not, be just or unjust, good or bad. A very large segment of the legislative aggregate can be regarded as morally irrelevant.

In the last one hundred and fifty years, in which legislation has increased in quantity, and accelerated in tempo, much of the new law is, quite simply, technical. Very valuable law, from the technical standpoint, is the codification of sale of goods learning in the Sale of Goods Act 1894. Marine insurance was codified in the same period.

Other codes include Companies Act, and Bankruptcy Acts, vital to the commercial community. Even more technically important have always been Conveyancing Acts. In the 1920s an enormous simplification of conveyancing law and property generally was achieved in the Law of Property Acts 1922–5, and the Administration of Estates Act, 1925. The 1925 Land Registration Act developed an existent scheme which has brought about, and will bring about, further simplifications.

In legislation of this type no ethical issues are involved. In Town Planning, another vast body of law, it may be said that there are assumptions, which are the assumptions of collectivism. To that extent there is moral relevance, but, the postulates being granted, the subject can be regarded as technical only.

In Rent Acts, which will be discussed later, argument is heard, at every legislative stage, on behalf of economic classes. Again, a social valuation is in the background. The same can be said of tax legislation, in which the principles of graduation are relevant to social welfare.

Paradoxically, moral decisions present themselves on the statute-book in small law reform acts, which abolish ancient doctrines of the law, without the publicity that might be expected to attend revolutions in our jurisprudence. As it happens, the publicity in morally relevant law is almost monopolised by Matrimonial Causes Acts, for, happily, sex is always with us. Let those matters be postponed.

From the foregoing description of legal changes, it is clear that in English law, as in all systems of law, ancient and modern, changes are brought about in two main ways; by legislation and by litigation. In legislation the public opinion of the country, as it happens to be expressed in the government of the time, expresses its demand for change, including moral change, as when, for example, capital penalties are abolished, or a new doctrine introduced into matrimonial law, or a new standard of care set in company practice.

When a legislative change is relevant to morality, that relevance is manifest in the Parliamentary debates and in the contemporary press. In contrast, the changes wrought in the law by litigation may involve moral decisions calculated to make their mark on the law, and may go unseen, because litigation is not debated in the press *pendente lite*, and civil litigation is little reported after the event; except in that branch of the Admiralty jurisdiction concerned with 'ships that pass in the night'. Yet it is in civil litigation that findings are made as to the duties *inter se* of citizens. Here, in the order of private rights, we learn about standards of conduct, and observe changes in the judicial statement of them. In this sphere much morality is pronounced and laid away in case law. 'And freedom slowly broadens down, from precedent to precedent.'

The changes effected in the course of litigation are of two kinds, technical and doctrinal.[6] A useful modern example is afforded by the practice of hire-purchase and the law relevant thereto, which will be separately considered.

Doctrinally, however, the great advances, or changes, are, in

[6] The above description is, it is submitted, more useful for the analysis of modern law than Sir Henry Maine's distribution of changes into legal fiction, equitable processes, and legislation. Sir Henry Maine was describing the history of institutions – and his description stands unchallenged. Analytically, however, legal fiction is one instance of legal improvements are equitable within the accepted connotation of that word.)

this century of Parliamentary activity, best achieved in legislation.[7] Legislation can make a total change. Thus not all the ingenuity of draftsmen, creating restraints on anticipation, could protect the married woman in the degree that was achieved in the Married Women's Property Act of 1882. Similarly, judges could not strain the law of contract to protect the ill-advised adult against hard bargains. The burden was on Parliament; and part of it was discharged in the moneylending laws of 1904 and 1927.

These examples suggest the desirability of mentioning (in anticipation of later chapters) some moral or quasi-moral trends. Dicey demonstrated, in a masterpiece of jurisprudence, how nineteenth-century laws for long were individualistically inspired, and (consequently – though this is not Dicey's statement) less rich in what we now consider to be ethical doctrine.[8] The ethical co-efficient of much of that legislation was the virtue of individual effort. Yet before half that century was past, 'protective' laws were being enacted, protective of women and children, protective of the poor, protective of public health.

This century, which has seen a retreat from *laissez-faire* in economics, has witnessed an immense growth of 'protectionism' in social relations. Amidst masses of laws that are 'ethically irrelevant', many emerge which have the avowed purpose of protecting the poor and the otherwise unprotected. These laws are part of a social movement against property, against capital – are, indeed, the English 'evolutionary' effort to ends that are sought elsewhere by revolutions. That distinction, be it said, is more than a nineteenth-century platitude. The 'accepted' revolutions, such as the French, inspired in a measure by English example and precept, were revolts against privilege, not primarily against property. Twentieth-century revolt, from the red of 1916 to the black of the 1960s, is precisely against property. England has been saved from this by economic developments which eventually rendered

---

[7] It was not always so. In the seventeenth century, the courts created equity, and legislation only served to force the lawyers into more ingenious treatment of it.

[8] *Law and Opinion in England in the XIXth Century.* The transition from individualism to collectivism has been made vivid in this century, less here than in U.S.A. – where New Deal legislation established itself only after a generation of old lawyers had died or retired.

the lower classes middle-class. But the impulse to condemn the private holdings of large fortunes is a continuous function of public opinion, even while large fortunes accelerate in their growth.

What others have achieved by expropriation, and the assumption of functions by states, which states are unfitted to fulfil, is partially achieved here by immense taxations, by death duties, for example, and other varieties of levy on capital; graduated taxations generally. Consistently with these measures, relief is given to the propertyless by free education (rooted in the 1870s) subsidised medicine, and by laws which protect the house dweller against the landlord, the borrower against the lender; the worker against the employer, the under-dog wherever a tail is wagged.

These things are of ethical relevance – but they do not exhaust morality, or its legal expression.

For over a century, the private lives of the citizens have been emancipated from a good deal of dogma. Sex is no longer an ugly word, though contemporary literature and art seek avidly to restore a pristine ugliness. Much law-making of moral significance is concerned with the control, or reduction of control, over sexual life. This, more than other important issues, has recently brought about new thinking (or revival of old thinking) on morality in the law.

FROM THE BOSOMS OF JUDGES

The suffusion of the Anglo-American legal systems with moral notions is easily understood when we learn that our judges are recruited from legal practitioners. These men have, in every generation, brought to the Bench a set of contemporary valuations. In the nature of things, the lawyer is conservative because the laws are self-limiting. Their scope is reduced by their reduction into words. Nevertheless the lawyer carries with him an awareness of the critical spirit of his age. When he is called upon to judge, he seeks in his bosom and finds sympathies with the demands and the protests that clamour round the seat of justice.

Clearly judicial morality is a variable in one sense at least, that judges are brought up in different periods. Few of them stand significantly above their contemporaries – or their classes.

Therefore it is to be expected that many judgments have been bad ones. In our civil system, which is to such a great extent judgemade, we find doctrines that are quite bad from our point of view. Thus twentieth-century legislators have had to abolish or modify rules of law such as the following: that any charge of contributory negligence completely defeats a claim for damages;[9] that joint-tort-feasors cannot claim against each other;[10] that a husband is responsible for his wife's tort; that a wife accused of crime alongside her husband is deemed to have been coerced by him (abolished 1925): that one spouse could not sue the other in tort[11] (modified now); that a child under twenty-one[12] is in the custody of a parent; that a workman cannot recover damages from an employer if the injury is caused by the negligence of a fellow-workman;[13] that death is not a cause of action. In a limited sense this, the rule in Baker v Bolton,[14] is still the law. Teachings such as these can all be explained in terms of period ethics. There was an awareness of one ethical argument, an occlusion of others.

In complex economic situations ethical merits can be differently assessed at short, as well as long, intervals. One example is afforded by a quite recent set of cases. In 1952 the plaintiff, D. C. Thomson (a publisher), failed in his action against trade union leaders who had brought pressure to bear on his suppliers causing them to break contract, because the court held that there was no evidence that the defendants had actual knowledge that contracts were in being.[15] In the 1960's in Stratford Ltd. v

[9] Based on a primitive concept of causation. The rule was modified in 1945 so that now a degree of fault mitigates the damages proportionately. See p. 48.

[10] The rule in Merryweather v Nixon (1799) 8 7.R. 186.

[11] Even though each or either of them was insured in respect of that type of tort (e.g. negligent driving). See Edwards v Porter [1925] A.C. 1 for the learning. A suggested exception (when the husband is agent for somebody else) in Smith v Moss [1940] 1 K.B. 424 is disapproved by the experts. For changes, see pp. 65–6.

[12] Recent statute has made eighteen the age of majority.

[13] Notwithstanding that, for that other workman, the employer would be liable to third parties.

[14] 1 Camp. 493.

[15] D. C. Thomson & Co. v Deakin and others [1952] 2 Ch. 646.

Lindley,[16] and in the Emerald Construction case,[17] the courts were less concerned to find such proof.[18]

These later cases, like the first mentioned, arise from facts that are described as secondary boycotts – where trade unions, or other organisations or groups, put pressure on businesses by threatening, coercing, or otherwise influencing, their customers, their suppliers, their contractors generally. In Thomson's case, during a period when 'the hand of the workman was uppermost', the court was more lenient than the courts of half a century previously.[19] But in the 1960s the courts were less sympathetic to the so-called 'under-dog'. They seem to have held that the interferer with contracts does so at his peril. He is made aware of ethical duty. An 'ought to know' is substituted for an 'actually knew'. Here we see a moral movement against unfairness. Trade union law is one of the fields in which judicial and Parliamentary legislation seem always to be ethically relevant, if not always ethically motivated. After a long period in which the hand of the worker was not uppermost, there was a trend, from the late nineteenth century, through the laws of 1906 and case law of the 1920's, to a justification of what might easily be condemned as unfair industrial action on the part of workers. The strongest case is reported in 1942[20] when the House of Lords declared a boycott of crofters to be justified because the trade unionists were animated by the reasonable desire to promote their own economic interests. If the Law Lords were pronouncing ethically, they were expressing the ethics of classes that had been oppressed and were achieving that economic strength which makes freedom a reality. That spirit had, possibly, animated the Liberal legislators of 1906.

Such ethical situations are inveterately ambivalent. From the standpoint of the ruined crofters, the Law Lords had declared, or legislated, a non-ethical or unethical norm. A later generation of Law Lords showed itself conscious of the ethical claims of

[16] [1964] 2 All Eng. R. 102.

[17] Emerald Construction Co. Ltd. v Lowthian and others. [1946] 1 All Eng. R. 1013.

[18] In the Emerald case the defendants knew that there was a contract in being, but did not know its terms.

[19] Quinn v Leatham [1901] A.C. 495.

[20] Crofter Hand Woven Harris Tweed Co. v Veitch [1942] A.C. 435.

those who suffered at the hands of labour leaders. In point is the case of Bonsor,[21] a man driven to misery and early death by the operation of a closed shop union which had wrongfully expelled him. The Law Lords, reverting to earlier learning, and over-ruling intervening case law, held that a union could be liable in contract to a wrongfully expelled member. The opinions may be nothing more than sound case-law, but the language sounds with ethical overtones. Similarly a consciousness of the concept of fair-ness is clear in the case of Rookes v Barnard[22] wherein the courts 'drove a carriage and six' through the protective language of the Trade Disputes Act of 1906.[23] The gap so disclosed was quickly fenced by a Labour government[24] in legislation which some would call ethical, and others non-ethical.

It may be asked, in this and other, context; when we speak of morals entering into, or suffusing the law, or when we speak of the moral principles applied by judges, what principles are being invoked? Since the law is involved with much that is ethically irrelevant, it is not easy to extract the moral coefficient. Let it be borne in mind that much of the task of the lawyer in the courts is in the form of problems of law and nothing else. A few instances, from recent (1970) litigation, may usefully be mentioned.

What is the effect of a conflict of powers, between town plan-ning and road development? (Westminster Bank Ltd. v Ministry of Housing and Local Government). To what extent does a later statute supersede or control a similar earlier statute? (Pattinson and others v Finningley Internal Drainage Board). Whose servant is the clerk in a Land Registry? (Ministry of Housing and Local Government v Sharp and others). These examples serve to show that law has much to do that is not concerned with morals. The problem is made harder by the fact that not only in our own age, though in our own age especially, the 'content' of morality, as well as the subsistence of morality, is for debate. How

---

[21] Bonsor v Musicians Union [1954] 1 All Eng. R. 822.
[23] To induce a breach of contract is unlawful. But the protective Act makes this not unlawful in industrial disputes. In the case cited the courts held that, nevertheless, 'to threaten a breach of contract' was unlawful. Some very subtle thinking and interpretation was involved.
[24] Trade Disputes Act 1965.

much of the law is moral, how much non-moral, how much immoral; how much of morals is legal, non-legal, illegal; these are questions to be answered by each according to his understanding, in descriptive or normative terms, of what constitutes morality, and according to his notion of law, and his degree of law-abidingness. Immediately we are plunged into a vortex of relativism, from which only those escape who are completely dogmatic or totally sceptical. Between these poles there is a range of practical difficulties, each arising when the advocate of some moral position says that the law *ought* to include morals in general, or his moral judgment in particular, and some lawyers, or a moralist with a different legal-moral view, would exclude what is sought to be included.

These abstract problems come to practicality when claims in the courts are not clearly covered by authority. The word authority, in the sense used here, calls for some explanation. Authority here means precedent; that is to say the judgments of courts and the dicta of 'authorities' (in this case the writings of recognised jurists) which are respected by the judge or court considering their words. Authority embodies many principles that cause the judge to be wary of departure from precedent, to be reluctant to find scope for his own discretion.[25] He is reluctant (in the language of Coke) 'to substitute the uncertain and crooked cord of discretion for the golden and straight metwand of the law.'

Frequently an observer of the law will say: 'how severe'. A judge refuses to interfere with a contract because it does not fall within the precedents of, e.g., restraint of trade. He will not interfere with an arbitration, however bad, unless a formal defect appears on the face of the record. In cases such as these the judge recognises no option as open to himself. There are, indeed, not many situations in which the judge is totally unguided. Much will be said of judge-made law; but let it be clear that only a small percentage of judgments afford the scope. What the scope is requires investigation.

From the fact that the state does not exhaust society, follows another fact of importance: namely, that the law, whether it be

[25] E.g. In the admission or exclusion of evidence.

religious code or the framework of a state, does not, cannot, regulate the whole field of human activity. English lawyers know that, in some of the simplest appearing aspects of life, such as the relationship inside families, the law still remains 'to be found'. In this century there have arisen questions about liabilities that were held in the last century not to exist; and the courts have extended the range of liability; extending, for example, the notion of duty to neighbours by restating the concept of neighbour.

This field is worth studying, because in it we see the operation of judicial legislation – and this interesting process, its scope and its limits, must be understood for the better understanding of moral factors in the law. Here we see the limits set by legality as such to moral purposings, and how these limits can be transcended.

Thus it is notorious that common law claims for damages must be based on some recognised legal relationship expressed in a form of action.[26] No remedy follows automatically on wrong; for wrong is only recognised where there is remedy: where there is a precedent form of action.[27] One of the general characteristics of the traditional forms of action is that there must be a proximity between the parties to actions. x 'injures' y only if y is the person with whom x makes some hurtful immediate contact; through personal assault, etc., through damage to property, through direct reference in deleterious words, etc., or through breach of a contract in being between them. Also, in most instances of tort, there must be 'fault', in the sense that what happens is intended or careless; and that conduct is actionable if what was done had

[26] The availability of the very useful concept of negligence is itself a late emergent from the strict writ of trespass, which gave, and still gives, a remedy for immediate, direct, physical injury. Trespass is rarely pleaded now in 'running-down cases', for technical reasons, including its inavailability for vicarious liabilities (for servant or agent). Also negligence, not trespass, is the plea against a surgeon, operating with consent. In the old days he could only be sued in contract (by the person who paid for the operation).

[27] Even in these less formalistic days, the unprecedented presents almost insoluble difficulty: as in the question whether a maker of drugs can be held liable to a very young embryo damaged by the drug. (J. v Distillers Co. Biochemicals Ltd. [1969] 3 Q.B. 1412.)

consequences that could or should have reasonably been anticipated and the defendant was careless not to do so.[28]

That was useful law before modern industrial development
created new relationships unrecognised by law: new situations
where wrongs went unrighted: when, that is to say, a fairminded
person would opine that less than justice had prevailed – that
there was moral inadequacy in the law.

In point are cases in which a manufacturer (or repairer) has
been careless in such a degree that he ought to have anticipated
danger; but the person injured is not his customer, only his
customer's customer. When the carriage wheel flies off and someone is injured (either the driver, or someone whom he is called
upon to compensate), who is liable? Not the person who sold or
hired out the vehicle, because he had no reason to suspect, or no
means of knowing, that the wheel had been carelessly affixed. He
had no fault. Not the manufacturer, it was held,[29] because his
carelessness was a breach of contract with the person he supplied,
not with a stranger.

It had been suggested in the nineteenth century by a lawyer
not sufficiently esteemed, Lord Esher, in the case of Heaven v
Pender,[30] that a person could be liable for the consequences of his
lack of care to the world at large. That proposition was not
adopted – was, perhaps, too wide. (It became notorious as an
advocate's *tabula in naufragio*.) The test of negligence, in the
first instance, implies that bad consequences should not be so
distant as not to be reasonably anticipated.

Earlier, in Langridge v Levy[31] a shop-keeper (not the maker)
had been held liable to a person injured by the explosion of a gun
that he had sold to another, only because he, the seller, had told
lies to his customer. That case was held to be one of the exceptions

[28] Some statutory duties (e.g. to fence machinery) are absolute. Not to
fulfil them is a wrong which is not only penal, but gives rise to an action
for damages. (The last was not always assumed.)

An absolute duty can be broken without any perceptible moral fault.
(Negligence has little enough in its definition.) *Inter alia*, few statutory
duties can be delegated.

[29] Earl v Lubbock [1905] 1 K.B. 253: an unconvincing case because
of the pleadings.

[30] (1883) 11 Q.B.D. 503.   [31] (1837) 2 M. & W. 519.

that test a rule. It was there (and later) assumed that a dealer was not liable for latent defects and that the manufacturer could only be liable (in contract) to the dealer, and would not be called upon to indemnify him unless he (the dealer) was called upon to pay damages.

In 1932, however, there came to the Law Lords a story of a disintegrating snail, manifesting itself in ginger beer from a sealed container. Evidently the seller could not be aware of the latent snail, nor liable for the hysteria induced in the plaintiff. Another remedy was sought. Wherefore the Law Lords were invited to hold, in an interlocutory process, that there was no cause of action against the manufacturer. This, however, they refused to do. That the manufacturer of unexaminable articles owes a moral duty to the world to be careful, few would dispute. Until Donoghue v Stevenson,[32] here referred to, that moral obligation was not translated into a legal obligation. In a classic debate between Lord Atkin and Lord Buckmaster, it was explicitly stated by the former that judges could change the law, and not merely articulate it by ingenious interpretation of the obscure.

The snail case was settled. But the legal approaches to that case are not more interesting than its consequences. The lawyers are conservative. It is the duty of whomsoever defends a claim of this type to resist the encroachment of social and moral values.

They treat every statement of liability at its minimum. Donoghue v Stevenson was an authority covering the negligence of manufacturers in circumstances where no one else would have opportunity to discover the defect. It could also be described as authority to cover liability for intrinsically dangerous chattels. Those are not very wide categories; and, though a Law Lord had pronounced that the categories of negligence were not closed, it was not without difficulty that the Court of Appeal held the repairers of a defective lift (not an intrinsically dangerous chattel) to be liable (after an accident) to the licensee of the occupier who had had the lift repaired.[33]

[32] [1932] A.C. 562.
[33] Haseldine v Daw [1941] 2 K.B. 343.
Semble, the 'repaired' lift could be considered dangerous, and the building occupier would not be able to become aware of the danger.

When it was sought to extend the doctrine, so as to make accountants liable for the consequences of bad advice which harmed a person not their client, the Court of Appeal refused. It was held that what applied to dangerous chattels did not apply to dangerous words.[34] Seventeen years later, the Law Lords appear to have overruled this finding.[35] But the sequence is of interest in order to show how the law develops. It develops slowly, and always with a restrictive approach to situations.

In fine, the opinions in Donoghue v Stevenson constitute a decisive restatement of many judicial contributions to the law. Some bad doctrines, as we have seen, like that of common employment; some good and bad doctrines in the categories of public policy; some undeniably good doctrines of equity, are all the results of judicial legislation. It follows that a study of some changes in the context of judge-made law should repay anyone interested in the relations between law and morals.

Not least of the discoveries of the researcher will be the fact that a great area of life is not covered by the law. We have, for example, no stated legal minimum in the duties of parents to children. There is a margin round every individual life of a certain freedom from legal control, a certain freedom to behave according to his will.

In the above mentioned fields of activity, clearly there is scope for the exercise, outside the law, of moral principles, and for disobedience to them. To define morality, for these purposes, is, in turn, more difficult than to define the law.

But some exploration of morals is necessary, if only to discover what ethics are likely to be or become legally relevant. Before that investigation is attempted, a general observation may be of interest.

Whatever rights exist between citizens, there is no law coercing a man into the exercise of his rights.[36] Who can compel him not

[34] Candler v Crane, Christmas & Co. [1951] 2 K.B. 164.

[35] Hedley, Byrne & Co. v Heller & Partners Ltd. [1963] All Eng. R. 575. In this case the claim was dismissed, because the defendants had expressly given their advice with disclaimer of liability. But the Law Lords made it clear, *obiter,* that otherwise the claim would have succeeded.

[36] Except, of course, in situations where the enforcement of a right happens to be a duty. In point is the executor or administrator.

to be generous?[37] In contrast, there may be rights in the exercise of which others can be injured. In point is the right to tell the truth for mischievous purposes. Here there is no legal prohibition available to inhibit the exercise of wickedness.

This topic is of special interest, precisely because it is an obvious field for legislation. If there is a margin round the individual on which the law does not impinge, who else may tread there?

In some jurisdictions there is a rudimentary right of privacy; e.g., *Persönlichkeitsrecht* in Germany and some Swiss Cantons. Some states of the American Union have enacted some limited laws of privacy. England (as will be seen later) is deficient in this sector. In England a journalist can resurrect the skeletons of a citizen's past, and escape penalty for the very bad reason that his 'libel' is true. Not so in many states of the American Union, though, even there, 'news value' can constitute a defence.

The domain of privacy has been said (wrongly) to be the realm of moral conduct. But certainly the privacy of public men is a target for the mischievous, and requires to be protected. Even that 'private place' which is the grave is unprotected against calumnies directed at the deceased. Just as death is not a cause of action, so the dead, by bad judge-made law, cannot be said to be defamed.[38] That fact is a true defamation of English law.

In mitigation, let it be said that the English law of defamation is severe, approximating, in some cases, almost to a law of absolute liability. The newspaper which receives from usually reliable sources the item that x was in female company in Paris has to pay damages when it transpires that at the material time x was with his wife in London. A lie by the subject of a photograph (a false name) has enriched, at the expense of the newspaper, the wife of the liar.[39]

[37] Again, with reservations. By the Bankruptcy Act he must not waste his assets to the detriment of his creditors.

[38] See R. v Ensor (1887) 3 T.L.R. 366: an amusing case where a lampoonist tried to show reason why a statue should not be erected to a deceased dignitary.

[39] Cassidy v Daily Mirror [1929] 2 K.B. 331. The man who posed as Corrigan with fiancee was a married man named Cassidy. Mrs Cassidy was defamed by the innuendo that she had been 'living in sin'!

Slighter errors than that are expensive. Nor does the Defamation Act 1952 materially alter the law. The principle, of course, is clear. The publisher of words, sounds, or pictures is under a very high duty of care, because whoever is injured is usually totally blameless. The result was summed up, years ago, by a melancholy editor, named Joy, who said: 'When I put the paper to bed at night, I am in the position of a man who has put into motion an immense chocolate machine, knowing that in the mass of foodstuff someone has dropped a pinch of arsenic.'[40]

NOTE ON CONTRIBUTORY NEGLIGENCE

This concept, ethically cognate to the rule as to Joint Tortfeasors, has been of harsh application. Claims have depended on the metaphysical tastes of judges. (Who did the first wrongful act? etc.)

The harshest application has been in Labour Law. Although the courts have expected less care from a workman, yet, contributory negligence being established, he was deprived of damages, even where the employer was in breach of absolute statutory duty (Caswell v Powell Duffryn Collieries [1940] A.C. 152).

In Admirality, joint fault has for long been expressed in a sharing of loss. In 1945, Parliament appplied this thinking to terrestrial tort. If both plaintiff and defendant were careless in the events that constituted the accident, the plaintiff is not completely deprived. He loses a proportion of his claim according to the degree of his fault. (Law Reform Act 1945). The judge is still called upon to think with great subtlety.

[40] It is of interest that the British press fears the citizen – not the Crown. Indeed 'the bright light that bears upon a throne' has become the lurid effulgence of the flashes of the yellow press. As for the government, it does not expect the press to be patriotic. But, in practice, the press of Britain is the most discreet (voluntarily) of all the world's presses. At times of public scandal it waits for a lead. Also, where defence etc. is involved, there is a working liaison between press and government, expressed sometimes in 'D' notices, which, however, are not threats of damnation. For a Note on the Press and the State, see p. 118.

4

A Semantic Exploration

SENTIMENT, CHARITY AND CHASTITY

Whereas the word law is a sort of sieve or pyx, the word morals is a container. What do we find in the container? And what do we find there that is not in the law?

An initial difficulty derives from the fact that morals change, sometimes less perceptibly than changes in law, sometimes quite evidently. But acceptance of moral changes is slower than the acceptance of legal changes, which is, *ex hypothesi*, immediate. Perhaps it is permissible to speak of an ecology of morals. In the socio-economic circumstances of the ancient East, of ancient Greece and Rome, and, later, of the southern States of the American Union, slavery was the background of civilised life. Humane persons saw no wrong in it. Aristotle thought it natural. The scriptors of the Pentateuch accepted it, even while declaring protections, controls and limits of duration. The Roman lawyers, in the Christian period, accepted it as *Ius Gentium* and so valid. But modern morality seems to declare, indeed to postulate, the immorality of treating a human being as a chattel. That is an extreme example. But in the theory of the proper treatment of human beings, there have been changes in British thought, all of them recognised by everybody, which restate the relationship between master and servant, between husband and wife, between officers and private soldiers, between teachers, or parents, and children, etc.[1] The present trend is regarded by many as a phase

[1] Only in this century has the wife ceased to be *sub virga viri sui*: and only since 1891 (R. v Jackson [1891] 1 Q.B. 671) has that Baconian principle ceased to have literal validity ('not to be entertained in a civilised forum').

in an ill-considered egalitarianism. But the positive merit is a diminution in the scope for cruelty, for man's inhumanity to women and children.

Some of the changes in thought (e.g. those above mentioned) are now absorbed in the law. Less perceptibly, the 'valuations' of an economically conscious society change – and not always in the same direction. Thus moneylending and bankruptcy which were anathema to the religious systems, and so to the people and the state, are now recognised as features of commercial life, and at the same time as potentials of abuse.[2]

Are the problems of the underprivileged a matter of morals, or are we speaking of sentiments – even of sentimentalities? Has the law merely been indulgent to a common sympathy for the unfortunate, whether by birth, accident or fault?

This apparently academic question became a lesion in our social consciousness when the world became acutely aware of race relations. Granted that a human being is an end in himself – not to be treated as a chattel – granted that slavery is immoral, does it follow that egalitarianism is a moral purpose, or even morally relevant? The question has been asked: were there not always hewers of wood and drawers of water? To English law-makers the problem is ever present and is two-fold: manifest in the need for decisions as to the attitude to be adopted towards nations which discriminate between the colours of people for administrative, or other, purposes; secondly in the particular policies of our own immigration law.

As to immigration, nineteenth-century Britain, religious and idealistic, and, it is fair to add, the *dives* of the nations, threw its doors open to refugees from oppression. Further, as the centre of

[2] Interest on money, in proper case, is, as Boehm Bawerck makes clear, a payment for economies in the way of time and organisation. It can, however, be a way of deprivation of assets, whether of individuals or of nations: a taking of advantage, and an increase of waste. This is particularly evident in India. The religion of the Hindus is mainly a theology. The ethical content is expressible as personal resignation. Therefore no Indian law, whether municipal or moral, restricts the avarice of the moneylender who has succeeded in reducing a high percentage of the population to a state where they cannot achieve economic increase.

the British Empire, it could accommodate the subjects of the Empire who sought education and improvement in the motherland. The 'colour problem' as it has come to be called did not arise in imperial times, because most 'participation' was white, and the claims of the backward lands did not achieve any dimension until years later, when (after the Second World War) the empire had finally weakened into commonwealth, and the function of unity was restated in terms of British nationality, and coloured subjects claimed the status that the denizens of the white dominions had been allowed to take for granted.

As a receiver of immigrants, Britain early became aware of limitation. The golden gossamers of Victorian idealism were blown to shreds on the industrial winds that began to howl round the turn of the century. The Aliens Act, and with it the zenophobia that influenced Parliament in its enactment, could be, and was, rationalised as a protection of our internal economic well-being. Over sixty years later that protectionism is still a potential of argument. Here we see an economic purpose obtruding itself among the ideals. With it is the pragmatism of those who hold that the purpose of government is to make the people happy, not to imbue them with ideals.

On a larger scale the pragmatism of governmental purpose gives some rationality to the states which are afraid to give power to their coloured majorities. To Africa and Rhodesia the British Government has assumed an attitude of moral obligation. It is at least arguable that the issue is one of sentiment, not morals, and that the ethics are not clear.

Nevertheless, a great deal of morality arises from sentiment. Whether or not one accepts egalitarianism as a moral desideratum, the social fact must be accepted that many persons, rightly or wrongly, have made some such sentiment into a concept of duty, and feel bound by it.

A further difficulty in ascertaining what are the moral principles which influence our law-makers and our judges is precisely that tolerance which goes with pragmatism. Tolerance, indeed, has respectable antecedents – the freedoms of speech and thought that give meaning to our respect for the human being. Even at a low level, the abolition of varieties of censorship is consistent, as an American jurist has put it, with the adult nature of the people for whom the laws are made.[3]

At the lower level, the pleasure world, including gambling, sex and drink, the world of licence and licensing, is no longer condemned by the sober-minded as the domain of the devil. Modern alchemy has exorcised him.

Let there be added to this the fact that we live in an atmosphere of scepticism as to obligation, and it will appear that specific statements as to the content of a positive morality are not to be uttered dogmatically; i.e. unless the dogma is explicit, and a postulate which its defender will not abandon.

Nevertheless, there is much common content. If, in modern England, the strictures of an Amos, or of a prophet called Isaiah, were pronounced, they would not evoke disagreement, though they might not result in prosecutions. The moral desirability of righteousness, and the undesirability of cruelties, are still present in the atmosphere of thought. On Bible lines, morality quite frequently takes the form of doing what is more than minimal: to go beyond the letter of the law in order to fulfil the spirit, or in order to add a generosity to a propriety. To be charitable is to behave morally, in this positive sense: not to be charitable is not to be immoral in the way that a positive malignant meanness is immoral. Then the axiological gears are 'in neutral'.

This morality of generosity, or, as it has been called, of 'aspiration', is not a morality that is expressed legally, except when the State behaves generously.

Charity is recognised and approved in laws that exonerate charitable funds from taxation, and except conveyances to charity from the operation of the rule against perpetuities.[4] But the citizen in litigation is not asked to perform duties beyond the strict obligation.

Yet even in civil claims, which are, as we have seen, limited in scope, the principle of altruism is not entirely legally irrelevant. When the vehicle driver is called to account for his negligence

---

[3] Mr Justice Cardozo in Butler v Michigan (1957) 352 U.S. 42.

[4] Charity, in these contexts, is strictly defined. The purpose must be benevolent, or educative, or religious, and untainted by political, or social pleasure, purposes.

– which in English law is breach of a quite specific duty to take care – is he called to account to the 'volunteer' who has risked his life, or lost his life, in the saving of somebody who was directly endangered? The obvious defence is *volenti non fit injuria*. But in this century the courts have held that a policeman was entitled to compensation for injuries received while trying to stop a runaway horse and cart.[5] More convincingly, in Videan v B.T.C.[6] the estate of a stationmaster was compensated for his death, caused while trying to save his very young child, notwithstanding that the baby was a trespasser. The baby, however, received no compensation, because he was a trespasser. Therein we see a paradox typical of the common law. The human consideration that a man should not lose by his heroism stands side by side with the inability of the law to extend more protection than is now available to trespassers, even to infant trespassers.[7] An Irish ingenuity (in Cooke v Midland G.W. Railway)[8] which made arguable a doctrine of allurement, for the protection of children who play with turnstiles, etc., has only enjoyed limited success.

The ethical relevance of the laws about trespassers, licensees, invitees, consists in the thought that English law is obsessed with material interest. To whom does an occupier of house and land owe duty, and in what degree? Commonsense (involving a generally accepted moral standard) would put in a claim for a protection of guests. But the word 'invitee', to whom the highest duty is owed, is not the guest, but the person who comes 'on business'.[9] The guest is a mere licensee. Of invitees one 'takes care'. Licensees one warns of concealed dangers. For trespassers one should not 'lay a trap' – and the law as to trespassers has changed little since the abolition of enclosure laws rendered 'trespassers will be prosecuted' into a 'wooden lie'.[10]

[5] Haynes v Harwood [1934] 1 K.B. 146.

[6] [1963] 2 All Eng. R. 860.

[7] Contractors working on land are liable, where owners are not liable. The following cases are relevant. Excelsior Wire Rope v Callan [1930] A.C. 404; Addie v Dumbreck [1929] A.C. 358; A. G. Moulton v Poulter [1930] 2 K.B. 183.   [8] [1909] A.C. 929.

[9] Indermaur v Daimes (1866) L.R. 1 C.P. 274, 2 C.P. 311.

[10] Only since 1861 has it been a crime to set a man-trap or a spring

The present state of the common law as to trespassers does not harmonise with the Occupiers' Liability Act of 1957 which did, at least, extend to licensees most of the protection that the law gives to invitees. Nor does legal 'materialism' of this kind harmonise with the trend to the recognition of human factors in other contests. In point is the recognition of psychological upsets as heads of damage.[11] The law was clearly stated, in 1925, as human enough to award damages for the injury which is the shock caused by peril;[12] and later allowed damages to persons whose shock was caused by distress, as when a hearse was involved in an accident – and horror was added to fear.[13]

Let it be conceded that the common law tries not to be sentimental. The degree of success in this effort is a function of 'period'. Recent cases are suggestive both of movements to sentiment and restraint on sentiment.

In Barnes v Hampshire County Council, [1969] 3 All Eng. R. 746, the court showed its care for children by holding an educational authority liable for injuries to a child who had been let out of school too early to be met by her parent. A heightened awareness, this, made possible by sentiment.

Some humanity is also to be observed in Levine v Morris and Ministry of Transport, [1970] 1 All Eng. R. 144, in which the court held the Ministry liable for damages when a car, negligently driven, went off the road and collided with a massive road sign set up by the Ministry. The court indicated that it is important to take into account the rule that people who are negligent are also entitled to protection.

In contrast, in Gallie v Lee and another [1969] 1 All Eng. R. gun. In this decade a man who set a trap for a burglar was not convicted of any crime. The shooting of burglars is not exactly a right, but is defensible conduct in some circumstances.

[11] Wilkinson v Downton [1897] 2 Q.B. 57 – in which damages were awarded for a breakdown in health caused by a false alarm.

[12] Hambrook v Stokes [1925] 1 K.B. 14.

[13] Owens v Liverpool Corporation [1939] 2 K.B. 394. But that seems to have been disapproved by the Law Lords in Bourhill v Young [1943] A.C. 92. But shock due to the seeing of a killing is a 'head of damage', as recently affirmed in Hinz v Berry [1970] 1 All Eng. R. 1074.

Shock, however, it was emphasised by the Court of Appeal, must be distinguished from grief, for which there are no damages.

1062, where money was imperilled, not life, the court was unsentimental. An old lady, without her spectacles, signed a document which she believed to be a deed of gift (of a house) to her son. Instead, it was an assignment of more than that to a rogue. The formula *non est factum* (this is no deed) was held not to apply. She knew the kind of document she was signing. Therefore it was not void, only voidable: which means that innocent third parties can avail themselves of the benefit of the grant if it has been made over to them. This finding (involving a fine analysis of the law) moves away, let it be said, from altruism.

Altruism may be classified in that section of morals which Professor Fuller has called the 'morals of aspiration'. Paradoxically, the principal claims of municipal law to participate in human aspiration has been made by post-Hegelian state worshippers, whose theology is an idolatry – sometimes described as ideology. We, in England, expect high morality to be displayed, not to the state, but by the state.

On the state is charged the duties, moral, quasi-moral, or social, which we know collectively as justice or fairness. These two concepts (not quite the same) include the belief (1) that persons should be treated equally; (2) that the game of law (and of life) should be played according to the rules. And there are always clients for mercy.

The greatest role in moral aspiration has been conceded to charity. The state is not normally described as a charitable institution, except by those whose theory of the economy calls for economy, or by those who know what a charitable institution is like. Our officials are not authorised to give alms. (Maundy money survives to remind us of older traditions.) Nevertheless, the prerogative of mercy, and the exercise of leniency by the courts, are charities now accepted as normal behaviour on the part of our rulers. Also, even if one assumes that welfare is the right of the citizen (and is not generosity, because it is paid for), yet one expects it to be generously administered. Hence the long and successful campaigns against 'means tests'; and now such a practice as the giving of relief to the dependants of those who forfeit wages by refusing to work. This last is an example of charity in the interpretation of laws.

Also among the aspirations is chastity, a control which is perhaps more valuable in its metaphorical applications than in the literal.

It is doubtful whether the word immorality is properly used as a description of hetero-sexual relations between those who are not inter-espoused. If morality includes honour, and we may assume that it does, then there are sexual relations which are immoral because dishonourable. Dishonourable conduct may consist, not in the informal nature of extra-marital intercourse, but in dishonesties that are practised by one or other of the participants. This is recognised in some of the states of the American union, where a marriage coerced by a false claim of pregnancy can, on that ground, be annulled. When adulteries and fornications are described as dishonourable, they are, in general, correctly so described in so far as they involve breach of agreements that are hard to enforce.

The notion of honourable obligation arising out of fornication, etc., is expressed in English law in the statutes that have made moral obligations of the fornicator into legal obligations, that is to say, in the Bastardy Acts, which enable the mother of an illegitimate to recover maintenance for herself and child from the putative father. (This law is also explicable as a relief to the rates.)

In an idealistic scheme it may, of course, be argued that any sexual intercourse of an informal nature is a betrayal of one's own personality. That is tenable, but only as dogma. Asceticism is similarly dogmatic.[14]

So far as the laws are concerned, it is difficult to extract from them any clear doctrine. Suffice it here to say that much has

---

[14] The argument for hetero-sexual intercourse between the unmarried is not based on mere hedonism. The divorce courts and the criminal courts are replete with evidence of the consequences of marriage in which inexperienced persons become involved. They marry because of sexual appeals which, in their innocence, they overvalue. When incompatibility in other aspects of life reveals itself, there takes place a desperate process of endeavouring to maintain an illusion, a process of self-seduction, which, when it is exhausted, leaves frustrations, cruelties, and much psychological and physical distress in its wake. Against this argument let there be set all the happy marriages between the innocent, all the unhappy ones where there is cynicism.

flowed under the arches since fornication was a crime. Adultery ceased to be criminal when the Ecclesiastical Courts lost their jurisdiction (in 1857), and when the crime of 'criminal conversation' disappeared from among the indictments.

The common lawyers, indeed, took little or no notice of sexual conduct, except as an element in public order. When divorce ceased to be a luxury that the rich could buy (in the form of an Act of Parliament) and became the subject matter of common law, there was manifest a cynicism redolent of the Restoration. A woman could be divorced for adultery – a man only for adultery plus cruelty. Only in 1923 was that inequality rectified. However, by making adultery a ground of divorce the law has at once adopted a moral standpoint (i.e. a standpoint within ethical theory), and may be said to have affected general morality. The divorce jurisdiction stigmatises adultery: and that stigma means that the law does not leave fidelity to private honour. Yet the legal and the honourable, for moral people, run in double harness.

This is manifest in the history of social and Parliamentary process. The Act of 1937 recognised that marriages could break down for reasons other than adultery. Desertion and cruelty and insanity became grounds for divorce. Cruelty was not accepted happily by the courts, which tended at first to require evidence of physical brutality. Later 'mental cruelty' (a Scottish phrase) became recognised, and that, after many years, was allowed to cover the case of a husband whose conduct was mere laziness.[15]

The latest statute abolishes all these refinements and treats a breakdown of marriage as an event in which no guilt is charged. After five years divorce can be claimed as of right.[16]

Apart from divorce law, there is no shortage of statute and case law on matters sexual. These call for special treatment. Suffice it at this stage to say that the legal attitude to sex is much misunderstood because of the failure to realise that many of the laws relate to the need for public order rather than to the desir-

[15] Gollins v Gollins [1962] 3 All Eng. R. 897. For the earlier learning see Jamieson v Jamieson [1952] 1 All Eng. R. 875.
[16] Even in this statute the occurrence of adultery is allowed to facilitate the freeing of the innocent spouse. (Divorce Reform Act, 1969.)

ability of chastity. A brothel is a 'disorderly house', associated now, as it was always, with theft. The prostitute and the importuning catamite are potentials of larceny and general disorder. This is what gives to 'illicit' sex its flavour of illegality. To encourage it would be against public policy.

The law regards as 'against public policy' many contracts. Not all of these are immoral or anti-social. (Indeed a contract has been held unenforceable because its language, making certain financial assessments unchallengeable, purported to oust the jurisdiction of the court.[17]) These include agreements deleterious to the state, or to the public weal (e.g. it is impossible to make an enforceable agreement not to join the army or not to marry). In the list are contracts for illicit cohabitation or ancillary thereto.[18] Also gambling contracts – which, in strange consequence, become matters of 'honour'.

The word honour is applied metaphorically to other contracts than the carnal. In the context of gambling the word is much employed, because, as most gambling contracts are not enforceable in law, there supervenes a sort of confidence in debtors. The word honour is here an over-statement. But the general principles against lying and deceiving are valid at all levels of conduct. There can be morality among the 'low livers'. Whether 'honour among thieves' can be called morality is debatable. Whether it exists is less than debatable.

[17] Re Davstone Estates Ltd. Leases [1963] 2 All Eng. R. 849. The facts of this case are different from those in agreements where the mutual intention is that the obligations shall not be legally enforceable (as in Balfour v Balfour [1918] 2 K.B. 571, a case of an agreement between husband and wife).

[18] Pearce v Brooks (1886) L.R. 1 Ex. 213. This holds unenforceable a contract to pay for a brougham to be used by a lady of 'doubtful virtue'. Followed in Upfill v Wright [1911] 1 K.B. 506. In 1956 in R. v Silver, (unreported) a landlord who charged extra money because of his tenant's immoral use of the premises was prosecuted for living on immoral earnings.

The judge ingeniously found that the earnings were 'his' earnings, not 'hers' – and directed an acquittal. Probably this would not have been done if the learned judge had anticipated the opinions of the Law Lords in Shaw v D.P.P. (see p. 117). It may also be thought that the use of 'morality clauses' as a device for extracting extra rent is a form of blackmail.

FAIRNESS, FREEDOM AND PERSONALITY

Below the level of aspiration, the individual and the state are aware of the notion of fairness. Some aspects of this will be considered in more detail under the heading of justice. At this stage, it is relevant to mention the difficulties that prevent the law from being uniformly fair. Fairness is seen in that principle of law which protects persons against legal surprise. The extreme case of this is retrospective legislation, which is very rarely allowed to be passed. Another aspect: it is fair not to blame the innocent party to a quarrel. On that principle is explicable much civil law: e.g. the notion of prior fault in negligence, made even fairer by the abolition, in 1945, of the doctrine that contributory negligence defeated a claim. (Now the damages are reduced.) Also relevant is nuisance, where he cannot complain who came to the nuisance. On that principle, when ruffians interfered with a Salvation Army parade, and magistrates bound over the Salvationists to keep the peace, the Queen's Bench overruled the order.[19] Similarly in Wise v Dunning[20] it was held wrong for Protestants to provoke Catholics with their parades through Catholic districts. But when a great Suffragist appeared before the Court of Appeal, the Lords Justices, without finding him guilty of provocation, yet held it right for his processions to be prevented. Since then (Lansbury v Riley[21]) expediency has gently obtruded morality from magisterial minds.[22]

In 'fairness' we approach valuable, if vague, concepts, such as equality.

[19] Beaty v Gillbanks (1882) 9 Q.B.D. 308.

[20] [1902] 1 K.B. 167. Consistent with the holding by many judges in homicide cases that there is a limit to the duty to retreat in order to avoid violence. The directing of juries on this topic is difficult. (R. v Julien [1969] 2 All Eng. R. 856).   [21] [1914] 3 K.B. 229.

[22] Comparable is the problem of picketing. After the prosperous rulers of 1875 had decided that the right to strike was fair, and after the legislators of 1906 had protected trade unions funds from civil litigation (a unique privilege this), it still remained doubtful to what extent pressure could fairly be brought against the non-striker. He must not be touched, nor his tools stolen. He must not be 'watched and beset'. But the Act of 1906 allows persons to attend on him with a view to 'communicating' and 'peacefully persuading'.

Is it fair that there should be one law for the rich and one for the poor? In recent years that question was raised in a narrow context. Was it fair to penalise street betting, available to the needy, whereas credit accounts were available, and lawful, for the rich and greedy? The collectivists, whose thinking echoes the paternalism that existed before the triumph of individualism, would find a paternalist answer, even while pragmatically allowing betting shops to come into being. But the prior question 'is it fair that there should be poverty?' is one that the law cannot answer. 'The poor ye have always with you.' Legislators cannot abolish poverty, though they can reduce privilege. Legal development, alongside an increase in the area of distribution of wealth, has eliminated many of the privileges which *de facto* were enjoyed by the rich. In Britain, now, a poor man can afford to be ill. He can also afford to assert his rights when he is wronged. Divorce is no longer a luxury in the form of an expensive Parliamentary process. Moreover, the ordinary petition is available to the poor. This, with other litigation, has been brought within the reach of all classes by the development, in this century, of legal aid. The Gallic sarcasm that England is egalitarian in that the millionaire who steals a loaf of bread is equally punishable with the pauper loses some of its sting when it is pointed out that both of them can now afford good defence when they are charged.[23] The British complaint is that an unfairness is left to be suffered, not by the poor, but by those classes, which, short of rich, are not sufficiently poor to be allowed the benefits of state-aided litigation.

Of equality and liberty, which are so emphasised among lawyers and laity alike, it is no longer arguable as to whether these are describable as moral ideas. In Entick v Carrington ((1765) 19 State Trials) moral attributes are attached to freedom from interference, to property, privacy, and the absence of privilege from the law. These principles are embodied in the American Constitution and Bill of Rights. Certainly they are values, at whatever level; and they justify, in this context, an inquiry into their legal framework.

[23] The English judge's observation that justice is free to all, as is the Ritz Hotel, is not yet met by the quality of Legal Aid.

Compendiously, freedom, as recognised by law, is describable in two main ways. Freedom is freedom from interference with the body and property of any person except through the proper operation of law. It follows that a person is free to behave in any manner which does not conflict with laws. A second mode of statement is that the law recognises that a person is free, within the law, and from the law. When the arm of the law interferes with the individual, the onus is on the officers of the law to demonstrate the claim of the state against the body or property of him with whom they seek to interfere.[24] At one level, the level of prosecution for crime, the law, as we shall see, offers protection to the accused person against itself. In case the Briton lays a flattering unction to his soul, that our common law has evidently been a moral law, let it be explained that in the past the common law was a very cruel instrument. In order to protect prisoners against the severity of the penalties that conviction would entail, the presiding lawyers legislated (judicially) into being a number of protections; a severe pedantry as to the language of charges; and considerable restrictions on the evidence that could be adduced against the accused – notably that his character was never allowed to be known to the petty jury.

That the prisoner was not called upon to give evidence was not a charitably motivated rule. The theory was that his evidence was suspect. For this theory the biblical system lent authority. Evidence was by witnesses other than the parties. In crime there is only one party; in civil litigation there are two. Civil parties, until the 1850s, were not allowed to give evidence.[25] Not until 1885 (Criminal Law Amendment Act – a 'sexual' statute) could a person accused of crime testify. Under that Act Oscar Wilde was prosecuted, and gave evidence, in 1896. Not until 1898, however, was the witness-box laid open to the generality of accused persons. When this was done, there was dismay among counsel, who could no longer say to the jury, in heart-wringing tones: 'my

[24] In Leachinsky v Christie [1947] 1 All Eng. R. 567, a Law Lord treated informality in arrest as inconsistent with our antagonism to slavery.

[25] Hence the absence from the witness box of those most desirable sources of testimony, Mrs Bardell and Mr Pickwick.

client stands mute. If he were able to speak what might he not tell you that would shed revealing and exonerating light. . . .' Indeed it was not until fifty years had passed that a prisoner was protected expressly by the bench (Devlin J. as he then was, in R v Adams) from the drawing of adverse conclusions from his failure to give evidence. Compendiously, by reason of protections that were proper when the law was severe, miscreants benefit now from protections against an altogether more lenient jurisdiction. The forces that saved his predecessors from the gallows now operate to save him from the fierce probation officer.

These matters are for other chapters. Meanwhile, questions are asked on the following lines. Granted that a person who commits crime is vested with protections in the form of freedom from the necessity of self-expression, what of the relatively law-abiding?

Is his house his castle, which can be broken (lawfully) by the minions of gas and electricity companies and water boards? and who needs a dozen permits before he can build a garage, and who may find his castle 'compulsorily purchased' for trivial compensation? Is he free who is not allowed to burn coal in his grate, to say nothing of emitting smoke from his chimneys? Is this the liberty for which Britons executed a King, and for which a drunken continental poet composed a broken-backed marching-song? Or which our own Wordsworth matinated in the hills and valleys of his lakeland?

The answer is that when a Briton thinks of freedom he does not think of untrammelled scope for self-expression. Admittedly, few in these islands would be content with the philosophic notion of freedom as an awareness of, and reconciliation to, restriction, which is the thinking that reconciles the citizens of slave-states to their servitude.

Conceding that some such philosophy may be called for, as consolation, to the private in the army, from the majority of the citizens no such intellectual effort is required. The Anglo-Saxon tradition is to protest against proximate impositions. When Patrick Henry said: 'Give me liberty or give me death' he was not expressing an heroic dedication to the schools of anarchy. He was more concerned with a rise in the price of tea, which indicated that somebody else was 'taking a liberty'.

Although we have had our revolutions (and those the most successful in the history of political upheavals) the issues have been practicalities – like taxation. Britons have not sacrificed their lives for abstract notions, for a 'freedom whose banner torn but flying streams like a meteor against the wind'. Nor have they asked anything of the mountains except privacy.

What excites the Englander is the proving to him that someone is enjoying a right that he himself is lacking. In other words, when he says freedom he means equality. In turn, when he says equality, he is not asking to be equal with all others as atoms are equal. Equality means an equal claim to the protections and the privileges that the law affords – in other words an equal degree of freedom. Succinctly, that 'equal freedom' – a very simple, but also a very sophisticated, notion – is the social demand, and the social value, that the legislators, parliamentary and judicial, have for long been called upon to provide.

In Britain few persons are restrained from expressing themselves freely, whether in public or private. Soldiers in service, by their status, and civil servants, by a sort of contract, are inhibited from political utterance. But any other restriction derives mainly from statutes, which are calculated to preserve public order, not to preserve the 'established order'. Relevant are statutes of the Lancastrians which enable justices of the peace to take steps to inhibit an incipient breach of the peace.

There is some common law, never invoked now, which treats as conspiracy, or as public nuisance, meetings convened for the purpose of rousing one section of the community against another.

In this century the practical law has been constituted by the Public Order Act 1936, directed against Fascist parades, and which enables police to close streets to processions. Also relevant are the laws as to 'peaceful picketing'.

There have been times (as recent as last century) when it could be said that the law was organised to protect the rich against the poor. Peterloo is the calendered example. This is no longer the case: and restrictions can fairly be classified as protective of order for everyone.

Incitement to Dissaffection of the Armed Forces is special law, cognate to the laws against treason, and to the protective laws (such as laws against the spread of alarm and despondency) which are enacted during wars. The observer of British life may find it quite remarkable that, in a highly regulated collectivist system such as ours, there has been little regimentation, and little propaganda to that end. Fascism, the vertical axis, as it were, of many socialist systems, has made little appeal. Perhaps it was British humour which disposed of the sanculottism of the variegated shirt. For the rest, the law seems to succeed in protecting the peaceful demonstrator against bullies (especially 'regimented' bullies) who try to shout him down and violently suppress him.

That, briefly, is what is meant by freedom of speech.

Of privileges, it may safely be said as a general proposition that no individuals enjoy protection from the law that others lack.[26] If we find a lack of right, usually there is an adequate explanation. Thus there are persons deprived of rights through their crimes. Prisoners constitute this class, though they continue to be able to litigate. Idiots and lunatics do not suffer loss of rights, even when they are confined to institutions, but their rights are maintained for them by custodians, by the commissioners in lunacy or by the public trustee.[27] Minors in the nature of things

[26] The last important privileges are those which inhere in the peerage. Thus it was a privilege (literally, private law) that a peer could only be tried for felony by his 'peers' (equals) in the House of Lords. He had a very large jury. Motor killing was the occasion of the last trial there, impeccably conducted, before the privilege was abolished in 1936.

It must also be called privilege that the male heir of a peerage acquires a seat in the legislature. The merits, or defects, of this tradition are observed by the wider debate as the need for a second chamber.

Most psephologists would agree that there should be a function of stability to deprive of ill effect the violent swings of the popular vote.

The Roman Senate was a better, and longer lasting, institution than the comitiae. In the British system it is accepted that the standard of debating in the upper chamber is higher than in the lower. But there is little opinion now in favour of the birth qualification. When, recently, Parliament enacted a right for a lord to abandon his peerage, some distinguished peers availed themselves of the right and now sit in the Commons.

As to Bishops, some of whom sit among the Lords, let it be said that their presence, in fact if not in theory, is due to a qualification better than birth. It is not easy to become a Bishop!

[27] The legal dangers of unnecessary certification and overlong confinement do, however, persist.

do not acquire full legal responsibility until they lose their minority, but, at least during the years of discretion (thirteen to eighteen), they can carry on business and make contracts for their benefit, and be bound by them.

'The widow, and the orphan', says the scriptor.

There is an equitable tradition in England enabling the court to look after orphans, who, in the past, if they were rich enough, became wards of court. That protection is now known to be available to all minors, and they can be put, even by their parents, into the tutelage of the judges. This can be done in order to prevent an elopement.

The criticism was as to the age limits. Since men can be conscripted at eighteen in order to fight, it was argued that twenty-one is too high an age for the termination of minority. That argument has been accepted, and eighteen is now the age of majority.

But the task of protection of orphans is submerged now in an immense welfare organisation, created in part by the Guardianship of Infants Act 1926, and the Children & Young Persons Act 1933 etc. which endeavour to cope with the problems of ill-cared for children. In an emergency, County and Borough Councils may assume the custody, and arrange for their accommodation with foster parents.

Widows were strengthened by the enactments which created and developed the right to compensation for a husband's death;[28] and they benefit as all women do from the Married Women's Property Act 1882, which enabled them to claim, even before the death of a husband, the protection of the court for their separate property. By that Act a wife can sue a husband, even in tort, where her property is concerned. Before that Act only rich women whose parents had made settlements (strengthened usually, by restraint on anticipation) could enjoy wealth of their own.

That Act has been said not to be a Married Man's Relief Act, for it did not rescue the husband from liability for his wife's torts. That was not done until 1934. Even after that it was the husband who was at legal disadvantage. He must pay her income tax. She might pledge his credit for necessities. In no case could

[28] A technical difficulty is due to the Statute of Limitations 1963. Lucy v W. T. Henley's Ltd. [1969] 3 All Eng. R. 456.

he sue his wife in tort. Yet she could sue him, as we have seen, in order to protect her property, also, exceptionally, for damage done to her before marriage.[29] (The position is altered now by a Law Reform Act of 1962, which almost gives spouses a normal position in litigation.) Women, for long, were lacking in full legal status – lost their property to their husbands, could not vote, etc. Of women it is now true to say that they are only at an economic disadvantage. Their complaint, a legitimate one, is that, as married women, they earn no salary, and do not earn a share in their husband's property. The 'housekeeping money' is the husband's money; so their savings out of it belong to him. In compensation they acquire widow's pensions – and for men there are no widower's pensions – but even these are not perfectly distributed. If a woman is under fifty at the husband's death, she acquires no pension. Also she suffers some disadvantage in the very complex taxation of joint income. But, generally, it may be said that women's disadvantages are in a class of economic shortcomings. The woman suffers when she is without assets, and because employers will not pay her as well as men are paid. On the whole her problems are not legal ones, but matters for economic negotiation.

In general the common law does not pretend to compensate the poor for their poverty. The poor man suffers little lack of privilege. He can vote – Gladstone and Disraeli between them abolished the lingering property qualifications. A non rate-payer will not be called to jury service. That lack of duty is not generally regarded as a serious social handicap. In addition to the common law of status, positive legislation has provided protections against the extremes of poverty. In one direction at least poverty has lost its worst feature. No one in Britain is lacking in medical care or treatment in sickness for want of money. Nor is their treatment of 'workhouse' standard. In this respect Britain offers to its resident what no other nation offers.

Thus it is clear that Britain boasts a high standard of 'fairness'. Departures from this standard are 'unfair' – 'unjust' – are favouritisms; are failures to play the legal game according to the

[29] Curtis v Wilcox [1948] 2 K.B. 474. An accrued right to damages for injuries incurred in a car accident is part of her property.

rules. If there is a properly called 'moral' element in their applications, it may be described as the demand for 'conscientiousness'. This word tells us something semantically important.

There are two aspects of morality. One aspect is the use of the word to describe objective rules; be honest, chaste, etc.

Another aspect is described when we speak of the spirit in which deeds are done. Perhaps this latter sense is one in which law can never be said completely to absorb morality. For, given obedience, the law is satisfied. There is then no legal need for inquiry as to the spirit of the obedience.[30]

Yet lawyers know the question not to be entirely irrelevant. At least one church schism expresses the difference of belief of those (Augustinians) who held duty to be of obedience to the laws, and the other (Pelagians) who saw virtue in the purity and strength of the will, whether in obedience to the laws or outside the laws. That distinction is appropriately mentioned here, because conscience has been a topic in English law. We see it, without recognising the relevance, when the oath is taken. More clearly, we saw it when the state set up tribunals to investigate the state of mind of conscientious objectors. Always the court insisted on the formal activity of conscience rather than on the content, in the shape of doctrines believed. Thus the fact that a man was a Marxist would be irrelevant. If a pacifist, then was it on the grounds of some doctrine such as Marxism, according to which the conflicts between nations are unimportant, or was it a conscientious objection to the spilling of human blood, in whatever cause?

This is perhaps the only case, since the abolition of religious tests in Britain, when the subtler issue of morality has come before the courts.

Apart from this, the relevance to the law of the conscience of the people is that the law does accept, even if it does not enforce, the moral principles of the people.

It accepts, for example, the value of truth; and that explains the absence of censorship.[31] All of us refine the duty of truth

---

[30] Note, however, the later discussed standards of obedience on the part of fiduciaries.

[31] That is to say, restrictions on the publication of truth. Restrictions on pornography are controls of conduct not of information.

telling when we consider that, for humane reasons, truth, though great, should not be allowed to prevail; or when, being trivial it should be forgotten. Better to deceive in the interests of peace, of human comfort, human life. There moral purposes are in apparent opposition, but situations are usually malleable enough for an intelligent man to be able to harmonise duties. Truth gives way, perhaps, to other values. One of these is discretion. This is particularly important to the legal profession, which could not function unless it had a duty not to reveal the truth.

But tyranny goes further and, pretending benevolence, advises concealment of the truth from the people. Facts, says the totalitarian, are misleading. Let our people wait till the total event has crystallised, and the fact is revealed in its proper perspective; and let us wait, also, for the recipient to be educated enough, sophisticated enough, not to be intellectually disorganised by difficult communications which corrupt morals as they traditionally corrupt manners. Here, at the hands of the state, moral values are twisted into the shapes of cynicism.[32]

To revert to the individual, a moral man recognises that rules should not be stated with rigidity, yet they should be stern and binding where there is no moral conflict. A moral man tells the truth to his own detriment, and does not speculate that the expediency of improving his livelihood may transmute untruthfulness into moral conduct if it enables him (after his lie) to increase the prosperity and comfort of his wife and children. That way materialism lies.[33]

[32] In Britain the government may conceal, may influence the press to conceal, but will not misstate. Even concealment is regarded as exceptional, because every government wishes to avoid the appearance of deceiving the people.

The concealments required by the Official Secrets Acts are in a different category from the ordinary topics of politics. This is not censorship.

Similarly, where defence secrets are in evidence, our courts will sit otherwise than with open doors.

[33] Truth is undervalued, also, by some who are not materialists. Thus Sir Frederick Pollock tells us of eminent Hindus who failed to appreciate the British rule of the acceptability of dying declarations. 'Why should a dying man tell the truth?'

If there is an imperative it is categorical. The difficulty is to know what is imperative.

There is no catalogue of traditional morals: and there is (as we have seen) evidence that the 'content' of morality changes. But some acceptances seem world-wide in the civilised world, and long-enduring in time.

A moral person is a responsible person, and 'responsibility' is, with few exceptions, the criterion of legal liability. There are exceptions in the 'absolute liability' cases which are discussed elsewhere in this book. They are explicable. Psychological states in which there is no responsibility (automatism) are exonerative of guilt. Diminished responsibility diminishes guilt.

For those of sound mind, the standard has been thought exacting. For long it was the law that if a homicide was done by one of many men engaged jointly in a crime, all were guilty, notwithstanding that evidence did not point to any particular member of the group. That law seemed to disappear – and, twenty years ago at Assizes, was found, in the Hanging Boy case (unreported), to have become obsolete. Nevertheless the standard of responsibility remained reasonably high.

Men were judged to be responsible for consequences which they were not proved to have anticipated, but which they ought to have anticipated. In consequence of some not very clear opinions of the Law Lords in Smith v D.P.P.[34] the legislature decided to alter the law. By Sec. 8 of the Criminal Justice Act 1967 'a jury shall not be bound in law to infer that he intended or foresaw a result of his actions by reason only of its being a reasonable and probable consequence of those actions, but shall decide whether he did intend or foresee that result by reference to all the evidence, drawing such inferences from the evidence as appear proper in the circumstances.'

Other 'human' aspects of the human being are also relevant to morality and to the law.

A moral person is loth to do a mean or cruel, or oppressive act (these expressions may well be invariants) even for an end which

[34] [1960] 3 All Eng. R. 161. A case in which the driver of a car drove on, with a policeman clinging to the front of his car, and so causing injuries from which the policeman died.

is noble. He holds that (*exceptis excipiendis*) the end does not justify the means. One does not steal for charitable purposes. If one respects human personality, one does not humiliate, bully, deceive, cozen, or cheat an individual because the person in question is behaving erroneously, and it would be a benefit were he thwarted. The end would have to be of an intense moral importance, and the dangers of general moral degradation great indeed, before there is justification for the thrusting of a person ruthlessly aside in order to secure efficiency or the rule of wisdom.

Perhaps this is one aspect of a conscientious attitude. Morality seems to be best understood by those who relate it (as Bishop Butler did in the eighteenth century) to conscience. Conscience is independent of interest, but is not anarchic. It is guided by the rules in which it has, in each particular case, been trained. These rules vary from generation to generation, but tend, in the long run, to express what we call the humane.

If men of conscience seemed cruel once, they tend now to regard any motive that can be called cruel as unconscientious.

From the legal end, cruelty has long been disapproved by the law; but it was long before those cruelties which claimed justification, were finally repudiated.

Thus the paterfamilias of the nineteenth century, even after wife-beating had ceased to be regarded as legal,[35] could behave with an oppressiveness which would now be recognised as cruelty by the divorce court.

Similarly the chastisement of children, recommended by one of the crueller sections of the Bible, can, when excessively carried out by parent or teacher, be prosecuted. (The problem now is the protection of the teacher.)

Logically, this leads to the proposition that a democratic state protects the dignity of human beings, and values human life. But that last value – to some the ultimate value – involves thinking that justifies separate treatment.

Postponing that, we should, nevertheless, be now in a position to consider some results of this excursus. What is a moral law as

[35] Blackstone's statement of the right to beat a wife with a stick not thicker than one's thumb was not officially overruled until 1891.

such, and how does it differ from, how is it related to, our municipal law?

Definitions remain difficult, but some relationships are clear. We have seen that the state, with its laws, participates in our morality, and our morality expresses itself, however slowly, however indirectly, in the laws that are the operations of the state. So a municipal law can coincide with a moral law.

Against this synthesis, it must be apparent that however man (the state writ small), is involved with the state (which is man writ large) their purposes are not identical; their range is not identical. The state does not consist of the total of persons in it and their total sphere of activity. It is as true now, when the state provides for people, as it was in the days when the state exploited people, that a one way control moves from the state to the citizen. Even when the government has accepted the citizen's valuations – and it is, of course, impossible for the government to adopt all the conflicting valuations of the citizens – the function of authority remains, to rule, and enforce the rule. Morals may help men to keep the law, but the law is binding in itself.

Law, then, whatever be its definition, moves from outside the citizen's domain into it. The citizen's behaviour, in his domain, is in smaller scope, is self-centred. Moral action is, admittedly, a type of action that the state can perform. But at that stage a metaphor is discernible. The notion of the state's morality is based on the notion of the citizen's morality; is, in so far as it is real, derived from the citizen.

Let it then be suggested. Law is a frame for social coherence, and that coherence makes it real. A man behaves legally when he acts out of respect for society; for the state, or any order of rules (e.g. religious) in which he is involved. Morality (whether participant in the social frame or not) is a framework for personality. A set of standards to be achieved; not a pattern of indulgence. A man acts morally when he acts out of respect for himself. When that notion of self-respect is analysed, the differences may come to be restated, for a person cannot respect himself if he does not respect others, if he does not respect some values which his friends and neighbours share; for, psychologically, he is part of the people among whom he spiritually lives.

5

Recent Dialogues

THE FIELD OF CONTENTION

Between law and morals there should be no conflict. Theoretically an exponent of hermitry can exclude himself from society and its laws. Equally, a legal system, pagan or materialistic, can outlaw morality, though efforts in this direction have been limited to campaigns against religion.[1] In civilised practice we have found that the two orders run in parallel, and in accordance with a harmony, but are not coextensive. There are laws which seem morally irrelevant; and there are moral purposes which are not affected by the law as it stands. Of the two orders at the practical level the moral is the more inclusive, because ethically minded people include in their moral duties the duty of obedience to the laws of the land in which they live. 'The law of the land is your law', pronounced a Rabbi of the Roman period, 'for were it not for the kingdom, men would devour each other alive'. That same tradition (and not, as some hold, an ascetic indifference) explains the dictum of Jesus (in Matthew XXII): render under Caesar the things that are Caesar's.[2]

The law offers no substitute for the higher purposes of ethics. Nor would the order of moral persons claim to be able to dispense with a secular system of laws. The impossibility of a substitution of morals for law was demonstrated in a strange context. The Russian revolutionaries of 1917 included many theorists, on whose

[1] From the Papal standpoint the English law Praemunire and the Act of Supremacy are such laws.

[2] The second half of the passage, be it respectfully said, should not be treated as a contrast. The duties to God must include the duties to man.

advice they abolished the entire corpus of Russian law. For Lenin, law was the otiose superstructure of a propertied capitalism. Once private property was abolished in essentials, the rulings that were to be obeyed would be the intuitive findings of the leaders of the proletariat. A proletarian, and empirical, ethics would render a legal system of the old type unnecessary. By 1923, supervening chaos had demonstrated the inadequacy of this ethical system, or absence of system; therefore Russia restored to itself a legal system which bore, and still bears, a superficial resemblance to Western codes. The differences consist in the immanent moralities.

In bodies of law which have grown in morally conscious societies, the two sets of rules of obedience run, as was said above, in double harness. Law drills into the many what otherwise might be the habits of the few.

In a practical way, moreover, the law relieves the burden of some moral duties. State charity takes away some of the burden that was morally upon the less poor to help the poorer. (Very great wealth is also exonerative!) In some systems supports are given to morality which other systems do not provide. So the Roman law contained provisions punitive, directly or indirectly, of ingratitude (on the part of children and freedmen). Our law relieves, in great degree, the duty of parents to educate their children, and makes child maintenance easier. In these and other ways the law assists in the living of the good life. Complementarily, ethics includes not only its own rules, not only rules similar to, or parallel to, municipal laws, but principles as to the mode of obedience. The moral man obeys the law even when he can evade it. So Socrates refused to avail himself of the chances of escape offered to him by his well wishers. Moral is the volunteer who does not await compulsion, does not avail himself of devices, however legitimate, which would exclude him from the class of conscripts. Moral is the person who prefers not to avail himself of a technicality.[3] At a lower level, there is a certain morality in

[3] Interesting is the case of Spencer v Hemmerde (1922) 2 A.C. 507. The defendant (eminent counsel) had borrowed money from a person who probably intended the loan to be a gift. But when the creditor died, his executors sued for the amount owing. On the advice of even more eminent counsel, the defendant pleaded the Statute of Limitations, and

the person who insists on paying his fare before descending from the vehicle; who will not take advantage of confusions and congestions in queues; who is, in a word, more strictly law-abiding than circumstances compel him to be. Even in the non-moral atmosphere of taxation, he will defend, but will not 'evade', for he sees no difference between outwitting the community and outwitting a simple citizen.

If, then, the lawyer and the moralist are enjoying a happy symbiosis, what is the motive in the agitation for the omission of moral rules from the law. The answer – like any treatment of an obsession – entails clarification. First, the context is sex, which, as was said previously, is not a monopolist of morality, nor, indeed, dominant in the moral constitution of the honest, the charitable, the strong minded, the good citizen, *integer vitae scelerisque purus*.

Secondly, the agitation is not truly expressed in the terms: 'You, the state, abstain from your powers and leave obedience to moral authority'. The agitator is one who wishes to extrude the discipline from the moral order as well.

The agitator of this type has been called (inaccurately) a sinner. In the better description, he is a heretic as to a whole body of doctrine. Perhaps his heresy is justified. But let not his purpose be disguised. He requires that freedom shall be granted for certain modes of conduct: and the emancipation is not from the law alone, but from the law and from morality. His clamour is only against the law, because only the law exercises the material sanctions that prevent him from enjoying, or obtaining for others, a total freedom.

Heretics of this class lay claim to a good tradition. Historic is Milton's campaign against the censorship, which that great poet and thinker held to be something morally weak – making only for a cloistered and fugitive virtue – as well as undesirable

---

up to a point that defence prevailed. In the Court of Appeal he was rebuked for (in effect) unethical conduct. Ironically, in the House of Lords, his defence failed because of a document which was held to be an admission of liability within the statutory period. The result was destructive of the career of the author of *Butterfly on the Wheel*. There are those who say that he ought to have known better. *Scilicet*, the law.

policy. But in this century the clarity of Milton is lacking: and other theories have been invoked. Consequently, since the 1890s, when the misfortunes of a much lesser poet caused many to think that the laws of England were unduly severe to homosexuals, a campaign has been waged, not, openly, for the desirability of total freedom (though the homosexual asks for this), but for the prohibition of this practice to be expunged from the rolls of the law. The intellectual authority of Bentham and Mill is invoked, and that ineptly, because these were more concerned with religious freedom, at a time when the law was oppressive of some religions. Those philosophers possibly over-stated their case. It is not desirable that the law shall be indifferent to religion. The law is, after all, required to protect religious groups from oppression; to protect their buildings from sacrilege. What the law should not include is a prohibition of free expression, within the decencies, of all creeds, of all attitudes to religion, including the extreme negative. One does not ask that the law shall be an atheist.

It is of interest to contrast the English system, in which 'an act of worship' is part of the curricula of all state schools, and the American system, in which this is prohibited. The American prohibition is motivated by tolerance of a variety of creeds. (What is apparently important in U.S.A. is for children matutinally to salute the flag. Britain makes no such demand.)

This 'tolerance' has strange consequences. By the 1st Amendment 'Congress shall make no law respecting an establishment of religion or prohibiting the free exercise thereof'. It has followed that, though the land is full of 'provided' schools, set up by religious denominations, it would probably be *ultra vires* for any State of the Union to establish such a school. How then can grants be made (as they are) to pay teachers, provide books, etc? The Supreme Court has been ingenious. This kind of aid is not for the benefit of religions but for the benefit of pupils. That benefit is constitutional.[4] Campaigns for freedom of religion have been serious, but their need disappeared a century ago when

---

[4] See Everson v Bd. of Education 330 U.S. (1947) and Bd. of Education v Allen 392 U.S. (1968).

Similar reasoning has enabled people to benefit from taxation allowances where donations are made to religious charities.

Catholic institutions were freed of restriction, when Rothschild was able to take a Parliamentary oath, and when restrictions, in the way of oaths, were removed from Oxford and Cambridge. Modern universities are obsessed, be it added, with different freedoms.

The agitations for the reform of the laws relating to sex are differently conceived. They are abolitionist, and are, properly, to be compared with agitations against compulsory vaccination and similar 'interferences' with individuals. Just as vaccination has public implications, so has sexual morality. That this nation regards sexual life as of public importance is evidenced by the unhappy Windsor affair, when the ethics of public men conflicted with their loyalties to the wearer of the crown.

In contrast to the 'conventional' attitude, the agitations for sexual freedom have, throughout, been abolitionist both in the legal and moral orders. The process of divorce reform has been, not a reference back of legal duties to the moral consciousness, but a response to a demand to relieve the human being of certain duties: the demand, for example, that a spouse shall not be tied to a partner he or she no longer loves; that the promise 'till death do us part' be remitted. The advocates of these reforms do not propose that a moral duty shall 'take over' from the law. The duties in question are thought by many to be morally unjustified; therefore they seek the abdication by the law of some of its protections of convention, and its preservation of social embarrassments.[5] A similar propaganda has been active as to the laws relating to a number of other vices.

In fine, what the legal attitude to sex 'should be' is a moral question, and a social question at the level of public order. No answer (at either level) is tendered here. Suffice it only to say, first, that simple distinctions, between the public domain and the private domain, are not valid, because they do not correctly describe the function of morality in the law; secondly, that nevertheless, a strong case can be made for modification of, at least,

[5] In our day people deplore the fate of men like Parnell and Dilke who lost their political futures because of their involvement in sexual affairs. More recently, it is not known whether the text of the Macmillan Bible was altered from *de Profundis* to *de Profumis*.

the criminal law, in which some sexual offenders, non-violent and not dangerous, are imprisoned together with killers, thieves, and all the classes of recidivist.

SIN ON THE THRESHOLD

The topicality for contemporary England may be said to have begun with an epigram. In 1957 the Wolfenden Committee[6] gave communication value to its thinking by presenting, in simple appearing antithesis, an interesting 'confrontation' between the orders of crime and sin.

'Unless,' the Committee said, 'a deliberate attempt is to be made by society, acting through the agency of the law, to equate the sphere of crime with that of sin, there must remain a realm of private morality and immorality which is, in brief and crude terms, not the law's business. To say this,' the Committee added cautiously, 'is not to condone or encourage private immorality.'

This compendious pronouncement, redolent of semantics and philosophy, has caused the stones to cry out from the walls of the law courts, and the beams of jurisprudence to reply.[7] But while the doctors have disagreed, a process of influence – even of causation – is manifest in modern legislation. For (apart from trends in mitigation of 'sin') the Wolfenden Report (enjoying more rapid fulfilment than is normal for Committees and Commissions) has been a major factor in the enactment ten years later of a statute which has pronounced homosexual practices conducted in private between consenting adult males no longer to be criminal (Sexual Offences Act, 1967).

This statute is consistent with, but not necessitated by, the

[6] On Homosexual Offences and Prostitution. 1957. Cmd. 347.

[7] In point are (*inter alia*) Lord Devlin's *Enforcement of Morals*, and some lectures by Professor Hart (*Law Liberty and Morality*, and *The Morality of the Criminal Law*). Of books on the topic written recently, but before the Wolfenden Report, very important are Professor Goodhart's Hamlyn Lectures (*English Law and Moral Law*) and a parallel set of lectures by Sir Alfred Denning, as he then was (*Freedom under the Law*.) Formal theories are well discussed in Professor Hart's *Concept of Law*.

Wolfenden conception of the proper function of the criminal law, viz.: 'to preserve public order and decency, to protect the citizen from what is offensive or injurious, and to provide sufficient safeguards against exploitation and corruption of others, particularly those who are young, weak in body or mind, inexperienced, or in a state of special physical, official or economic dependence'.

This description of the function of the criminal law justifies some digression and anticipation of later argument. Certainly the criminal law serves the purpose described: but this, however 'public', is a moral purpose, as well as a social or political one. We shall see, further, that the criminal law is hardly definable without reference to the indignation that bad conduct evokes, or the retribution which it entails. This bad conduct cannot be described as 'public' rather than 'private' because no barrier can be erected between the two realms. Husbands ill-treating wives, parents ill-treating children, wrongful carnalities, frauds within families, destruction of wills, etc., these can all take place within an apparently private domain, but they are not less public in their mischief than is a murder committed in the dark.

On the subject of privacy there is much confusion. We know that there is, in a sense, a margin of privacy, by reason of the limited scope of government. The state does not exhaust society. Nor do religious systems claim an all-embracing control. Much that a man does is legally irrelevant, and, in that sense, not of public interest. We know also that there are aspects of life which the law does not protect. Privacy can be infringed by malicious persons by words and writings which, for one reason or another, do not fall within the category of provable defamation. But within that same private realm there are interferences which the law can prevent or penalise. The concept of privacy is, then, evidently a very loose one, and insufficiently exact to assist in any description of morality. Moral and immoral conduct may take place behind closed doors; but what conduct behind closed doors can fail to have repercussions outside the house?

Moreover, even if a person could describe accurately his margin of privacy, what conduct or thought takes place within it which is not determined by his relation to the external world? His thoughts, his behaviour, are the products of his environment;

of the thoughts, the customs, of the laws manifest in the society in which he lives. His mind built of those bricks: or, as a famous cleric expressed it, 'no man is an island.'

All that can be conceded to the advocates of a distinction between a private moral realm and a public legal realm (and be it noted that the Wolfenden advice is not dependent on so explicit a distinction) is that the law does not interfere in many matters, public and private, which moralists regard as important. So the state is more concerned to suppress brothels, which are relatively public, than to penetrate into private houses; and, similarly, more concerned to suppress gaming houses than to prevent gambling.

Before laws of this type are discussed at length, it requires to be said that the Wolfenden epigram is unfortunate for some other reasons. First, it suggests the compresence of two static sets of rules, which can be treated in isolation from each other. That is not a true account of the long-growing, historically-changing English law, nor of the Judaeo–Christian religious system which suffuses it, and which also grows and changes. Secondly, it is dogmatic in the assumption that, in a proper use of words, we can equate 'sin' with the allegedly non-criminal manifestations of a private sexual immorality.[8] There are many who hold that sin connotes more serious misconduct than those misbehaviours that the report would call 'merely immoral'. There are those who would describe as sin (and as a high degree of immorality, public and private) all the greatest betrayals and slayings condemned in the Scriptures (Hast thou murdered, and also inherited?)[9] to say nothing of those modern holocausts unimagined of the Scriptors. Yet are these not crimes? (Even across the borders of nations, they have been so held.) To persons who think and believe in terms of conscience, whether religiously or humanistically, whether in a Pelaggian way, or as the disciplined instrument of

---

[8] The Wolfenden text becomes more reasonable if the word 'vice' is substituted for 'sin'. The word vice can, indeed, describe very bad conduct. The word 'vicious' is usually very pejorative. But 'vice' also includes the 'bad habit', as when we say that smoking is a vice, that gambling is a vice, etc. There are no religious systems known to the author which extend commination to all the weaknesses of the flesh.

[9] Elijah to Ahab.

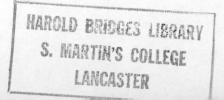

articulated authority, the criminal who wreaks murder, mayhem or rape is laden with a guilt which can properly be called sin.

Certainly, it would be absurd to equate crime (in general) with sin, if only because trivialities irrelevant to conscience – or moral laws, whatever they are – can be crime. The criminal law is disciplinary in relative trivialities, as well as retributive in the graver issues. Offences against Highways Acts and Vagrancy Acts are legal misdemeanours only. Parking a vehicle among city traffic can rarely have endangered an immortal soul. (One distinguished the legal parking that takes place on a campus!) Among the more serious offences, negligences of a criminal degree are not always sinful. But there can be little doubt that, for anyone who does not accept a rather naïve positivism, there are forms of guilt, described by religions as sins, and also described by religion-influenced lawgivers as crimes. Such are the violences and the frauds which arouse indignation. In religious terms, there are forms of spiritual merit and defect, corresponding to, even if not identical with, the condemnations and approbations that are stated or implied in municipal law.

To isolate categories of municipal law and moral law as unrelated sets of obligations, unrelated modes of obedience, is, it has been submitted, an unrealistic, verbal, analysis. The obeyer may be obeying a law which is municipal and moral and/or religious. He may be obeying a law religiously or morally as well as municipally. The other approach ignores the content of obedience, and loses the immanent values. Not only does such an approach lead too easily to a more than relativistic scepticism, indeed to a total heresy as to unforced obligation, but, like this scepticism, it is unscientific. The data of law consist in the laws obeyed and not in the outside form only. And one datum of morals, as Kant makes clear, is that people obey. If their values are, ultimately, illusions, these illusions for us frame a real world of activity. In discriminating the forms and modes of that activity which is obedience, let us study the obeyer when he obeys specific rules or principles.

Why does a man not steal? Conceivably, he may be deterred by the prohibitions and penalties which are the Larceny Acts (and now the Theft Act). Conceivably he does not steal because the

Bible forbids theft.[10] Or he may be a person to whom the idea of taking what is not his would never occur: and even though there are experts who would dismiss this virtue as the result of training, or as acquired habit, it cannot be disputed that the mode of obedience here is not a simple compliance with criminal law. Nor, indeed, would the life of the nation be happy if only the sanctions of the Larceny Act protected property; for it may confidently be said that the person who refrains from stealing because of the criminal law is a thief.[11]

Have we, then, in the Wolfenden text, a subtle theology distinguishing between sin against God only, and sin against man and God, or, if possible, against man only?[12] A casuist might delight in the writing of such a commentary. Can any one be sure that such a theologian would not classify private male homosexuality in the second category rather than the first? Significantly, we find in the Bible, in a chapter (Deut. XXII) setting out many precepts which, by any semantics, are moral precepts, that the practice of transvestitism is 'rejected of God'. There is, perhaps, here an ill-defined but clear concept of naturalness (implied though not expressed at several levels of the Pentateuch) that men are reluctant to exclude from the theological – or, for that matter, the social – virtues.

This reflection introduces a concept which is made the more

[10] Not in the 'Eighth Commandment' specifically, because, in Rabbinic opinion, that is a law against kidnapping; but other commandments and many other passages in Scripture are available in condemnation of the varieties of larceny and fraud.

[11] One of the features discernible in contemporary anarchism is precisely the misbehaviour which takes place when the law is not on guard: e.g. the looting (with the vandalism) which too many psychologists would exonerate as the consequence of unhappiness. Whatever the causation, the facts of irresponsibility and dishonesty seem to be increasing. That the criminal law is involved in great activity, showing that the state cannot trust its citizens to behave well, is a criticism, not of the law, but of a society too liberated. Functions of freedom, such as money and transport, serve to facilitate in the twentieth century conduct reminiscent of early biblical times when 'each was a law unto himself'.

[12] This, for anyone in the Judaeo-Christian tradition, is not an absolute distinction.

topical by contemporary municipal legislation as to drug consumption, and by contemporary religious legislation (or restatement of law) as to contraception. Instead of distinguishing between the standards of established laws, and the eccentricities of the private domain in which, according to the Wolfenden Committee, the law should not intrude, should we distinguish between the realm of the natural (preserved in a natural law) and the realms of deviation? In other words, are those thinkers right who condemn the Wolfenden recommendations because the established law is true to nature?

A defence of homosexuality cannot, it is submitted, be refuted (or established, as psychologists seek) by an appeal to nature. In every important phase of legal change men appeal to nature for guidance, and fail to find it. Nature is undiscoverable beneath accretions, if they are accretions. 'Nature is made better' [or worse] 'by no means but nature makes those means'. When the Sophists, in their critique of the state, declared (rightly) that the state was a creation of law, not of nature, they were telling us only that we are concerned with human conventions and values, which can change. Again, the Greek tragedian declares that the laws were given by Apollo for the benefit of property owners; and that thought is echoed by the Marxist who regards 'property' as a transient phase in the evolution of institutions. Is our morality then unnatural in so far as it makes a general respect for property ethical? The answer is that, for the purposes of ethical realism, the naturalness is of human nature, with which we live. Institutions and customs are facts that we must accept. Superstructures let them, by all means, be called. Behind or above or below the surface constructions, there is no model or pattern. The early natural order, if it included a shape of society, was probably a chaotic state, as Hobbes taught, with man solitary and poor, his life nasty, brutish and short. That life may or may not have been homosexual.[13]

[13] The story of Sodom (from which is derived the word sodomy) and the similar story of the concubine at Gibeah (Judges XIX) – both from low strata of the Old Testament – show homosexuality to have been rife in early urban communities.

It may be worth observing that though a theory of social contract (explicitly adopted by the American Fathers) can be anthropologically

The issue in terms of English law is probably nothing other than the acceptance or repudiation of the Biblical tradition in our jurisprudence. English judges, seeking in their bosoms for guidance in their treatment of cases of first impression, have invoked a natural justice, which, in reality, is a blend of Biblical and Roman ethical and legal thinking. It is to be suspected that when they refer to the reasonable man (who, as Lord Devlin points out, is not the 'rational man', but rather the right-feeling man) they mean the moderately religious man. Similarly, the canon law, from the days of Gratian onwards, has looked to nature for indications of propriety: (Aquinas is responsible for a masterly analysis). That they have failed to find any guidance other than the behaviour of the conventionally chaste we learn from the recent Papal encyclical *Humanae Vitae*. Of this, suffice it to say that the appeal to nature, the appeal to human beings to follow some natural pattern, if there is one, has failed to prove (to those who are concerned with population problems) that nature can indicate what is good or what is bad.

What applies to contraception applies to homosexuality. It can be maintained that, since all habits are learned, acquired rather than innate, conditions may produce that oxymoron, the 'natural pervert'. But nature will not make him bad, or good. What we do know is that there are social traditions that will make him an object of pity or antagonism. Whether that attitude is true morality is another question. Without doubt, it is relevant to the law. The 'moral' of the story is that important axiological distinctions are not to be drawn 'in brief and crude terms'.[14]

refuted, yet it expresses a truth, similar to Aristotle's thought that men form states in order to live well.

[14] Perhaps the proper epithets for the 'privacy theory' are 'plausible' and 'specious'. It appeals, but analysis exposes the inutility. Let one clear case suffice. If a law is to be applied against racial discrimination (and there are statutes in U.S.A. and in Britain (1965), with that purpose), then the law is involved with personal, private, tastes; with dislikes, hatreds, obsessions; inducible, perhaps, from conduct, but nevertheless features of a private world. How terrible the private world can be was revealed in the 1930's. Then the simple hatred of Germans for Jews, the simple Franco-British distaste for, or lack of interest in, Jews, were causal factors in the rise to power of a creature of nightmare, and a creator of nightmares that came true.

6

Condemnation and Tolerance

MORALS AND THE CRIMINAL LAW

Without the aid of some 'moral' ideas, the understanding of criminal law would be difficult. This justifies, perhaps, a technical digression.

Everybody has a rough and useful idea of what is meant by crime and the criminal law; but lawyers are hard put to it when they attempt a definition. The layman would see some of the difficulty if he were privileged to sit as juror both at the Old Bailey and in the Strand. If he were very fortunate he might hear closely related argument in both courts. In point is libel – with its pleas of privileges and justification common to both jurisdictions. There are formal differences (e.g. in the jurors' oaths; and between the words prisoner (or accused) and defendant); but the content of the cases sounds similar. Then what formally distinguishes this trial on a charge of criminal libel and that civil action for damages for defamation? Is it that the one can end in a sentence of imprisonment, and the other only in an award of damages?[1] Criminal libel so often ends in a fine. Also this juror has heard of imprisonment for debt, which he knows not to be a crime. Again, what differentiates a civil plea of trespass to the person from a charge of assault, especially as here the criminal charge (if brought before magistrates) can result in the payment of civil compensation? These considerations cause lawyers to seek

[1] Criminal libel is a species of breach of the peace. Civil libel is an injury to reputation, calling for compensation. The main difference of 'content', so to speak, is that, whereas in the civil action, truth is an absolute defence, in criminal libel truth, as a defence, must be supplemented by proof that the publication was of public importance.

refuge in technicality. They say that crime is what is dealt with by the criminal law, and that criminal law is the law relating to crimes. This, like any other circular definition, is mathematically – and legally – satisfactory, but, for purposes of communication, unhelpful. Also, as we shall see later, even this tautology can be misleading. However, when the layman is told that the obstruction of a highway is a common law felony, and that the exacting of high rates of interest from the widow and the orphan is (*pace* the Scriptures) a civil issue only, he becomes aware that, in searching for criteria, the would-be definer has problems.

In ancient systems, including the Biblical and some early West European, the difference between tort and crime was almost non-existent. Most wrongs were righted by self-help, including the haling of a wrongdoer by a complainant before some seat of authority. Yet there are instances (e.g. the rebellion of Korah), and there are dicta in the Bible, which do suggest that there can, for some wrongs, be no private remission or condonation. That type of wrong (whatever it is) has a public importance.

Similarly the modern state, once kings had ceased to be private persons, could never treat treason as a private wrong. Nor could a monarch prevail unless he had it in his power to control depredations against life and property, and to exact fines. We know how Henry II made crime a Crown interest by setting up Assizes. Gradually the expanding state has declared its special interest in a large number of wrongs, and has created, for dealing with them, tribunals that we call (collectively) the Criminal Courts. Description of these institutions is relatively easy. Yet it still remains difficult to define the nature of the criminal law. Is it something enforced (and process initiated) directly (rather than indirectly) by the Crown? The ghost of the old common informer (now extinct) survives to blur that otherwise acceptable definition. Is it that only the Crown can terminate the process before verdict? A hard criterion: especially when we learn that the Crown proceeds civilly in revenue claims, and negotiates settlements as a private plaintiff would.

Another difficulty is as to penalties. Admittedly a difference exists between the sending of a person to prison for a crime, and the mulcting of a person in damages for a civil wrong. But

imprisonment is not the only penalty. Since prison building became a housing problem, the courts are less chary of 'letting the
accused off' with a fine. Also a number of technicalities bring
about similarities in difference. Suppose that a criminal court
imposes a heavy fine on a person charged with fraud, and that the
person wronged also recovers heavy damages against the same
person. The sufferings of the culprit are separate sufferings.
Intriguingly, he can now be imprisoned in two separate jurisdictions, though not without technical difficulties. He may be liable
to imprisonment if he defaults in payment of the fine, and he
may also find himself pressed for the civil liability by Judgment
Summonses, which are enforceable (in proper cases) by imprisonment.[2]

In that example we have peripheral coincidences, which are
calculated to make formal distinctions difficult. But we have
already seen that the content of law is more important than its
forms. From that standpoint, looking at the content of the
criminal law broadly, and considering heads of crime like murder,
manslaughter, mayhem, rape, arson, theft, etc., one must realise
that these are in a different category of wrongs from the civil,
even if it happens that some of them also entail consequences in
the form of civil liability. And if one looks for common factors in
serious crimes, are they not to be found in a sense of the gravity
of the conduct vis a vis the whole public, as distinct from the
seriousness of injuries which are the bases of civil claims?

Then the question arises: what public reaction is relevant to
conduct, when the conduct under scrutiny is criminal? Undog-
matically, let it be suggested that in behaving criminally the
criminal is arousing a social indignation. He is to be punished

[2] Pursuant to the Debtors Act 1869, and other statutes. The resident
population of British prisons always includes many persons who are
'imprisoned for debt'. A high percentage of these consists of men who
have refused, or failed, without good reason, to pay maintenance to
their wives pursuant to orders of civil courts. In contrast, bankrupts
who have wasted their assets, or who fail to comply with duties declared
in the statute, are imprisoned as criminals, not as debtors. Imprisonment for debt is now rationalised as punishment for contempt of court:
but historically it is continuous with enslavement for debt among the
ancient peoples.

rather than called upon to pay compensation. The payer of compensation is, it appears, in the position of a respectable citizen, discharging something like a contractual liability to society. He is a subject of the law behaving according to law, rectifying any balances that he has disturbed. The criminal is dealt with not as a subject of the law, but as an object. To speak of him as paying a debt to society is to use a bad metaphor. Once convicted, his treatment is calculated to demonstrate that society is angry with him. Against him is exacted retribution – and all forms of punishment, whether described as preventive, deterrent, reformatory, or educative, are also retributive, because the fact that society is angry and is vengeful is precisely what prevents, precisely what deters, precisely what is calculated to reform or to educate. There is a logical continuity between the burnt child that fears the fire and the arsonist who suffers the rigours of gaol. Punishment is the infliction of suffering. With the punishment, and perhaps this is not the least part of it, goes disgrace. Disgrace, which is not usually suffered by the payer of damages, can also be suffered by the payer of a fine.[3]

What is here submitted is that the notion of crime, properly understood, is a moral notion; its consequences show society, through the law, 'punishing', not merely arbitrating or compensating.[4]

Imprisonment constitutes, of course, a higher degree of disgrace than does a fine, and is a more immediate manifestation of retributive 'pain and penalty'. This is why, when Parliament enacted trading restrictions during and after the Second World War, both Parliament and the judges endeavoured to show their

[3] Even by the paying of a small fine for an indiscretion such as urinating *coram publico*.

[4] Incidentally, a recent development has been governmental acquiescence in the demand that persons injured by criminals in the course of their crimes should be compensated by the state. Under old statutes, public authorities have been liable to pay for damage caused by rioters. But only within the last decade has the government (by order, not by statute) declared itself liable to compensate the sufferers of personal injury inflicted by criminals. The principle is still a narrow one, because the personal injury compensated is injury to 'person', and not damage to property, or loss of property, which are 'personal injuries' in the law of tort.

disapproval by inflicting sentences of imprisonment instead of the fines that are normal in regulative discipline. There was an element of justice in this policy, because no great sanction can be experienced by a man of means when, in his efforts to be richer, he loses money.

Such a decision seems to be just. Nevertheless, it suggests some difficulties, not in the theory of punishment, but in the moral application of it. Thus there are differences in criminality; between, it may be suggested, the 'civil', in the sense of urbane, and the 'uncivil', unurbane. In the latter class are the violences including the robberies and the crude larcenies from house or person. Fraud, embezzlements and conversions are also immoral; and not less immoral on occasions when the person swindled is the impersonal state or some great corporation. But the person who does such things may well be morally incapable of violence, and would never do wrongs involving personal contact. Then is it proper to lodge such a one among the ruffians and the yahoos? Snobbery is out of place in morality; but charity endeavours always to minister to the poor in the light of what they have lost. Charity is class conscious. The charitable would endeavour to restore poor persons according to their status; and would probably hold that punishment of an embezzler, e.g. by putting him among the exponents of grievous bodily harm, is punishing him more severely than does disgrace and the deprivation of liberty. This conjures problems of administration: and there is something to be said for a division of servitudes, or of places of incarceration, restoring, to an extent, the old system in which the debtor's prison was clearly separate from the felon's prison.

Problems would still be left unsolved, because there are degrees of immorality. Some 'urbane' villains are as cold blooded and cruel as any ruffian, and it is fortuitous that life has given them different opportunities, and a different technical equipment, for the manifestation of their callousness.

In both classes of crime there are degrees of wickedness. Sympathy is available for the hungry thief; incidentally a rarity now when so many youths arrested for larceny are from good homes and from schools inferior to Borstal only in discipline.

Among the urbane the differences of degree are more perceptible. Corruption (bribery) is a crime; and an immoral act. The person bribed is taking money or favour for betrayals ranging from the commercial to the political. The briber, for his part, is evidently a corruptor. Yet men have been found guilty of corruption who, being agents, have accepted presents from their principals' customers, without intending any disloyalty. The Prevention of Corruption Act 1906 (strengthened in 1916, in respect of government employees) is evidently a good measure. But it illustrates the difficulty of framing laws so as to account for differences in ethical situations. 'An agent who accepts or obtains or agrees to accept or attempts to obtain' [clearly there is difference of degree here] '. . . an inducement or reward for doing or forbearing to do . . . any act in relation to his principal's affairs or business or for showing favour or disfavour to any person . . .' is guilty of a misdemeanour. The law is beyond criticism in so far as it suppresses a mischief; yet is unsubtle because it does not account for the agent who is approached with commercial propositions which will be beneficial to his employer and beneficial to the second party. Is he so wicked in working for both?

In contrast the criminal law makes no provision to protect industrialists against the sale of their secrets by persons who have left their employment. These are disloyal, yet commit no crime with their disloyalty.[5]

Clearly there are difficulties in the notion of punishment when the criminal law, which used to deal only with the simpler categories of crime, including forgeries and the better known frauds, has to cope with the administrative task of enforcing such laws as the Purchase Tax Regulations and the duty to pay wireless licences.[6] What was easy when the accused was guilty of a clear Thou Shalt Not, is difficult when the crime is a breach of Thou Shalt.

In modern times the task of the criminal law has been increased by the demands of collectivism; especially the demand for the control of what was once uncontrolled. An extreme case

[5] Government employees are controlled by the Official Secrets Act.
[6] There always has been excise law; but there is a distinction between smuggling and unpaid-for listening.

is to be seen in the history of the 18th Amendment in the United States, a period when the consumption and/or provision of alcoholic refreshment was a crime. In Britain one advance in social morality or social wisdom can be seen in the development of an awareness that alcoholism is bad conduct. Whether the ethical or the economic motive was causative has been debated. It is of interest that the Licensing Act 1911 was passed into law under the aegis of a strong exponent of Welsh Methodism and a pioneer of modern administrative action for the amelioration of the life of the poor.

Britain did not illegalise the consumption or provision of alcohol, but made it subject to restrictions and to licensing.

By the Act of 1911 the worker's opportunities for consuming his earnings were reduced. This was 'one law for the poor', and, in the best opinion, justified. The legal consequences is that to drink in clubs or public houses 'after hours' is a crime; and the law puts the providing publican among the sinners.

The concept of licensing is not limited to the field of licence. To do something not quite proper subject to control is one right for which one can be licensed. Other licences are granted to persons engaged in many industrial or commercial functions which are under government control, to say nothing of the acquisition of wives or dogs.

The semantic problem suggested by this is not socially important, but it presents itself. Is a provider of drink after hours a criminal? Few would so describe him. Perhaps the solution is offered by the fact that the penalty he incurs is a fine – not imprisonment. At this stage it is desirable to narrow the frame of reference. In considering crime, we must exclude much that has come within the scope of the criminal law, but does not seem to be criminal in the way that ordinary people think (and think correctly) of crime. The immense complexity of modern traffic and trafficking throws onto the state the duty of organising these things for whatever social purpose the state recognises as important. Failing the state, who will enforce sanitation, safety in factories, safety on the roads, economic protections, etc., etc.? Thus the machinery of the state lends itself to the prevention of chimney-fires by the punishing of those who allow them. Yet no one thinks of this offence as crime, and there is no recorded case of any suicide brought about by the imminence of that particular prosecution. Although boundaries are hard to draw – e.g. in which category is drunkenness? – let it be suggested that much disciplinary law, involving as it does none of the stigma of crime, is only called criminal law because courts that deal with crime deal also with this, and our legal vocabulary is inadequate to afford alternative terminology. In practice the word 'offence' is used, and the offender is called a defendant, rather than an accused person. Also these matters are for the most part dealt with by a petty magistracy.

That this petty magistracy plays some part in crime proper reminds us once again of semantic difficulties. The point of the excursus, however, should be clear. There is crime – with stigma. There are offences – without stigma. If we inquire into the nature and reality of the stigma we discover that what we are looking for is a moral criterion.[7]

Taking for granted a well-known, though ill-defined, group of moral ideas, and applying them, it seems that all 'real' crime consists of conduct which the moral person would not perform. He would not kill, he would not steal, he would not ravish, he would not wilfully wound, forge, defraud, etc. Because morality has included these prohibitions, therefore has the law retained them.

When morality has changed, the law has tended to follow. Both changes are slow. Until the first quarter of the nineteenth century England was a cruel country. Morals improved, and the laws changed. Before they had completely ameliorated the prospects of the felon, who might be a hungry child stealing bread, they introduced legal pedantries protective of criminals. Subsequently, cruelty to animals became a crime; this in the 1830s. Children continued to be slaves in factories. Fifty years later cruelty to children became a crime.

England, be it remembered, was for long a flagellant land, and

[7] Relevant to this is the brilliant speculation on the concept of crime to be found in Samuel Butler's *Erewhon*. In *Erewhon* people were imprisoned for illness, 'treated' for crime; and the former, not the latter, involved shame. Butler's essay affords, incidentally, a *reductio ad absurdum* of much modern psychologistic criminology.

its sports were bear-baiting, cock-fighting and prize-fighting. The poet Blake, in the eighteenth century, had condemned the caging and torture of animals. His was not common opinion. The nineteenth century, horrified by what Burke and Hare did to human beings, became, at the same time concerned with the growing practice of vivisection. That propaganda attracted more attention than cruelty to the beast of burden and the domestic animal. But the law finally condemned all the varieties of this genus of cruelty. When the ill-treatment of animals first became recognised as a crime the offence was made indictable. By the Protection of Animals Act 1911, the importance of the offence seems to be reduced because, being now magisterially punishable by three months of imprisonment, the charge is no longer indictable (i.e. chargeable in front of judge and jury).

Some sentiment in this context can be discounted as sentimentality, because, after all, animals are a main source of food; and experiments on animals have been of immense value in the science of medicine. There is, however, evidence here of some moral consciousness, and this is one of the many ways in which the morality of England and the English law can be seen to have changed and improved.

On cruelty in England a long treatise could be written. Few realise how recently it is that the morals and the laws of England ceased to be tolerant of, even acceptive of, much conduct that would horrify us now. Less than two hundred years ago hangings, and worse, were public spectacles. One hundred and fifty years ago all felonies were capital; and those accused of felony could not be defended by counsel.[8] One hundred and twenty years ago (i.e. until 1853) there was still a penalty of 'transportation'. Until 1870 there were forfeitures as well as executions for treason, and the Act which abolishes these, preserves a royal prerogative of ordering the drawing and quartering and other mutilations of the traitor.

Until less than a century ago it was not a comfortable thing to be a soldier or sailor. The underpaid, three-quarters starved,

[8] At the lower level, misdemeanour, prosecutors in the eighteenth and nineteenth centuries made great use of a concept of conspiracy (now much restricted) in order to have strikers imprisoned.

heroes of Trafalgar and Torres Vedras were under a discipline which contemplated as much as eight hundred lashes as a proper penalty for disobedience (including the stealing of food). This discipline was modified; but not abolished until late in the century; and not until the end of World War I was flagellation abolished in the navy. Not until the 1870s, be it added, was the system abolished by which captains bought companies and were left free to feed or starve them.

On the domestic front it was not until 1891 that the courts finally pronounced against wife beating. Not until after the Children & Young Persons Act of 1933 had become part of life, did judges take seriously the limits on the rights of parents or teachers to chastise children.

To sum up: this has been a cruel country, and that has been an important series of developments in the national morals and the law which has resulted in the elimination of many cruelties by the criminal law and from the criminal law. By way of re-action, the present fault is excess of sentiment. Criminals are treated now with a 'sympathy' which recalls the Rabbinic pro-nouncement that if you start by being kind to the wicked you will end by being cruel to the good.

NOTE ON THE INDIGNATION OF THE COURT

In the award of punishments modern judges are much more inhibited from the expression of their feelings than were the judges of earlier centuries. Those were fierce; and even tortured juries into desired verdicts. (Ten years ago a petulant threat that they might be forced to stay over-night was condemned.)

Penalties are now limited by statute. Moreover, an empirical practice, manifesting itself in the dicta of the Court of Appeal, ensures that very few punishments are maximal. Nor are appel-lants (however impudent) against sentence to the Court of Appeal faced with the old threat of increased sentence.

The residual (and very important) power of the judge to vindi-cate the law to his taste consists in the power to commit persons to prison for contempt of court.

One species of contempt is civil, and is instanced by the wilful failure of a person to obey an order of the court: e.g. to honour an injunction, to produce a document, to answer a question etc. (Editors have been known to suffer for this last.)

The other species is illustrated in the terrible fate of the man '*que jeta un* brickbat which narrowly missed'. This is called criminal, *can* be tried as a crime; but in practice never is tried by judge and jury, and is not recorded as a criminal conviction. Those who are violent in face of the court, or who express outside court, orally or in writing, insults to the court, are sent to prison by the judge concerned: and if it be said that he judges in his own cause, the answer is that he is vindicating, not himself, but the court and the public that uses the court.

Theoretically, in both classes of contempt, the prisoner lies in gaol until he has purged his contempt.

Paradoxically, it is in the civil order that the sentence remains theoretically unrestricted. In the criminal order, authority has declared a maximum of six months (Att. Gen. v James [1962] 2 Q.B. 637).

In the recent interesting case of Morris and others v The Master of the Crown Office [1970] 1 All Eng. R. 1079, it appeared that a number of juveniles had disturbed an English court in Welsh and had been promptly sentenced in English to three months of imprisonment. On Appeal (itself a modern feature) it was argued that since this was 'criminal', the appellants should enjoy the benefit of the Criminal Justice Act 1967 which enacts that all sentences of six months or less be, in the case of first offenders, 'suspended'. A far cry, this, from the days when the criminal was suspended! The Court of Appeal, while exercising great clemency (a binding over) yet refused to accept the argument addressed to them. Consequently, contempt remains the only punishable conduct which is not a crime.

THE VALUE OF LIFE

If a spectator chances into a civil court at a moment when damages are being awarded to widow and orphan on account of the loss of their breadwinner through somebody's negligence, he may hear quite large sums being awarded (to the dependants) as an assessment of future earnings, which were earnable by the deceased, and have been lost; and, then, an award to the estate of the deceased – loss of expectation of life, £500.

If he thinks that this is a very small recompense (if it can be regarded that way), then it is desirable to enlighten him and say: there was a time when death paid no dividend.

Lord Ellenborough put it succinctly in 1808 when he said: 'In a civil court the death of a human being cannot be complained of as an injury'.[9] This rule, which has been described as a fine example of the maxim *communis error facit ius* (common error makes law), was probably wrong, even in 1808, being a confusion of two principles (1) (no longer true) that after a killing the civil suit must abide the result of a trial for felony: (2) that a personal action dies with the person suing or sued. Neither of those rules is justification for holding that dependants cannot sue for their loss. Yet so it was held until statutes provided otherwise. The common law rule that killing is not a legal injury to the person killed has not been abrogated by generations of lawyers 'letting decisions stand', nor even by the statutes and cases that give death a financial significance.[10]

The result of the old rule was the absurdity that for a tortfeasor it was cheaper to kill than to injure.[11] The law was changed

[9] Baker v Bolton (1808) 1 Camp. 493.

[10] What adds to the absurdity of the rule that actions die with persons is the consideration that the law recognizes that an 'estate' survives the deceased and remains 'his estate'; so that if an assignment under deed has failed, the property can revert; and so that creditors can claim under contract. Why, then, should the 'estate' not claim or pay damages? This aspect of the rule in Baker v Bolton has been almost legislated away. Moreover, at common law, the death of x can be a head of damage in an action for breach of contract by y. So when a wife was fatally poisoned by food that the husband had bought, the husband recovered damages for the loss of his wife's services and consortium in consequence of the breach of contract (Jackson v Watson & Sims [1909] 2 K.B. 193). That was a 'discovery' in 1909. Later statute and case law combine to enable the executors etc. of a poisoned person to sue on behalf of the deceased (for pain and suffering and loss of expectation of life) even if he or she had not personally paid for the food. That would not have been possible in 1909.

[11] That is still the case, but at a different level. Very high awards are now made to persons crippled for life (as when paraplegic effects

by Lord Campbell's Act (Fatal Accidents Act) in 1846, under which the near relatives of the deceased can sue for their loss, whenever the death is so caused that, had the deceased person been injured and not killed, he would have had a right to damages. (It may be of interest to note that by an amendment in 1934 (Law Reform Act) the list of persons who can sue – parents, children, etc. – is extended to include illegitimate children.)

Notwithstanding Lord Campbell's Act, the House of Lords in 1917[12] upheld the doctrine that death, as such, is not an injury to the deceased. This is still the law: but Parliament and the courts have been ingenious. First came the Law Reform Act 1934, which abolished the doctrine that actions and causes of action die with death. Parliament left in the old category certain very personal actions, such as breach of promise of marriage and defamation.[13] The effect of the Act is that, if the deceased has rights accrued in tort, his death does not terminate them. His injuries would ground an action on behalf of his estate for his suffering, but not his death. However, in two cases, Flint v Lovell[14] and Rose v Ford[15] the judges discovered, or created, a claim available to any person injured, including persons killed, for damages for loss of expectation of life. That was creative law: and for some years insurance companies paid very large sums under this head of damages. But, eventually, in Benham v Gambling[16] the House of Lords reviewed the principles; and the spirit of Lord Ellenborough seems to have brooded over the assembly. Reducing a figure of £1,000 (awarded by a jury in respect of a young child) to £200, the Law Lords opined (adopting the views of Lord Goddard in the lower court) that they were in fact awarding, not a recompense to the deceased, but a solatium to the relatives, and possibly creating a fund available (in the case of older deceased) to creditors. Philosophically, the Lords expressed their doubts as to the cer-

obtain); whereas the combined total of loss of earnings and loss of expectation of life very rarely approximates to the 'paraplegic' awards.

[12] The Amerika [1917] A.C. 38.

[13] This exclusion makes it impossible to bypass the rule that there is no defamation of the dead. The recent posthumous assassination of Churchill by a vengeful German therefore goes unavenged.

[14] [1935] 1 K.B. 354.
[15] [1937] A.C. 826.   [16] [1941] A.C. 157.

tainty of happiness for anyone. Nor should account be taken of possible duration of survival in the vale of tears. What has to be measured, and that objectively – i.e. in the same terms for all classes and persons – is the 'prospect of a predominantly happy life'. They advised judges and juries to abandon any attempt to equate incommensurables, and to give quite small sums. In this way they made the world safer for insurance companies.

In this evolution of the civil law two trends may be discerned; the trend to individualism, which carries with it a high valuation of human life; and the trend, due to growth of population and the collectivist theory which it fosters, to preoccupation with large groups, and the consequent devaluation of individual rights.

So far as the individual as a moral unit is concerned, he is necessarily remote from most kinds of conduct that could be relevant to decisions affecting life as such. Kant has told us that an OUGHT implies a CAN. This corresponds with moral experience. Hence the despairing note, so often heard; what can I do about it? What can the individual do if a casual spectator dies and the football match goes on? What can he do to stop a system of transport which seems inevitably to cost thousands of lives per annum? Nor are these the worst features of the backcloth of the modern 'human comedy'.

Just as eighteenth-century faith was shattered by the Lisbon earthquake, which was large-scale death, corresponding to no discernible wrongdoing, no probable sin, so the immensity of the movements of states and the carnage that results, even from the acts of the least barbarous, has made our recent generations sceptical of any basis, in the natural world or beyond it, for the high estimation of life. If millions can die at the hands of a mass-murdering nation, if millions can die in a famine, if myriads must be killed in merely defensive fighting, life seems to lose its high price and become cheap. The individual is forced to shrug his shoulders and say with Voltaire: All I can do is cultivate my garden. So the modern Candide finds himself abandoning theoretical inquiry, and deciding that he may leave his morality to the law; and (amorally) accept the expediencies that are forced upon the state.

If life is 'in issue' the citizen is rarely relevant. The judge, the occasional juror: these are few. The voter, even the member of Parliament, these can only remotely and incompletely control decisions whether or not to kill. For himself, the ordinary man will not kill, because he does not think of doing so, because he is physically unable to, because there is no reason to; but he makes no decision, and the decision is taken out of his hands by the law which either tells him not to kill, and makes clear its sanctions, or instructs him to kill, as in war, and, again, displays its coercive power behind the verbal authority.

As for religious authority, and the sixth commandment, his interest in this particular commandment – Thou shalt not kill – must be academic, except when he uses a vote which, directly or indirectly, will affect the subsistence of a capital penalty, or the manufacture of very destructive weapons.[17]

To overthrow a government which undervalues human life is self-evidently beyond the powers of ordinary men. The duty to rebel, which at one time was said to be implicit to the American Constitution, is, in these days at least, one of those duties which can hardly be morally binding. There is no 'duty' where there is no 'ability'.

There are, however, occasions, in the lives of individuals, when a man can defy the authority of the state in refusing his own obedience. In point is the martyr. Jews and Christians of old refused to commit idolatry or bloodshed even if their own lives were sacrificed. These occasions were exceptions to the Talmudic rule that 'the law of the country is your law', or, as Jesus put it, 'render unto Caesar'. To command murder (*sci* – assassination) or idolatry was not conceded as a right to Caesar. The subject so commanded must 'be killed and not sin'. This is martyrdom. The martyr's 'can' includes his ability to sacrifice his life for what he 'ought'.

Martyrdom is a rarity these days, but the question is not academic. What of the soldier who is ordered to kill civilians? The principle was accepted at war crime trials, after both world

---

[17] In the present state of Parliamentary party opinion, no such vote is available. Only a referendum would give articulation to public opinion on these topics: and referendum is anathema to British party theory.

wars, that a soldier must disobey a patently unlawful order according to the laws of war. The position of the soldier is difficult, faced as he is with the danger of the charge of mutiny. Not every soldier has the courage, the education, the social position of Colonel Wolfe who refused to obey the Duke of Cumberland's order to shoot a wounded man. Nevertheless, the principle declared in the war crime trials is not new, and not unjust. Only by the exercise of such principles can the horrors of war be limited to military necessity – and only in this way can the concept of what is militarily necessary be stated with a minimum of barbarity.

At a lower level than martyrdom is the position of the objector to military service. The laws of Britain and U.S.A. do not permit exemption because of a person's political views. Does he object to the war in Vietnam? That is not his concern. The state decides whether the war be waged; and his conscription is pursuant to law. His martyrdom, if he refuses to obey is, happily, only imprisonment. But if his objection is a conscientious one – to all killing – then the religious traditions of the Anglo-Saxons give him the privilege of asserting – and proving, so far as they can be proved – his principles; and they are respected.

The above cases are not the normal of civilian life.

Perhaps the ordinary voter, though remote from power, can find moral problems developing, if only seminally, when he votes.

Yet, as it happens, unless he be a member of Parliament the citizen does not enjoy a direct opportunity of expressing himself on the value of human life.

Even the member of Parliament is remote from decisions as to war and peace, which are executive decisions. All he can do is refuse to vote the funds called for by the government. In our time this refusal has never been a practical proposition, though the opposition came near to it at the time of Suez (1956). It is a very important feature of our law that Mr Gaitskell, on that occasion, was not guilty of treason. Members of Parliament enjoy rights against the government. They rarely have to exercise them; and they are rarely called upon to debate the great values. Yet great questions are raised whenever the issue of capital punishment is argued. On the one hand, to kill by 'justified homicide', as the executioner does, is an act from which the ordinary person recoils in horror. On the other hand, it has been thought, perhaps by the vast majority of mankind, that this kind of killing does something to maintain the value of life, in so far as the penalty is a deterrent; and, at least, to assert it.

Perhaps this moral conflict would seem less acute if, instead of thinking in terms of life and life ('life for life') a distinction were drawn within the category of human life. Is that a false egalitarianism which esteems all life equally highly? Certainly the danger of not doing so is evident, because once differences are stated, then the way is open to a dialectic of *Herrenvolk*. Certain facts, however, require to be faced.

First, neither here nor abroad does the valuation on human life that was set by Western religion enjoy universal acceptance. Nor (secondly) is the religious assessment quite so dogmatic as religious people believe.

'The beast shall perish, and the man shall perish with him'. We who have come to believe that killing is too severe a penalty for the crime of bestiality, are yet made aware, by the Biblical pronouncement, that there are persons in the world who disgrace the world. More clearly there are some murderers, and evil persons other than murderers, of whom one can say that it is not fitting that this person should be allowed to stay in the world which he has so defiled. Even it is arguable that the child-ravisher could reasonably be removed from a world in which his survival would be a source of terror and shame to his victim. There are civilised states in which rape, in certain circumstances, is capitally punishable.

That we do not cause the bestial man to perish is consistent with our law as to insanity. English law does not attribute responsibility to persons lacking in the mental ability to make a rational decision. Such a person is not 'responsible'. The test was always an 'intellectual' one. As the McNaghten rules have it, the insane person is a person who, by reason of disease of the mind, does not know what he is doing (the nature and quality of the act) or does not know that what he is doing is wrong.[18] That person, charged with murder (or any other crime), could be

[18] As, e.g. if he thinks that spirits are commanding him to do the act.

found (pursuant to the Trial of Lunatics Act 1883) 'guilty but insane'. Not, be it noted, 'not guilty because insane'. The point of the verdict is that the court should have power to inflict the sentence of detention during His Majesty's pleasure.[19]

The result of this rule is ambivalent. Certainly there are creatures entitled to pity, and it would seem cruel to kill them. There are, on the other hand, creatures whose insanity is so terrible that, in the opinion of many humane persons, society should be liberated from them completely. (Should other prisoners, it may be asked, be condemned to live with them?)

That, however, is not the accepted view. Insanity is an exoneration from guilt, though not from control. What agitated the reformers was the belief that the category of insanity as the law described it, was too narrow. There are persons, it was maintained, who, although they knew what they were doing, and that what they were doing was wrong, were yet impelled by an uncontrollable impulse. Some support for the claim to extend the category of insanity in order to accommodate 'uncontrollable impulse' is afforded by the phenomena of epilepsy and *petit-mal*. In 1957 the legislature accepted the argument and created a defence of diminished responsibility, which reduces murder to manslaughter, treatable by detention during the Crown's pleasure.

An effect of this enactment has been the finding of manslaughter in many cases that used to be murder, and many cases which still are.

Given guilt, without the mitigations of psychiatry, the question of the capital penalty involves a discussion on the value of life as one value among other values.

That human life is the ultimate value (as distinct from the highest in the scale of value) would not be maintained by any of

---

[19] Interesting is the defence of automatism, raised in R. v Kemp [1956] 3 All Eng. R. 249, and considered by the Law Lords in Bratty v Att. Gen. for N. Ireland [1961] 3 All Eng. R. 523.

It appears that if a person could prove that he was, in effect, unconscious at the time (totally drunk, e.g. and not merely drunk and amorous as in R. v Beard (1919) 14 C.A.R. 110) then he could claim an acquittal. The position is not clear, because usually the proof of 'automatism' will be a medical proof of disease of the mind – i.e. insanity.

those martyrs who have preferred death to indignity or loss of integrity. Nor could a humane man resent the destruction of any being that constituted a threat to the decencies without which life can seem worthless.

Human life is the highest-assessed in the scale of value, but is not an ultimate, because in ethics there are no demonstrable ultimates; that is to say, no values that supersede all other values. Nor, in religion, is individual life more than a worldly potential of spiritual values.

So far as the British legal system is concerned, the foreground is dominated by triumphant abolitionism, which is embodied in statute. The death penalty for murder has been abolished in Britain. This bare statement leaves the uninformed with the notion that the English law used to value life so highly that it declared a *lex talionis* (life for life). The historical fact is that the death penalty for murder was a surviving death penalty from a period when all felonies (including small thefts by small boys) were 'capital'.

Nevertheless, it can fairly be said that, for all the period from the 1830s to the present, the laws, as they stood, residual but not irrational, embodied a fairly simple principle of retribution: that violence should be met with violence, killing with killing. The abolition of these examples of retributive law is of great significance, because it coheres with a psychologism which seeks to abolish the distinction between the wicked and the good. From the premise that 'the spirit of the heart of man is bad from his childhood', they deduce that it is the purely fortuitous effect of environment that men grow up to be murderers and villains. That the law should, therefore, be exceedingly merciful to sinners is, however, an inference that not all thinkers would accept.

The argument, in England, has moved from the retributive to the deterrent. Does the capital penalty prevent murder? Statistics seem to show that the abolition of the capital penalty is not followed by any significant rise in the murder rate. What the analysts of statistics overlook includes the following considerations:

(1) That in a period where there is no abject poverty, and when matrimonial law enables many unhappy alliances to be dissolved,

and when education is increasing, one would expect the murder rate to fall sharply. That it has not risen is, therefore, unconvincing.

(2) If murder has not increased, manslaughter has increased, and much of what used to be called murder is now, through changes in the law and in the attitude of juries, called manslaughter.

(3) Crimes of violence, involving weapons, have very much increased. This is a possible indication that people are influenced by the thought that it is no longer so dangerous to use a weapon as it was.

There are lawyers who think that comparable argument is valid for the restoration of flagellation for the major violences.

There are, apart from valuations, other difficulties which deserve mention. They derive logically from the language of the statute (of the 1830s) which restated the capital penalty for murder.

This law was re-enacted in the comprehensive Offences against the Person Act 1861. '(1) Whoever shall be convicted of murder shall suffer death as a felon. (2) Upon every conviction for murder the court shall pronounce sentence of death. . . .'

Subject to alterations in the form and ceremonial, that act remained in force. Consequently the judge had no option, no discretion. When the jury brought in the verdict of guilty, the death sentence was automatic. Clearly this could be wrong. The killer of a villain, in circumstances which fell short of provocation, must be different ethically, and should be different legally, from the planned murder for money. Moreover, provocation, which reduced murder to manslaughter, was held to be a causal factor only where the killing was in hot blood, and done at the moment of the provoking act,[20] which could be an assault, attempted theft or arson, an attack on a member of one's family, an outrageous insult involving striking or spitting, etc. Until 1957, words alone, whatever message they conveyed, could not be provocation. Because of the narrowness of the categories of provocation, many persons were found guilty of murder whose

[20] The learning is summed up in Holmes v D.P.P. [1946] A.C. 588.

conduct would, in ordinary language, have been described as provoked.

Further, the use of weapons would, in many cases, disqualify the prisoner from the plea of provocation. An unhappy example of the limits of the law occurred in the case of Mancini (1941) where a club owner, in the course of an attack on his premises by villains, killed one of them with a knife.

The plea was self-defence, and that failed because, at the moment of killing, he was not in danger. Because he was badly defended, this prisoner did not succeed in putting before the jury a very arguable case of provocation, and the jury were insufficiently directed as to this. But, because the judge had presented the prisoner's bad defence sympathetically, neither the Court of Criminal Appeal nor the House of Lords would interfere with the verdict.

But more dangerous than the risk of bad defence which could hang a man, what of evidence that could be wrong? Identifications, since the days of Adolf Beck, Oscar Slater, and Steinie Morrison, have been notoriously unreliable. Circumstantial evidence, in contrast, may provide a moral certainty. Errors, however, can be made.[21]

Two arguments emerge: (1) That death was, in many cases, too severe a penalty. (2) That the death penalty could be inflicted in error.

These arguments would lose their force if the death penalty were not automatic. The technique of reprieve has always been available, when even quite remote possibilities of error could be indicated. As for the possibility of awarding less than the death penalty, it was argued (against) that to allow this was to put too great a burden on one man (the judge). The answer to this is, obviously, that we do trust judges with lives. Does not every sentence of imprisonment carry the possibility of the ruin of lives? In the event, after restricting the capital penalty somewhat anomalously in 1957, and after successive Home Secretaries had

---

[21] Let not too much sympathy be wasted on those (such as Evans) whose voluntary (perhaps false) confessions have hanged them. These have used the law (as others have used the railway system) as a means of suicide.

granted many reprieves, Parliament finally abolished the capital penalty for a trial period of five years, and has now made the abolition permanent.[22]

This decision, whether good or bad, is interesting, because it was the result of one of those 'free votes', which occasionally present themselves in order to refute the sarcasm that politics is the mobilisation of bias. (It still remains the science of the superficial!)

So much for the state.

As for individuals, the moral situation of the individual who is obsessed with the value of life is not only a difficult one, but is an unreal one. He protests against an order of things too big for an individual's control. This is a world in which there are needs, wants, and wars. Let him be vegetarian and advise those who would starve without animal food; and argue with those who claim (and prove) that plant life is continuous with animal life. His greater difficulties will be due to the bellicosity of peoples. Nations attack nations.[23] Wherefore pacifism becomes a difficult policy. The pacifist has a moral problem. He will not kill, but will he accept a responsibility for the loss of life that failure to defend a land can involve? Not even the fakir-culture that suffuses Indian democracy has proved itself equal to the abandonment of the helpless in order to save the lives of the wicked or the feelings of the sentimental. The legal situation of the pacifist is that the law was kinder to him in 1939 than in 1914.

It may be said that Britain has been preservative of this 'valuation' in that conscription is not the normal policy of British governments. That is typical of a democracy which does not thrust patriotism on its citizens.

Unimperial now, we discover that these are times when what the government ought to do is controlled by what it can do.[24]

[22] I.e. for murder: not, apparently, for treason, piracy, or setting fire to naval dockyards.

[23] Sometimes understandably, as when water supplies are in issue.

[24] No modern British government has ever departed from the internationally valid distinction between just wars and unjust aggressions. But they cannot always act on it. Many individuals are normally myopic (or hypermetropic) enough not to see the difference. No citizen of Holland (the land of Grotius) would have been so blind in 1940.

Of human life, the preservation of the sanctities is beyond the scope of governments and individuals alike in a world where the machinery of social organisation is irreversible. As a voter in the political entity the citizen finds himself called upon to decide whether he approves of weapons that can kill millions. If he decides against them, he may find no recipient for his vote. He is answered by those who say to him: this is not a moral issue for you, but a practical one for us. We who defend you must choose the most effective weapons.

At this phase we are moving from the order in which an individual can be moral, into an order where his morality is irrelevant, because the decision is not his. We are also moving into an order where it has been claimed that no moral law prevails; an order of pragmatism and expediency, that is to say the world in which the units are large groups – states, for example – as to which it has been claimed that the duties of their leaders and their organisers cannot in the nature of things be moral duties.

The theory of the non-moral state may or may not be valid somewhere. Certainly it is not valid for England. Machiavelli does not speak to the Queen in Parliament who is Elizabeth II.

On the other hand, the British government of today is not in a position to express in arms the kind of indignation that Gladstone expressed in words against the unspeakable Turk.

When issues are clear, as they were (notwithstanding the historians who have obfuscated them) in 1914 and 1939, our state has acted. When less clear and imminent threats to international morality obtain, the risks of conflict outweigh the calls of indignation. The best that can be done is in the form of gestures. The present position is that men, inside and outside government, must frequently find themselves wondering whether the world, or even their own friends, will thank them for giving economic hostages to values that may no longer prevail.

Imagination, even political imagination, is not equal to large numbers or far distances. Effective political agitation is domestic. Most recent is our concern with the value of the life of the unborn.

As to the killing of the newly born, this is, and always has been, murder. But statute has allowed a modification of the criminal laws, so that a woman, who kills her child while suffering the disorders that can accompany and follow parturition, may be charged with infanticide, a crime of lesser gravity.

According to many, abortion of a formed foetus is murder. The legal practice was, of old, to charge manslaughter. But the Offences Against the Person Act 1861 made it possible to charge, or accept pleas to, the 'unlawful using of drugs or instruments'. The records show that the penalties were usually sentences of nine months imprisonment!

That abortion was justified in order to save the life and health of the mother was always an accepted view. Could the right be applied in the interests of the psychological welfare of the mother? That was discussed in the case of R. v Bourne ([1939] 1 K.B. 687) when a most distinguished obstetrician aborted a young girl who had been ravished by guardsmen. The surgeon was prepared to stake his liberty on the psychological purpose, but the court insisted on finding that he saved the girl's physical health.

Other arguments for abortion include the economic – that a child, born to parents who cannot afford to maintain him, is not entering a desirable life. This proposition has not been accepted by the legislature. But an Act has been passed (1967) which widely extends the discretion of surgeons. Abortion is allowed if two medical practitioners certify in good faith 'that the continuance of the pregnancy would involve risk of the life of the pregnant woman, or of injury to the physical or mental health of the pregnant woman or any existing children of her family, greater than if the pregnancy were terminated, or that there is a substantial risk that if the child were born it would suffer from such physical or mental abnormalities as to be seriously handicapped'.

In considering the woman's physical and mental health account may be taken of her 'actual or reasonably forseeable' environment.

If one medical practitioner, in good faith, thinks that immediate action is necessary to save the life of the woman or to prevent grave permanent injury to her physical or mental health, he can act at his discretion. (As Bourne did.) It is still not the case that abortion is legal as a remedy for the failure of contraception. On the other hand there is no restriction on abortion (subject to discretion) in the case of a spinster. There is further evidence that the state is not concerned with the virtues of chastity. That 'seed should not be wasted' is not part of our law. Other states are said to have suffered (notably, France in 1940) because copulation had not supplied population. But the British legislature has, perhaps, not needed to take seriously the equation of the 'could be born' with the born as lives to be protected. Recreation without procreation has never been a secular crime.

SEXUAL LAWS

To the modern indictment that the criminal law has usurped the realms of some private morality or public theology, the student of law can reply with a motion to quash; for what is charged is not an offence known to jurisprudence.

We have seen that criminal law embodies moral rules. All the laws against violences and frauds are grounded in the morality of the people, and, in turn, the morality of the people is influenced by those laws.

In the field of sexual conduct, criminal law is clear and limited; and its changes have kept pace with conventional morality. Of rape and unlawful carnal knowledge of girls below the age of sixteen,[25] the laws are severe and generally considered to be justly severe. Over adulteries and fornications, the already obsolescent jurisdiction of the Ecclesiastical Courts disappeared in 1857. The common law crime 'criminal conservation' (i.e. adultery) had by that time become forgotten among obsolete indictments. One reason for this is to be found in the emancipation of women; that is to say, the increasing recognition that woman is not property to be stolen. The civil law still retains, be it mentioned, writs that are founded on that doctrine.

A man can sue the lover *quod abduxit uxorem cum bonis viri sui* – that is the action of wife-enticement.[26] The important loss

[25] Very important in these days of coeducation. A youth under 23 (and that means that he has not turned 24) can plead ignorance of the girl's nonage – an older man must ask for a birth certificate.

[26] Place v Searle [1932] 2 K.B. 497 is the last case in which this cause of action was analysed.

is the loss of the wife's *servitium* – her household work. Her *consortium* counts for little as a head of damage, less if it be lost through her abduction than through her injuries.[27] The same reasoning is seen in the action of seduction. There a father sues because, through his daughter's pregnancy, he has lost her services. He proves that she used to prepare his tea, and hopes that the jury will put a high valuation on that service.

Compendiously, it may be said, that fornications are less seriously regarded now, because women are held to be persons not chattels; and adultery, if important, is remedied in the divorce jurisdiction. Here the change in the moral atmosphere is perceptible in the almost cessation of desperate fights against the accusation. The 'stigma' no longer operates as the incitement to perjury which at one time it understandably was. These changes in the moral atmosphere are expressed in the law, particularly in the discretionary concessions: the 'discretion' granted to a petitioning spouse in respect of his or her own adulteries. Also the judges no longer automatically treat as 'condonation' the fact of intercourse after a matrimonial offence has been committed. That doctrine, be it added, operated for long to keep unhappy marriages in being.

In these ways the law expresses morality, and, in so doing, fulfils a proper function of the law, just as it does in the unsexual fields of fraud.

In sexual matters, public opinion runs ahead of the law, and the law eventually overtakes it. The social history is that great increases of population, competitive, have been accompanied, in the intellectual field, by strong developments of individualism, of the notion that self-expression is good, inhibition slavish. Increases in wealth, the ability to travel (even over short distances), make pleasure-seeking and finding at once normal and easy. Other factors are the rise in the age at which marriage is economically possible. (It is no longer usual for males to wait until they have reached their apparent maximum of earning

[27] Best v Samuel Fox & Co. Ltd. [1952] 2 All Eng. R. 394. Hare v B.T.C. [1956] 1 All Eng. R. 578. In this context, the husband's action in respect of his wife's injuries is separate from the wife's action, and is not affected by her contributory negligence.

before marrying.) Add that most females work, and we have the explanation of much informal 'labour' among liberal women.

These developments, these integrations, have so changed the generally accepted averages of conduct that no one, without admitting great dogmatism, would condemn 'irregular' intercourse as wicked. Here, then, says the superficial critic, is an abandonment by the law of a field of private immorality. The answers to the proposition are (1) that it is not at all certain that the expression immorality is properly used when applied indiscriminately to all 'free love'. (2) That 'free love' never was acceptedly criminal in all its manifestations. (3) That there is much private conduct (involving cruelties) which, by all standards, is immoral and is illegal.

That some sexual licence is immoral would be conceded by most people. An example is dishonourable betrayal.

The betrayal which is at once dishonourable and criminal is bigamy. Clearly there are cases where the male bigamist is achieving rape – sexual intercourse, with consent being obtained here by fraud. A female bigamist can be achieving a seduction. Therefore the law punishes bigamy. In the past the penalty of imprisonment was inevitable. But in our day more allowance is made for the realities; has anyone been harmed? In our day, that Lord Russell, who married, in the 1890s, while his lawful spouse was alive, would not have been sent to prison. He had obtained a divorce in an American State, where grounds of divorce were accepted which the English law would not accept. He deceived nobody. Nevertheless he was imprisoned. By modern law he would probably still be found guilty, but no substantial penalty would be inflicted.

One is aware of the stigma that attaches to bastardly proceedings. But here no violation is alleged. These (civil) proceedings[27a] enforce the payment of maintenance by fathers of progeny inseminated by them in women who are not their wives. Some stigma attaches to such conduct, usually surreptitious, irresponsible, suggestive of lack of self-control. Religious traditions are relevant here. Their effect is less fortunate in the social con-

[27a] With high standard of proof, corroboration is required; and opportunity is insufficient.

demnation of fornicators than in condemnation of the unwanted progeny. In ancient systems, as well as modern, the bastard is a victim of society – even of societies that are proud of their kindness to orphans.

In England the bastard is *filius nullius*. This means (what is not generally known) that he not only lacks a father, he lacks also a legal mother. The bastard 'begot in nature's lusty strength', and conquering his environment, would be found, when he died rich and intestate, to have no next of kin. His mother could not inherit his well-gotten gains, until the law was altered by the Legitimacy Act of 1927.

Significantly, industrial laws, such as the Workmen's Compensation Acts, are mainly responsible for changes in the status of the illegitimate. Under those acts (workmen's compensation commencing in 1896) the expression 'dependant' included illegitimate children and unmarried bed-fellows. Since that time, such statutes as the Children's and Young Persons Acts give the same protection to unparented children as to all neglected or ill-treated children who come to the notice of police or local authority.

The illegitimate, parentless, is normally left in the care of the female. Lawful progeny of unhappy marriages can be worse off – because their custody belongs in law to the male parent. But there has been much modification of the common law by Matrimonial Causes Acts and the Guardianship of Infants Act. The courts now aim at achieving the welfare of the child in the circumstances. The 'natural' claim of the mother to be the proper custodian of the very young can fail. In an extreme case preference can be given to the claim of a male who is in prison.

In the light of the effects of illegitimacy, it is wrong to refer to all heterosexual conduct as taking place within a domain of privacy. Certainly more privacy attaches to unconsequenced sex, or sex protected against, or prevented from, consequences. But the law has not receded from interference with sexual conduct, merely because of a concept of privacy. Notoriously the English law knows little of privacy, as a right. The distinction between 'public act' and 'private act' is, if it exists, unimportant. In fact, the law includes restrictions on much conduct that takes place in relative privacy – e.g., privately organised prize-fighting, bear-baiting, cock-fighting, duelling, etc. – to say nothing of private torturings beloved of modern novelists. These are crimes. Nor does consent prevent the conviction of, say a successful duellist from prosecution for inflicting grievous bodily harm. In point, also, is incest.

The law, between 1857 and 1908, when the Punishment of Incest Act was passed, is believed by many to have left incest unpunishable. In the better opinion, incest was always a common law crime. The modern statute is probably declaratory.

Incest and bestiality constitute special problems for the jurist-moralist because, theoretically, they can be practised in private without apparent deleterious effect. The important question, however, is not whether the law is usurping morality. The question is, rather, whether the attitude of the moralist who condemns incest or who condemns bestiality is morally justified, and whether the law should be altered because the moralist who inspires it is, himself, in the wrong.

Let us frame this question in the legal-moral situation as it has been described. Laws change, as to their moral content, when public opinion, expressing itself through parliamentary legislators or the minds of judges, carries into the law the conviction that what was thought to be moral is now, or is now known to be, not moral: that what was thought immoral is now, or now known to be, not immoral. One factor which influences the public, and eventually the law, is the notion of personal harm – not necessarily public harm, except in the sense that it is ultimately in the public interest for individual persons not to be harmed.

In respect of incest, the condemning moralist rationalises his valuation by pointing to harm; the possibility of progeny which is biologically suspect; or the prevention of persons from forming the extra-familial attachments which lead to marriage. Also it is arguable that much incest (of male parent and female child) is not performed without cruelty; not to mention the fact that incest often coincides with the crime of unlawful carnal knowledge of a female nonager.

In the case of bestiality, which is intercourse with animals, the moral, legal, attitude is of disgust. Whether law is justified as an expression of disgust is arguable; but few will maintain that law is bad law only because it expresses a social disgust.

Buggery, a practice attributed to, and named after, the Bulgarians[28] (the descendants of the wild Phrygians), is cognate to bestiality, and legally has been defined as intercourse per rectum. It can be committed on the body of a woman, and is then a crime, even if the woman be the performer's wife.[29] It can, accordingly, be argued thus: as many wives may have submitted to demands of this order, and have not complained to the courts, and as these practices go unnoticed, how can a condemning law be practical? To this the answer is that law does not depend for its validity on its practicality. Yet there is an element of reason in the view that the offence is not important until someone complains. Complaint would imply that the crime was accompanied by cruelty.

As between consenting males, if the catamite is of mature age, and does not complain of the conduct of the pederast, then, too, we have a situation to which the law will be blind. To this the moralist will answer that, if the conduct is bad, the public knowledge of it is irrelevant. The issue may well be a conflict between dogmas. On the one hand we have a theory that sexual abnormality is bad, not merely abnormal; on the other, that the normal is only a phase in the gamut of abnormalities: that sexual development can take different forms from the heterosexual, that condemnation is therefore not justified.

The condemner of buggery is, however, reinforced by ancillary considerations. It is notorious that men have been known to seduce boys of immature age. It is also notorious that professional catamites are apt to be thieves and blackmailers, so that the practice is deleterious to public order.

It is in the light of law and order that the critics of the law make an arguable case. If there is conduct which will not lead to public disorder, or to other crime, should it not be ignored; treated, like onanism, as a mere vice? In support of this argument comes another, as it were from the equality of the sexes. If lesbianism is not a crime, why should intercourse between consenting males be punishable?

Crime, then, or vice? The law has now been enacted which

[28] In the eighteenth century a male homosexual was called a buggarer.
[29] Lord Audley's case (17th Cent. 3 State Trials 401).

translates the crime into mere vice: and perhaps that is consistent, not with any arbitrary limitation of the functions of the law, but with the realistic recognition of limits.

The morals with which the criminal law is concerned are the morals of society – public and private. Those immoralities which the criminal law ignores are ignored because, on the whole, public opinion does not cry out for any vengeance – does not cry out for suppression.

Also the arm of the law is too short to stretch everywhere. As a matter of organisation, and not by theory, the law is better equipped to deal with what the public can see than with what it cannot see. Nor is the public greatly concerned with what it cannot see. Let Shelley run naked through his drawing-room. But a man who finds himself compelled by nature to defecate in public is behaving in contravention of the criminal law. Much that the law has suppressed in the sexual context can be classified as disorderly conduct. This has come to include the notions of disgusting conduct and corrupting conduct.

If a man finds himself compelled by nature to take a woman into an hotel, that is not a public indecency. He must, however, be careful not to enter a false name into an hotel register because that can be a breach of the Aliens Act!

The lower limit of the criminal law proper is in laws against the improprieties. A male exposing himself to women is not ravishing them; but he is insulting them, and that causes indignation. Evidently here is stigma. That stigma should attach to defecation in public is a fact of psychology, not of morality. In this context the law is concerned with conduct which, while venial, is yet resented by many. We are moving into the area of indiscretion and vice, and out of the field of well recognised crime.

VICE[30] AND THE LAW

If there is one area of the law in which an administrative distinction can be drawn between the public realm and the

[30] The word is here used in its ordinary sense, whatever that is: not in the special sense of the term 'vice squad'.

private domain, this area is the area of the vices. On vices the views of law makers and moralists differ; and moralists differ *inter se*, because vices are not all admitted to be immoralities.

Drink has been considered a vice, but nowadays only 'excess' is regarded as an excess. More in point is 'gambling'. In the past it was worse regarded than now. The religious authorities of Jewry and Christendom regarded it as a means of 'unjust enrichment'. This coheres with the opposition to usury, which is characteristic of those religions. Alternatively it is condemned Rabbinically as waste of substance ('throwing one's money onto the horns of a stag'), and waste, like games in general, of time that should be used for the betterment of the world. The dice-player, in Talmudic law, together with the pigeon-fancier and the usurer, was unacceptable as a witness. The canon law adopts this thinking, and early (Puritanical) Protestantism adds to it.

In these condemnations there is psychological truth. Many lives are wasted in the pursuits which are said to be followed by 'the needy and the greedy'. But gambling, in the sense of playing games of chance – the English legal criterion – is also 'playing'. In days when 'protective' legislation was limited in its scope to the poor, the leaders of the nation spent their leisure, as well as their assets, in Bucks and Whites and Beefsteak Clubs, without incurring animadversion.[31]

There have, admittedly, been periods when work was regarded as a value in itself. (Strangely, now that the capital of Britain is its labour, this valuation is not universal.) Moralists who have valued will-power, courage, etc. – and certainly these are moral values – have condemned play of all types. But the law, in the past, was not play-conscious, unless cheating took place. In this century we live, particularly at night, in realms that the muses of play have created. An atmosphere of self-indulgence is regarded indulgently. Play as use of leisure, is respectable. Even, it can be regarded as praiseworthy, as when it is athletic; and there are those who think (not wrongly) that athletics are characterised by moral effort. This is the effort that ancient Greece expected from, and rewarded in, its atheletes. These games, ceasing to be pleasures, come to fall under the aegis of stern duty; become

[31] E.g. The celebrated Charles James Fox.

legally relevant, as when footballers litigate against their clubs.[32]

Once it is conceded (and the world now concedes) that leisure is a value, and that play is a legitimate use of leisure, the indulgence extends beyond athletics. Then card-playing ceases to be regarded as an invention of the devil. The effect of this attitude on the law is less violent than might be expected. According to English law, since the days of the Protectorate, card-playing and gambling generally have not been illegal; though not activities which could create legal rights. Only that gambling which could be called a nuisance was relevant to the preventive aspect of the law. The distinction is not between private immorality and public illegality, but between that which concerns peace and order and that which does not patently disturb the peace.

The law does not 'approve of' gambling – whether private or public. Gaming contracts are still unenforceable at law; and there is no need 'to plead gaming acts'.[33]

But laws against gaming were laws against gaming houses, and street betting. Race-courses were found early not to be gaming-houses.[34] But only in the 1960s did gambling clubs and betting houses become legal. The theory about gaming houses is that they have been thieves' kitchens. The criterion of the gaming house, for the purposes of statutes from the eighteenth century to mid-nineteenth century, was that in them unlawful games were played. An unlawful game is a game of chance played for money. But once it became established that a game of chance was being played for money on premises used for that purpose, then any other game played therein became an unlawful game. This had the amusing result that, though High Court judges in the 1930s thought bridge to be a game of skill – for most of them played contract, or was it tort? – bridge players found in poker clubs were held guilty of unlawful gaming.

[32] Eastham v Newcastle Football Club [1963] 3 All Eng. R. 139.

[33] The courts have, however, listened to claims against Pools promoters. These claims have failed on the ground that they are based on agreements which are expressly said not to be binding in law.

[34] Powell v Kempton Park [1899] A.C. 143, a case in which H. H. Asquith was Counsel. Neither the course nor the bookmaker's umbrella was described as 'a place' kept for gaming, for the purposes of the Act of 1853.

Compendiously, the law against gambling is a department of the law of public nuisances and breaches of the peace. A similar classification fits the laws about drugs and the laws about sexual 'misconduct'. Significant is the expression 'disorderly house' to describe a brothel. The phrase sounds an echo in Shakespeare, where Falstaff exclaims: 'This is a bawdy house – here's larceny'. Sir John (in whatever infernal ale-house he now inhabits) would undoubtedly be intrigued to learn that in the twentieth century, when prostitutes were being regularly fined £2 for solicitation (which the old warrior would not have regarded as a social evil), the important prosecutions (and those have been many) were for larceny. In near-by Paris the law recognises, as a head of crime, *vol à l'entolage*: which tells us that in France, as in Britain, the street-walker cannot pay for her clothes, her drink, and her *souteneur*, as well as excessive rent to a blackmailing landlord, out of her meagre earnings in a competitive profession.

Probably the law as to brothels, the keeping of which is criminal, was first designed as a law to restrict the scope for larceny. Similarly the crime of living on the immoral earnings of a woman owes its origin, not to the chivalry of the legislators, but to their knowledge that the man so living can also be a 'bully' engaging in theft and blackmail.

An interesting statement of the legal attitude to the life of the half-world is provided by the Law Lords in Shaw v Director of Public Prosecutions [1961] 2 All Eng. R. 446.

The background of the case is that, though to be a prostitute is not criminal, and though private premises are not necessarily brothels because their occupiers are 'immoral', yet anything in the way of solicitation is illegal, and any advertisement is likely to turn a prostitute's premises into a brothel.

Therefore a magazine – a 'ladies' magazine' – which contained thinly disguised notices of addresses that might appeal to the amorous, was held to be the product of a conspiracy to break the relevant laws. What surprised the legal profession was the finding that the editor was guilty of 'living on the immoral earnings of women'.[35]

The 'common prostitute' (i.e. common law prostitute, crudely

[35] See p. 58.

describable as a woman who makes her private property public property) has not been oppressively treated.[36] Under laws modelled on S.28 of the Town Police Clauses Act 1847, she was arrestable and summarily punishable. The punishment before 1959 took the form of a fine of £2. The police of London seem to have regarded themselves as enforcers of payment for a sort of 'licence'. They have been accused of choosing their 'subjects', proving them to be common prostitutes[37] who at the material time were soliciting; and refraining from further action after the magistrate had imposed the conventional fine. By the Street Offences Act of 1959 the technique is changed, so as to accommodate the solicitor not known to have been convicted. The police are allowed to 'caution' women; who may, if they so desire, apply within fourteen days for a note to be made that the caution was unjustified.

The statute says that 'it shall be an offence for a common prostitute to loiter or solicit in a street or public place for the purpose of prostitution.' All that requires to be proved, as to her status, is the caution. The maximum penalty has been raised to £10. If it be proved that she has one previous conviction, the fine can be £25. If she has more than one then she qualifies for a fine of £25 and/or three months' imprisonment. This last provision means that she is dependent on the justice of magistrates, and cannot elect to be tried by judge and jury.[38] There is a police power of arrest without warrant on reasonable suspicion.[39]

Two things are observable in this statute; first, that it operates against the professional, not the amateur; secondly, that it does not operate against men, whether they solicit women or other men.

There is, admittedly, a clause in the Sexual Offences Act 1956 which enacts that 'it is an offence for a man persistently to solicit

[36] The Latin suggests offering for sale. In English law she can be a virgin, pandering to male carnality without intercourse. (R. v Webb (1964) 47 C.A.R. 265.)

[37] One of the rare instances where past history (previous convictions) is admissible in evidence for the prosecution.

[38] She can appeal against magistrates' findings to higher courts.

[39] It is not clear how this is to be reconciled with the need for proof of 'caution' or previous conviction.

or importune in a public place for immoral purposes'. But the scope of this section is not clear. Some have thought that the reference is to male homosexuals. Also the word 'persistently' seems to exclude the casual accost: and it has been held that 'kerb-crawling' in a motor-car is not an offence against this section.[40]

Apart from details of possible unfairness, the statutes are clear as to one effect: that it is not a crime to be a prostitute: fornication for money (or gratis) is not a crime. All that the law is concerned with is the impingement of vice on public order and/or 'the peace'.

This is coherent with the policy of a legal system which insists on cleanliness and sanitation in its housing, health, and factory laws. Compulsory cleanliness does not, perhaps, amount to an assumption of a moral rule by the law; but is acceptable to a society which is not without godliness.

A more controversial question is as to the propriety (in a controversial sense) of laws which concern the cleanliness of the contents of reading matter. That topic calls for separate treatment.

THE OBSCENE AND THE IBSCENE

The concept of good order as a pattern of conduct is the matrix of much law that the moderns regard as unduly restrictive. The censorship of plays derived from the power of the Lord Chamberlain, in the days of the first Elizabeth, to license theatres. He was concerned with the structure of buildings, as well as with the claims of rival companies to play within the metropolis. He was more concerned with the morals of the players (easily classified as vagabonds – for few, indeed, of them had fixed abode) than with the ethical quality of the plays that they performed. The modern rules by which, until recently, plays were submitted to the Lord Chamberlain, is a byproduct that kept a worthy official profitably engaged, long after his original purposes, arising from the desire of the Royal Court for amusement, had oblivesced.

[40] Crook v Edmondson [1966] 1 All Eng. R. 833. The word 'persistent' is notoriously difficult – e.g. in matrimonial law as to 'persistent cruelty'.

(The office of Lord Chamberlain was abolished in 1968. He never controlled films, which are subject to a censor who determines the age groups to which specific films can be shown.)

To laws of public order and conduct 'against the peace' we owe the cases and statutes that constitute the law as to obscenity. It was not a literary exploit for which, in 1663, Sir Charles Sedley was fined and imprisoned. That gentleman had stood naked on his balcony and urinated his contempt of the public.[41] But when in 1708 Read, the author of *15 Plagues of a Maidenhead*, was prosecuted for the publication of 'a lewd licentious libel',[42] Sedley's case was distinguished as being in the class of offences *vi et armis*. Read was acquitted because (strangely) it was held that his work, though bawdy, was not a libel.

But later prosecutors availed themselves of the Sedley precedent by pleading, in their prosecution of pornographers, that the conduct of the accused was 'against the peace'. So Curle was successfully prosecuted in 1727 for his *Venus in her Cloisters* and pilloried. In the same period, Cleland was fined by the Privy Council in respect of *Fanny Hill*.[43] So the notion of 'breach of the peace' was extended to include in its scope the varieties of scurrility.

The prosecution of the scurrilous continued through the seventeenth and eighteenth centuries, because some of the most scurrilous writings of that period were directed against King and Church and Government. A censorship, instituted by the Long Parliament with political motive, had been abolished before the end of the seventeenth century, by reason of a public opinion that owed much to John Milton's *Areopagitica*. The eighteenth century was concerned with defamation.

It was left to nineteenth-century lawyers to isolate the category of obscenity. That century begins with John Bowdler's society for the suppression of vice. The Bible and Shakespeare suffered. The

---

[41] This kind of conduct would now be prosecuted under Vagrancy or Municipal Acts.

[42] In those days 'libel' connoted publication, not necessarily to, or about specific persons: and criminal libel was not necessarily defamatory, of specific persons. 'Social' invective was enough.

[43] A book reprinted, and proceeded against, over two hundred years later. Strange immortality!

common law as to obscenity was re-stated in 1857, in Lord Campbell's Obscene Publications Act, which remained in force until
replaced (largely re-enacted) by the Obscene Publications Act
1959.

The other notable restriction on publications was the common
law against blasphemy. That was rendered a dead letter after the
prosecutions of Bradlaugh and Annie Besant. Law against blasphemy is still (theoretically) in being; and it is not without
interest to speculate that a more intelligent prosecution might
well have used, at least, the concept of blasphemy when *Lady
Chatterley's Lover* came before the court. It implies no religious
bigotry if offence be taken at the description of a male organ as
the 'King of Glory', and an act of intercourse be described in a
quotation from the Psalms.

The law as to blasphemy has been stated by an atheist, at
Hyde Park Corner, in the words 'Thank God this is a free country'. True, but not accurate.

Time was when blasphemy stood as the accusation which
defenders of the faith (whatever faith it was) levelled at all dis-
senters, all schismatics, all heretics, all reformers, however spiritual
and however restrained; and the scoffer at religion was a lesser
object.

It is still the law of England, preserved in dead-letter statutes
of William III and George III, that the denial of the Christian
religion in writing is a crime – 'stockable', pilloriable. Also punishable are spoken words denying the existence of God and His
Providence, deriding the Christian Messiah, bringing into dis-
belief the Bible and the Book of Common Prayer.

Let it be said that the desuetude of these laws is consistent
with acceptable laws which protect religious services against
disturbance. Among the advances of nineteenth-century law are
the extensions of this protection to the Churches of Roman
Catholics (1829) and to Synagogues (1846); this last measure
owing much to that great intellectual and moralist, Lord
Macaulay.

A century of rationalism had been completed when the prosecution of Bradlaugh in 1878 and 1882 demonstrated that the law
was inept in the context of serious thought, however 'negative'.

The famous judge-historian, Stephen, expresses the evolved legal position: 'Blasphemy . . . is the publication of matter relating to God, Jesus Christ, the Bible or the Book of Common Prayer intended to wound the feelings of mankind or to excite contempt and hatred against the Church or to promote immorality'. Already it is clear that the modern law is not defending any theology as such, but is concerned with the social decencies. Stephen continues: 'Publications intended in good faith to propagate opinions on religious subjects which the person publishing them regards as true, are not blasphemous within the meaning of the definition merely because their publication is calculated' [i.e. likely] 'to wound the feelings of Christian people, or because their general adoption might tend by lawful means to alterations in the constitution of the Church as by law established'.

Sir James Stephen's statement expresses a change in the law from the postulates of previous centuries that Christianity was part of the common law of England. Stephen's view received authoritative confirmation in Bowman v Secular Society, in which the House of Lords held that a bequest to a secularist society is not invalid by any reason of public policy or because of any wrongful purpose latent in secularism.[44]

Since that time prosecutions for blasphemy have ceased. One reason for this is that blasphemies such as those rather cheap jibes that disfigure James Joyce's *Ulysses* have evaporated in the 'obscenity' which used to be the atmosphere attributed to that interesting thought-land voyage.

The law relating to literary obscenity emerges (as a law of obscene libel) from the general condemnation of 'criminal libel', a category which is now much narrowed, but which included the law as to blasphemy. The classical case on obscenity, R. v Hicklin, (1868) L.R. 3 Q.B. 360, arose from scurrilous attacks on the Roman Catholic confessional.

In that case (an appeal from a Recorder who had refused to hold the articles obscene) the court stated what was meant by

---

[44] [1917] A.C. 406. It is noteworthy that charges of blasphemy are framed in terms of the author's intention. In obscenity charges this is not the practice. That is one reason why, given a choice, the prosecution alleges obscenity.

obscenity in the common law and in Lord Campbell's Act passed
a decade earlier. A writing, picture, etc. is obscene if 'it has a
tendency to corrupt or deprave those whose minds are open to
immoral influence'. That criterion (appropriate to blasphemy) has
since been applied to erotic and physiological fiction, as well as to
tales of violence and drug addiction. A law, in fact, to prevent the
promotion of onanism and other malpractices deleterious to society.
The judges of the United States appear to have regarded this as
molly-coddling. Joyce's *Ulysses* was allowed to enter America on
the pronouncement of a judge that the thing was 'an emetic not
an aphrodisiac'. Thirty years later in Butler v Michigan[45] the
Supreme Court went further, and held *ultra vires* the 14th
Amendment a law of the State of Michigan against the publication of 'obscene, immoral, lewd or lascivious language'. Frank-
furter J. described the statute as 'the quarantining of the general
public in order to shield juvenile innocence'. This, he added, was
like the conduct of Elia's Chinaman who burnt down houses in
order to obtain roast pork.

The English courts have not been so reliant on the robust
masculinity of the reading public. Pornography is unlawful. Even
while the Law Lords were expressing tolerance of what has been
called blasphemy, the Chancery was dealing severely with the
very mild eroticism to be found in the pages of Elinor Glyn's
Three Weeks. That author, a philosophy graduate of an American
University, had described a marital desertion and an adulterous,
if romantic, liaison, but with none of those physiological data
which are the *sine qua non* of the modern lucubrations. Evidently
what lasts three weeks cannot be as 'physiological' as what lasts
three minutes. Nevertheless, when the lady sought a remedy for
breach of copyright, the learned judge who had felt it his duty to
read the book, refused her a remedy on the grounds (*inter alia*)
that a contract connected with a work of that type was void by
reason of public policy.[46]

It is doubtful whether all the later courts would have approved
the learned judge's condemnation of Miss Glyn's 'romance'. But
in 1959 the legislature seems to have taken the view that prurience

---

[45] (1957) 352 U.S. 42.
[46] Glyn v Western Feature Film Co [1916] 1 Ch. 261.

has not changed since the days of Hicklin. The definition of obscenity given in the Obscene Publications Act 1959 is 'that an article shall be deemed to be obscene if its effect . . . is, if taken as a whole, such as to tend to deprave and corrupt persons who are likely, having regard to all relevant circumstances, to read, see, or hear, the matter contained or embodied in it.' These words add little to Hicklin, except that they enable a court to distinguish between the conduct of a bookseller who sells *Aristotle's Anatomy* to small boys in a back street and the conduct of a bookseller who sells them to medical students in a better class back street.

The statute restates the two modes of procedure already existent: (1) that copies of obscene books can be seized, brought to a magistrate, and (if he so rules) forfeited; (2) that charges may be brought, before magistrates, or judges and jury, against (a) any person who whether for gain or not publishes an obscene article or (b) who has an obscene article for publication for gain (whether gain to himself or gain to another). The maximum summary punishment on conviction of such a charge is £100 fine or six months of imprisonment; on indictment the court can inflict an unlimited fine and/or up to three years of imprisonment.

As already pointed out, the law against obscene publications makes no clear reference to the intentions of publishers or authors. By their works ye shall know them. That exclusion is consistent with the policy of the law in the field of the decencies. On that principle are prohibited advertisements relating to certain diseases; on the same principle the reporting of sexual cases is strictly controlled. On the same principle also was enacted the Horror Comics Act (Children & Young Persons (Harmful Publications) Act 1955) which makes it an offence to have for sale stories 'portraying the commission of crimes, acts of violence or cruelty, incidents of a repulsive or terrible nature in a way that the work as a whole would tend to corrupt or deprave a child or young person into whose hands it might fall.' [Thereby a monopoly was created for television.]

The doctrine that intention is irrelevant is now modified, to this extent, by Section 4 of the Act of 1959, that a social purpose can be pleaded: there is no penalty and no forfeiture if 'it is proved' [the onus being on the defence] that the article in question is justified as being for the public good on the ground that it is in the interests of science, literature, art or learning or of other objects of general concern'. On this the evidence can be adduced of 'experts as to the literary, scientific, artistic, or other merits' of the article.

The statute does not seem to allow psychiatrists, the *fontes* of so much pornographic content in modern writing, to explain to the jury how an article works through a mind (if that is the proper word) in the process of corrupting or depraving. There is doubt (and the law is debatable) as to whether any such questions can be asked of any witness, because (this may not be a good reason) it is the precise question to be decided by the jury.

In the statute what the law does not achieve, perhaps because it cannot, is a precise description of the tendency to corrupt or deprave. The question is left to judge and jury. The judge can, in a proper case, hold that the work in question cannot be in the guilty category. But most cases are improper cases, and application is less difficult than the verbal forms suggest.

We are concerned with 'dirt', which has been neatly described as 'matter misplaced'. No one is concerned with any misplaced matter in the text of the Bible, Shakespeare, Dean Swift, Laurence Sterne and a host of other great masters. But Rabelais presents a problem – for that great thinker indulges in words replete with an awareness of the excretory-genital system, which is the inspiration of most European 'swear words' and bad language. This question is probably academic now, by reason of Section 4. And Section 4 would probably now save the previously condemned Boccaccio, whose pornography only differs by reason of literary merit and subtlety from the crude stories of some private detective who counts a day lost if in the course of it he has not seduced a debutante, debauched a wife, wrestled for his virtue unsuccessfully against a nymphomaniac, and drunk himself into final insensibility.

To works with social propaganda, or tragedies illustrative of sordidities such as Aristotle would have excluded, few would attribute obscenity. Marie Stopes[47] added many technicalities to the law of libel by defending her biological writings against such

[47] Sutherland v Stopes [1925] A.C. 47.

an accusation. But fiction is harder to vest with virtue. Is it obscene or, more respectably, ibscene?

A study in the pathos of lesbianism was condemned in the 1920s. Thirty years later a male, Kaufman, writing in *The Philanderer* more explicitly and with more detail, gave expression to his sexual vagaries. This came to the court in R. v Martin Secker & Warburg Ltd.[48] in which the presiding judge, in a summing up of monumental irrelevance, dealt with the aesthetic values patent or latent in nudity, but also asked one pertinent question, the critical question – 'corrupt whom?'

In the terms of the later statute, who are 'the persons who are likely, having regard to all relevant circumstances, to read' the article? Are we to consider the *homme moyen sensuel*, or the academic, or the immature? the ordinary reader, or the person who haunts the back street hunting the lascivious? Or has the statute, following Hicklin, misstated the common law, by omitting the notions of disgust or offensiveness, such as was aroused by Sedley urinating *coram publico*?

Undoubtedly the statute has made life easier for many 'realists'. How much easier was, unfortunately, not decided in the case of R. v Calder & Boyars, wherein an American book was considered in which the author described in great and gross detail, and in relatively filthy language, the otherwise unspeakable life of the denizens of Brooklyn. Obscene or ibscene? Unhappily, the case 'went off on a technicality'. The Court of Criminal Appeal quashed the jury's verdict of guilty because the judge had omitted to direct the jury's attention to arguments of great importance on the meaning of the statutory words.[49]

The law is, therefore, left in an empirical state, which is the normal state of English law. The moral standpoint of the public is more tolerant now than it was when Elinor Glyn wrote *Three Weeks*; and that tolerance has, in some degree, permeated osmotically into the law. Enlightened opinion, being the opinion of literary persons, is antagonistic to restrictions even upon classes of writers whom they would never wish to emulate. The writer of polysyllables will fight to the death for the right of the moron

[48] [1954] 2 All Eng. R. 683. Before the Act of 1959.
[49] (1967) 52 C.A.R. 706.

whose vocabulary is limited to the quadriliteral. Yet on the whole the law expresses the opinion of a majority which is not literary and which retains a belief that the sexual is a reserved topic; and that the profane should not traffic in those secrecies.

NOTE ON THE DEFINITION OF OBSCENITY

In the author's submission the law has been much obscured by a definition adopted from the quite different law of blasphemy. What the court said in R. v Hicklin had a meaning in the context of blasphemy, where it was desirable to narrow the scope of prosecutions for criminal libel.

In ordinary usage, obscenity is a clear concept. That is ob-scena, in front of the stage, which should be behind the stage. The basic notion is of disgust. If someone introduced into the street a model of a rampant penis, or a picture of an act of excretion, the presentation would surely be described as obscene, notwithstanding that none could be corrupted or depraved by it.

In other words, the rule in Hicklin is inappropriate, and has had the effect of rendering the law relating to obscenity narrow and difficult.

It may be of interest to observe that similar narrowness of definition has bedevilled other departments of the law. Defamation has been described as that which exposes someone to hatred, ridicule or contempt. Yet if that were adhered to many libels which are annoyances would not produce damages. E.g., when Princess Yussupoff recovered damages for the allegation that she had been ravished by Rasputin, could it be said that an allegation of being victim of a crime could cause, in reasonable people, hatred, ridicule or contempt for the victim?

Analogously, here, by thinking in terms of corruption and perversion, the lawyers have forgotten the wide notions of indecency which are part of the common law. Consequently, it is more difficult to judge obscenity. Were the law stated in terms of, say, disgust, it would be relatively easy to inquire whether the subject matter was mainly disgusting, or whether it had a value redeeming it from any element of the nauseating. That, it is submitted, is the essence of any legal appraisal.

7

Blossoms on the Tree

STANDARDS OF CONDUCT IN THE CIVIL LAW

In the heavy undergrowth which is English case law many a
branch is to be found in which an exploring moralist or man of
religion might each claim to recognise his own 'Golden Bough'.
Without dogmatism as to origins, let us rather invoke a poet
(incidentally the poet of morality) and describe the benign
growths of doctrine as 'intertwisted fibres serpentine, inveterately
convolved'.

In the law of contract, overlapping into the law of tort or
misfeasance, there are two discernible traditions of honesty. There
is a tradition of the strict interpretation of obligations, with
judicial interference only in the event of proven frauds or deceits.
The second tradition is one of conscience, in which the law
operates for the protection of persons at disadvantage, and for the
control of those in fiduciary positions (entrusted with special
duties). The second tradition, equity, derives from the chancellors, men of conscience[1] who took interest in documents in days
when the persons affected were likely to be illiterate. The chan-
cellor was concerned with fraudulent conduct in a wider sense
than is used in the common law; not only with forgeries, but with
all manner of mean advantages. Therefore he became the protector
of *cestui que* trust against trustee, beneficiary against executor
or rival beneficiary, mortgagor against mortgagee. Against wrong
behaviour, he enforced, not only payment of damages, but rectifi-
cations of deeds, and specific performance of undertakings, in-

---

[1] Said to vary as the length of their feet.

junctions mandatory and prohibitive; and his jurisdiction eventually extended over the whole field of real property.

Since the Judicature Acts of 1871 and 1875, the Chancery and the common law courts are no longer divided in a 'separation of powers'. Only a division of labour persists, because it is convenient for the topics invested with equitable doctrines to be dealt with by specialists in that learning. And no profane juries enter those austere realms. In the common law courts many cases are dealt with in which there is no relevant doctrine of equity. The law then is conscientious: but demands on conscience are not made.

Light may be shed by an illustration. A person makes a contract to sell a house. Now, after the purchaser, with his permission, has incurred expenses in decoration, etc., can no longer resile from the bargain on mere payment of damages. Against him the court may order 'specific performance', because damages would not constitute *restitutio in integrum* (restoration of the position as it was before). On the other hand, if x has contracted with y to do work and labour and finds that it pays him to break the contract, and pay calculable damages, while he gets on with more profitable work, he can do so. Against him there can be no order of specific performance. Nor will the court add any animadversions to its award of damages.

In contrast, in a Chancery court there appeared an executor who found the estate of his testator burdened with a difficult contract. There is legal thinking that a contract is a group of mutual rights and duties which include the right to fail in performance and pay damages. That 'failure' would have been the easy, and cheap, course for this executor; but the court prevented its adoption. 'The legal duty', said the presiding judge, 'in this instance is identical with the moral duty'. The court valued higher the duty of honouring obligations than the adventitious benefits of legatees. (Cooper v Jarman.)[2] Let it be added that, though in the intervening years the theory of contemplated breach received the considerable intellectual support of no less than Mr Justice Holmes, of the United States Supreme Court,

[2] (1866) L.R. 3 Eq. 98.

yet in 1938, the 'moral' doctrine was seen to be applied by the Privy Council in a similar case.[3]

That case suggests a high level of morality. But this is law of fiduciary persons. They are not the normal among litigants. Litigants in the common law, however, must not be misled in a dishonest way.

For the general parallelism, or pre-established harmony, between the common legal and the moral, reference may profitably be made to the lines of learning in which the courts worked out the essentials of the action for damages for misleading words, and, later, the development of the concept of unjust enrichment.

First let it be said that most of our earlier law is concerned with acts, not with words. Promises, in the old Year Books, feature mainly in debt. Most of our early authorities are occupied with the development of the law of trespass. Words first became important as causes of breach of the peace. Only later, in a more sophisticated society, is it important to define the legal significance of words as constituents of commercial relations. The early nineteenth century consolidates learning on this. So well established was the doctrine of liability for false words that, already in 1862, the question was whether conduct, in lieu of words, would be wrong in law; and it was held that any conduct designed to deceive another by leading him to believe that a certain state of facts exists, 'is equivalent in law, as in morals' to a statement that such a state of facts exists.[4] Here we have a notion which is expressed, in ethics and in law, in the same word, deceit. (Not the only 'term of art' which is also an ethical term.)

But if we follow the learning in this branch we encounter a distinction and a break. By unfortunate chance the authority of the House of Lords on the whole topic was invoked in a case relating to the prospectus of a company – in those days a new phenomenon. The facts are suggestive of negligence on the part of the promoter rather than wickedness. Accordingly the Law Lords, when asked to hold the promoter liable in damages to a

---

[3] Ahmed Angullia v Estate Trust Agencies (1927) Ltd. [1938] A.C. 624 P.C.

[4] Horsfall v Thomas (1862) 1 H. & C. and cases cited in Salmond on Tort in that context.

buyer of shares, refused to do so, and defined the scope of action for misleading words as follows. An action of damages for deceit lies at law when one person makes a wilfully false statement [in words or conduct] with intent that the other person shall act in reliance on it, and with the result that the other does so act and suffers harm in consequence.[5] A century later that doctrine was followed in the Court of Appeal when damages were sought against accountants for losses incurred by reason of their negligent advice (Candler v Crane, Christmas & Co).[6]

In that case the Court of Appeal refused to extend the doctrine of duty to neighbours from the physical order into the verbal. The accountant had a duty to his client, not to strangers. In the United States there have been similar refusals. The great American jurist Cardozo expressed the view that to make people liable to third persons for misleading words would be to extend the notion of deceit beyond its definition in Derry v Peek. A decade later, a House of Lords which regarded itself as able to overrule its previous rulings (a new doctrine this) held, *obiter* but convincingly, that such misleading words are actionable, and treated Derry v Peek as a limited authority.[7]

One simple inference serves, meanwhile, to show a limit to the moral duty as described in Derry v Peek. If the second person, though deceived in mind, yet does not act on the strength of the false statement, but relies, for example, on the honest, though mistaken, advice of someone else, then he cannot recover damages from the dishonest one. The moralist, to whom the dishonest effort is a wicked act, whether successful or unsuccessful, finds here an instance where ethics and law run in parallel, but not all the way.[8] At this point he learns, at a level deeper than the superficial, something of what is meant by the proposition that the

[5] Derry v Peek (1889) 14 A.C. 337.

[6] [1951] 2 K.B. 164.

[7] Hedley Byrne v Heller & Partners Ltd. [1963] 2 All Eng. R. 575. The Law Lords' opinions are too important to be classed in the ordinary class of *obiter dicta*. Incidentally, this thinking had been anticipated by Law Lords in Nocton v Ashburton [1914] A.C. 932, an action for damages against a solicitor.

[8] For a development in the criminal law (Trade Descriptions Act 1968), see p. 17 *et seq*.

court is not a court of morals. He will also know that, while legal rules and moral rules are not coextensive, yet the legal system is not, in general, anti-moral, or non-moral, or always, in the popular (and unfortunate) phrase, ethically neutral. He has seen an instance of the law operating so as to cause a man to behave conscientiously; he has seen the condemnation of immoral conduct; and that these manifestations of law are 'moral'. Morality is a dimension of law, not measurable in all the law's phases, but not to be thought away. Moreover, because the law is much involved with morals, it has been possible to suggest the operation of what the scientists describe as a 'feed-back', a process by which law, making men more aware of dangers, strengthens their morality. A recognition of higher standard is to be found in the recent House of Lords opinions, already referred to, that bad advice can, after all, be tortious.[9] This is very important socially; for it helps people to become aware that a lack of care for other persons' concerns is also an ethically bad attitude. Similarly, the quantity of recent legislation relevant to the promotion of companies, is calculated as a discipline from which may emerge a clear moral standard. Then promoters and directors will not need to ask whether the eye of the law be on them.

To return to the topic of deceit. Here we have one instance of the general proposition that the law is much concerned with honesty. So is the man in the street. Not everyone would admit his sexual deviations to be immoral; but no one, however opinionated, would seriously maintain that his lies for profit, his false promises, his traps for the unwary, are not immoralities, however they be regarded by the law.

Now it is observable in this century that the law endeavours to continue its parallel course with morality. To that end, gaps in the law are being closed. Deceit, under the title Fraud, was always so seriously regarded that it was classified among crimes as well

[9] Hedley Byrne & Co. v Heller & Partners Ltd. [1961] 3 All Eng. R. 891 in which the plaintiff only failed because the bank that gave the misleading information did so expressly without responsibility. Relevant is the case of Osman v Ralph Moss Ltd. (unreported) in which an insurance broker was held liable for misleading his client as to the solvency of the company in which he had caused the latter to be insured for motor risks.

as among torts. But the essence of the crime, as of the tort, was false statement of fact. A false praise of goods offered for sale, a false proposition about their value, carried no legal consequences. In 1968, false representations short of intentional misstatement of fact – that is to say, false praises, false valuations – have been declared criminal (Trade Descriptions Act 1968). This is a policy, perhaps, to be expected from a government pledged to the defence of the poor against their exploiters and against their own ignorance. But it is consistent with other legislation, parliamentary and judicial, to the credit of all parties.

Again, company law, after the opinions of the Law Lords in Salamon v Salamon ([1895] A.C.) offered opportunities for irresponsible traders who limited their liability by the forms of company law. Even if he was the virtually sole shareholder, his personal assets were immune from the attack of the disappointed creditor.[10] In this century, the law has required disclosures of the true state of company ownership, company assets, company affairs generally, which give the information to traders that will help to keep them from falling into the trap of the bogus company. Where the buyers of shares are concerned, the law protects them against the misleading prospectus – not only against its false statements, but against its concealments. That was demonstrated clearly in the case of Lord Kylsant, in the 1920s, where a chairman of shipping lines was imprisoned for non-disclosure of the fact that the apparent profits of his companies had been enlarged by the use of reserves. Since then a series of Companies Acts have made the issue of prospectuses into so serious an undertaking that most degrees of carelessness can be treated as criminal.[11]

Always there is scope for improvement in the law. Thus a serious ethical defect in the law of fraud is implicit in the proposi-

[10] For an expression of doubt as to the universality of the rule in Salamon, see the complex and interesting tax case, Littlewood's Mail Order Stores Ltd. v McGregor [1969] 3 All Eng. R. 855, in which an *ad hoc* company was a link in a chain of assignments calculated to avoid tax liability.

[11] The protection of shareholders or sharebuyers is achieved, in a degree, by the Register at Somerset House. Observe, however, that provident societies, being used as property-companies, are under fewer duties of disclosure.

tion that deceit, or fraud, consists in a false statement of fact. Not a statement of law, be it noted (i.e. not a false claim). Also, not a false promise. It follows, from the last, that one who dishonestly obtains credit on a promise to pay, or issues a cheque which comes to be dishonoured, is not, apparently, guilty of a crime. And, in a sense, that was (until very recently) the law. Nevertheless, a doctrine has developed that the issuer of a cheque that is dishonoured can be found guilty of a false statement of fact as to his intentions.[12]

Now by the Theft Act 1968, the law has been rendered considerably stricter against the 'irresponsible'. It is now a crime if one 'by any deception dishonestly obtains'. This also rids the law of an old technical distinction between larceny by a trick (violating possession) and obtaining by false pretences (procuring the property without violating the possession). On that distinction many indictments had foundered. Now the law is easier.

Clearer now is the notion of deception. Deception is deceiving, whether deliberate or reckless, whether by words or conduct, whether relating to facts or law or to the present intentions (i.e. expressed in promises) of the person using the deception or of any other person.

Deceptions are punishable even if, short of money and goods immediately taken, they obtain pecuniary advantages such as overdraft facilities, insurances, enhanced opportunities of earning, and opportunities for wagering.

Other changes in commercial law can be described as laws protective of buyers: not without moral overtones. Thus until recently an innocent misrepresentation could give rise to an action for damages, but not for a rescission of the contract. Also, if the innocent misrepresentation were embodied expressly in the actual agreement, there could only be an action for damages in contract.[13] By the Misrepresentation Act of 1967, these two limita-

---

[12] This seems to be the *ratio decidendi* of R. v Kritz [1949] 2 All Eng. R. 406.

[13] In some cases this could be advantageous to the plaintiff. Thus a purchaser of a picture which was innocently represented as a Corot would be better off suing in contract. He might recover what it cost him to buy a Corot. In tort the damages would be his money back.

tions on the rights of buyers were removed, so that now the doctrine *caveat emptor* has evanesced almost to vanishing point.[14]

From the above examples of case law and statute, it is safe to conclude that the law requires the citizen to be honest.

But honesty is an ambiguous word. Some use the phrase 'be honest' as an order not to do certain acts, such as the taking of another's property, the making of false statements, etc. Others would include in the notion a duty to do positive acts – volunteer information, etc. The law stops short of that except where fiduciary persons are concerned. But note the law of finding i.e. the duty to hand over to authority any object found if there is likely to be a discoverable owner. Stealing by finding is a 'head of larceny'. That need not be an addition of DO to DO NOT. What has attracted attention, however, is the occurence of overpayment in error. Must the worker who receives more in his pay packet than his wages, restore the additional money? The courts, since R. v Flowers (1886) 16 Q.B.D. 643, have not gone to the extent of holding that a thing innocently received becomes stolen when the receiver retains it.[15] Is it finding?

By the Theft Act 1968 S.5(4) 'Where a person gets property by another's mistake and is under an obligation to make restoration in whole or part, then' [in effect] if he does not return it he commits theft. But the question whether there is an obligation to return is one to be 'found' by the court in the particular case.

So far we observe the laws of commerce and ordinary life – what Cardozo called the 'law of the market place' – expecting from the citizen 'honesty' rather than 'conscientiousness'; and that holds good even if one adds the law about agents who are punished if they take a commission from the other side.

But the law has not in the past been protective of ordinary contractors who find that someone, without breach of law, is able to 'take advantage' of them; that someone is 'unjustly enriched'. If someone enters into an agreement for, say, work and labour, or sale of goods, without realising that he has omitted to consider certain expenses that will be involved, he is not able to have the

---

[14] It never meant, either in law or Latin, that the buyer should 'take chance'.

[15] Moyne v Coopper [1956] 1 All Eng. R. 450.

contract altered, or rescinded, on the ground of mistake. The commercial man pays for his mistakes. Only a mutual mistake (a comparative rarity) affects the duty to perform the contract. Similarly, frustrations are hard to plead. A change in circumstances is not enough. It must be the case (as found by the judge) that it was the intention of both parties that certain events should exonerate; so that if a busybody had asked: what about situation x, they would both have replied: thus and thus.

There is, however, one class of failures of foresight on which the law has recently been changed so as to prevent a person from profiting from a change of circumstances. Thus it happened that the coronation of King Edward VII was cancelled. People had booked seats on other people's property. Some had paid; some had not paid. The law knows a claim for the return of money paid 'on a consideration that has failed'. But the 'consideration' is the *quid pro quo*. The booked seat was there, available. When the matter came to the courts it was held that 'the loss lay where it fell'. Who had paid could not recover: who had not been paid could not recover. In this there is defect of logic as well as of ethics. That rule, the rule in Chandler v Webster,[16] stood for nearly forty years; and, by the principle *stare decisis*, seemed part of the law. But in 1942, in a case arising out of the interferences of war, the court held that, notwithstanding terms in a contract of sale calculated to allow for delay in delivery due to war, a total interference making the future unpredictable exonerated the buyer, and entitled him to the return of his money.[17] The Law Lords overruled Chandler v Webster, and thus removed an unfairness from the law.

This change in the law is not precisely an introduction of a conscientious motif. Rather it removes an unfairness of the type that is said 'to cut both ways'. Not unrelated is the effort of the court to allow a 'composition'. At common law an agreement to accept less than one is entitled to is unenforceable, because it is an agreement without a 'consideration'. Some inroad was made on this legal resistance in the case of Central London Property

[16] [1904] 1 K.B. 403.
[17] Fibrosa Spolka Akcyjna v Fairbairn Lawson Combe Barbour Ltd. [1942] 2 All Eng. R. 122.

Co. v High Trees House Ltd.[18] though the extent of this en-croachment of common sense is still uncertain.

These matters are victories of common sense, not of conscience in high degree.

Conscientiousness enters the law prominently with the trustee and other 'fiduciary persons'.

The 'law of the market place' is not ethical in any high sense. The normal is the strict letter of the law. That is connected with the requirements of commerce, which is 'hot for certainties'. Therefore, there is no relaxation of contracts because someone has done a bad bargain.[19] Mistakes (as has been said) receive no mitigation. Only a fundamental error, shared by both parties, will cause a court to interfere with the strict terms of a bargain. But the letter of the law is not allowed to cover the wrong that can be done by the fiduciary person. In this context the law does not resign certain functions to conscience, and retain certain functions to itself.

Thanks to the Chancellors of the seventeenth century (for all the elasticity of their consciences) the law now governs two realms. The history of equity shows a strong claim to jurisdiction over, and with the aid of, conscience. In equity there is a departure from lines of learning where the court has expressly refused to take into account a state of mind. Also there is more of pre-occupation with individual persons and not merely members of a class. There is here discernible a clear difference in the legal spirit, which is yet explicable in terms of jurisprudence.

The meaning of equity was made clear at the time of the civil wars when land-owners, involved in political loyalties, had to fear

[18] [1956] 1 All Eng. R. 256.

[19] The exception to this is moneylending contract, e.g. the contract that anticipates inheritances. But there is no sentiment for heavy losses in ordinary trade. Thus when Waterlows, innocently but negligently, manufactured forged bank notes for the state of Portugal, the fact that they had been misled by swindlers in the Portuguese cabinet did not exonerate them. (Banco de Portugal v Waterlow [1932] A.C. 1.) Another exception is in the law against Restraint of Trade. A contract which causes a man to refrain from his normal work (e.g. on dissolution of partnership) is not enforced if it effectively puts him out of business for too long – by reasonable standards.

the consequences of defeat, which were not only execution and torture, but forfeiture of property. So that their children should not suffer the poverty consequent on forfeitures, they assigned their property to neutrals. To be legally effective the devise had to be highly formal: by deed.[20] That the intention was for the property to go to the son of the assignor was a secret between the parties. If it was expressed in a document, that document (by law of evidence) was irrelevant to the title.

Therefore an unconscientious assignee could hold the land for himself. Then the old Chancellors addressed themselves to these unscrupulous fief-holders: 'Yes, you do own that land in the legal sense, and your deed cannot be upset by the circumstance that you were entrusted with this land by a man who, going to the wars, was anxious not to incur the forfeiture that would follow defeat. Nevertheless,' pronounced the Chancery, 'unless you, the feoffee to Uses [i.e. the trustee], give that land to the son of that now executed warrior, you will be put into prison for contempt of court.' (To be observed is the rule *in personam*, more direct than is a normal civil award.) In that way originated trusts, which constitute perhaps the most original contribution, and certainly one of the most important contributions, of England to jurisprudence. That seventeenth century spirit still prevails, late in the twentieth century, and illustrative cases are of frequent occurrence. Indeed, the courts tend now to go further than their predecessors.

A recent example is the case of Beswick v Beswick:[21] in which it appeared that a person had assigned his business to a nephew, agreeing with the nephew that the latter should give him a weekly allowance and, after his death, £5 per week to his widow. This transaction was embodied in a document to which the wife was not a party.

The rule of law is that a contract cannot be enforced by one who is not a party. (To put it technically, there is no *jus quaesitum tertii* in English Law.) In the Court of Appeal the claim of the widow was enforced in language that seemed to overrule that

---

[20] Cf., now a settlement *inter vivos* calculated to prevent the incidence of death duties.

[21] [1966] 3 All Eng. R. 1 (C.A.) and [1967] 2 All Eng. R. 1197.

doctrine. The House of Lords, however, did not adopt that thinking, but applied to the document (as the Court of Appeal had done) a section of the Law of Property Act 1925 which up to that time had been thought to be evidentiary law only, and incapable of adding a party to an agreement. In this way they enforced an informal trust.

But even in the realm of conscience there has been a countertrend to 'legality'. A trust has become a very formal affair. Informal understandings, for example, are not enforced. In the absence of writing, very clear inference is required to create an implied trust. Indeed the learning on trusts, implied, constructive, resultant, etc., is a very technical branch of law. And technical, too, have become all the rules relating to notice: what gives notice of a prior obligation to buyers of land; and the rules for the giving of notice of obligations when an estate is to be wound up. In these, and in most cases where maxims of equity are cited, it will be found that specific precedents are involved, and specific forms to be observed. Similarly, equity relieves from many 'forfeitures'; but not all.

Again, some of the maxims of equity are rather more widely stated than applied. To say that equity looks to the intent, not to the form, does not mean that forms lose their importance. Let it rather be said that some forms lose their finality. Some formal requirements, such as the need for a deed rather than parol (verbal or written) evidence, can be compiled with after the event, and persons can be ordered to perform the technical requirement. But complete informality finds no equitable remedy.

Compendiously, it may be said that equity has almost congealed into a system of law, though the law into which it is congealing is itself less rigid than it was.

At times, the rigidity of the equitable rules (even the less formal ones) can operate unequitably on persons who have behaved in a trustworthy manner. One rule is that which operates against unjust enrichment on the part of fiduciaries. In point is the case of Phipps v Boardman[22] in which a trust was rescued from financial disintegration by the skill of the solicitor to the trustees. He, with a beneficiary, entered into enterprises which the trustees

[22] [1966] 3 All Eng. R. 721.

would not contemplate. They bought the shares of a company in which the trustees held some shares, and used the assets of that company in order to make fortunes for themselves as well as for the beneficiaries of the trust. Their conduct was at all times fair. Yet it was held that they must surrender their well-gotten gains because a fiduciary must not make a profit out of his obligations.

This is one instance of what has been described as 'a trend to legality'; to the strict letter of a law which itself purports to express spirit rather than letter! A moment's reflection shows the inevitability of this process. In a world where economic life is geared to deeds and documents, the niceties cannot be too nice. The technique must be followed. In this world a mortgage is a business transaction; the sentiment for the borrower is out of place.

Here we encounter an inherent difficulty in the nature of our legal system – indeed of any legal system. Law, to be satisfactory, must be universal and must be certain. That carries the consequence that judges cannot, except in special contexts, such as that of trusts, ignore legal formalities. Even there the scope for deviation is small: because trusts have concretised in commercial machinery.

To call the law sub-moral on that account, is unjust.[23] Accurately, the law includes much doctrine which is distilled from morality; but the framework of law, being rigid, will always present appearances of indifference to ethical values.

Instances of the 'moral inadequacy' of the municipal legal system can be multiplied. Instructive is a situation made possible by the terms of the Wills Act. A beneficiary has made the mistake of witnessing the will. This deprives him of his portion. A resultant position is reached in which other beneficiaries, taking his lost share, may, or may not, feel under moral obligation to fulfil the testator's intentions. But the law is powerless. Here there is a

[23] Amoral is a permissible word if it be understood as describing situations (of which several have been mentioned) in which the argument is, e.g., as to the meaning of words, the scope of precedents, the strict effect of a statute, etc.

Morality enters when there is room, or when judges manage to make room, for an ethical determinant.

very clear contrast between orders of duty. The Wills Act was not unethically intended. Indeed its purpose was the righteous one of protecting testators from undue influences. It happens, however, that this law necessitates judgments which are inadequate to the ethical situation.

To cope with the failure of testators, either intentionally or accidentally, to make proper provision for dependants, Parliament has enacted Inheritance Acts of 1938 and later. These fill a gap, but they do not purport to close every conceivable gap through which estates pass into the wrong hands. In the last analysis there is no legal substitute for care and conscience.

THE POOR THAT YE HAVE WITH YOU

The revolution of the twentieth century is, it has been said, against property. The evolution of English law owes much to a general recognition of the needs and the dangers; to an awareness (on the part of 'those who have', even before they were joined in government by those who have not) that disorder and revolt only take place when many people are driven to desperation and find leaders who make them more conscious of it.

To such governmental recognition we owe our ancient Poor Law, which was old when the ministers of the first Elizabeth reconstructed it. In the first quarter of this century when the social 'id' could not be canalised into work, because there was no work, unemployment assistance came into being; an ingenious but unsatisfactory system which bridged the gap in time until a wiser economy, and impending wars, brought a prosperity in which all could share as wage-earners, and unemployment sank to a percentage which could be dealt with adequately by the varieties of social insurance.

Poverty corrupts, and absolute poverty corrupts absolutely. But with the high degrees of poverty the English legislature, and English economy, have coped. They no longer rely on doctrine that 'He made them high and lowly, He gave them their estate'. Instead they furnish welfare, so that none of the minima of living are beyond the reach of anyone; and the minima, be it added, are not minimal, since the services, including the medical, educational, etc., are of quite a high order.

There remains relative poverty, when the relationship of rich and poor is exacerbated by the circumstances of dependence; as when a dweller in a house is dependent on the owner of the house, as when a borrower is dependent on a lender, a trader on a grantor of credit, an employee on an employer. From the point of view of the courts at the beginning of the century, there was little or no protection for the dependent person against one whose rights of exploitation were well precedented or statutory.

The normal process of English law is a co-operation between judiciary and legislature. It is a postulate of the law that the statutes are binding on the courts – and the courts will enforce them, even if the statutory law is distasteful to the judge because it appears to work hardship. Then, if ingenuity fails to 'avoid', *obiter dicta* are pronounced to condemn.[24] But 'nothing can be done about it.'[25]

Fortunately legislation in this century has been characterised by a tendency to protect the poor and the improvident against those who seem to, or are in a position to, exploit them. Thus the Moneylenders' Acts of 1904 and 1927 insist on the registration of moneylenders, restrict the rates of interest that moneylenders may charge, prohibit the charging of compound interest, and also protect the borrower with formalities – including the need for a document in which the precise rate of interest is set out, with its changes from time to time as principal is reduced. The courts have enforced these protections, even at the expense of appearing legalistic in favour of defendants lacking in merit.[26]

It is to be remarked that, as often when poverty is catered for, less than poverty, even little less, is not catered for. The woman in the backstreet who lends 2s 6d for a month at 6d interest, is

[24] As in the famous satirical pronouncement of Maule J. when sentencing a poor man for bigamy in days when divorce could only be achieved by private statute.

[25] Contrast the situation in America where the Federal Court can, given principles, overrule in the light of the Constitution, not only laws made by individual states, but the laws made by Federal Congress itself.

[26] Congresbury Motors Ltd. v Anglo-Belge Finance Co. Ltd. (*Times* 29 June, 1970).

charging a very high rate of interest, but receives very little. Her contracts are roughly treated. But the small trader who deals with a bank can suffer a hard fate, because the bank, unlike the registered usurer, can and does charge compound interest, and that at half-yearly intervals, and frequently finds itself able to enforce mortgage obligations by the sale of the security, the debtor's house, or shop, for example. Probably a great deal of national wealth is lost in the forced sales. Nor, contrary to popular belief, is a bank prevented from charging rates of interest much in excess of 'bank rate'.

The above, however, is not said in defence of moneylenders, but to illustrate the proposition that not all classes are protected when laws are made to help the poor.

Of employer and employee, two processes have raised the legal and social level of the latter.

Governmental interferences, back in the nineteenth century, and continuing, have rendered places of work safe, and clean and healthy. 'Truck' has been abolished; so that an employer cannot regain the factory wages in the factory canteen.

The second factor is the success, after long struggle, in the courts and Parliament, that has been achieved by trade unions in the struggle for influence; until now (indeed since 1906) these institutions enjoy privileges in the way of legal immunity that no other institution enjoys.

A third potential exploiter is the landlord. Against him the tenant for other than a fixed term settled by contract has no common law defence against ejectment. The property is the landlord's; he can do what he likes with it.

Here we have another example of 'progress on the wheels of warfare'. When the comforts of the working-class became a national interest, during the first world war, a Liberal government (already responsible for much in the way of 'welfare'), enacted the Rent Act of 1915, one of the most important of enactments, and only less badly drafted than most of the 'amending acts'. The Rent Act virtually abolished the power of the landlord of unfurnished premises to eject the tenant without the mediation of a court order. This, too, has been quite strictly applied by the courts against the landlord: and the discretion which is left in the court to decide what order to make (eject-ment, postponement, etc.) has been generally exercised so as to protect the tenant.'[27] The 'merits', however, are not all on one side. Landlords are not all extortioners; nor are they all rich; nor are tenants always deserving of sympathy. Then the strict rights can be declared, in a proper case, and discretion applied against the tenant.

But such decisions are, in fact, a rarity. The County Court bench has been, in general, more sympathetic to the have-nots than to the haves. There has supervened, accordingly, an ebb and flow of statute law, granting 'decontrols', restricting decontrols, extending landlord's rights in exchange for his duty to provide alternative accommodation; and the tide has not ceased its ebbs and flows. A tributary of the law also flows from a series of Land-lord and Tenant Acts (starting in 1927) which make clear the landlord's obligations of repair, and granting remedies to the tenant for the landlord's failure (on proper notice) to effect repairs. This department of law is too large for compendious treatment.

Mention should be made, however, of one essential feature of Rent Acts in which the technical element in law reveals itself.

The statute protects 'unfurnished letting'. 'Lodgings' are not unfurnished lettings, and much disputation has taken place in connection with the degree of isolation required to make the user of some rooms in premises a tenant rather than a lodger. [E.g. what parts of the house does he use other than his own room or rooms and the approaches thereto?] Nor are furnished apartments included in the category of protected dwellings. What constitutes a furnished letting? Do a few unimportant sticks of furniture create that effect? The cases indicate that here, at least, an effective legal fiction is not easy to fabricate. But if there is sufficient furniture to constitute the letting a furnished one, not

---

[27] Discretion, like equity, tends to follow precedents and principles. In general, failures to pay rent are not treated as grounds for automatic eviction. The court will make an order allowing the payment, in instal-ments, of arrears. The delivered notice to quit having been deprived of its effect, the tenant remains a statutory tenant and, given what the court regards as reasonable efforts to meet his liabilities, he stays. And his widow after him.

all the sympathy felt by the judge personally will allow him to give the tenant before him the protection of the act.

In this instance is revealed once again the technicality of the law. 'The law is not in heaven'. It is not characterised by the purposes of human aspiration. On the other hand, the law, in its nature, is limited by its own language and its traditional forms. Duties cannot be imposed, or rights granted, which the law does not impose or allow. Social purposes, as apprehended by the judge, are as irrelevant as the paramount purposes of states were shown to be in the seventeenth century.

Therefore, for a different class, for the occupiers of furnished dwellings, law was enacted, in the 1940s, not restricting directly the right of the landlord to raise the rent, but creating tribunals to which the tenant could appeal. Those tribunals, which still exist, have the power to fix a reasonable rent – and to protect the tenant from victimisation for his having appealed.

At a higher economic level other Landlord and Tenant Acts prevent exploitation by landlords when contracts of tenancy have expired; also exploitation by freeholders when long leases 'fall in'. In this way persons are protected from being left 'shopless' as others are protected from being left homeless.

Thus far, the obligations that relate to land. But chattels, too, are important. These, the refrigerator, the spin drier, the washing machine, the radiator, the television; may be said to constitute the home. Add to these the motor vehicle which is a condition of freedom that prevents the home from becoming a prison.

These chattels are normally bought on credit terms, and the most interesting of credit terms, from the legal point of view, is hire-purchase.

Hire-purchase, a device thought to have been invented in nineteenth-century America, is not precisely a legal fiction, but is a technicality of similar utility. The trader has the problem that, when he sells goods on credit, he parts with the property in the goods. If the buyer defaults in payment, the seller's only remedy is by legal process against the buyer for payment. Even if he were content with the return of the goods, the buyer may have parted with them, or so used them as to make them unreturnable; and, as for the money, the buyer may prove to be a man of straw. But hiring is different, in that the hirer only borrows goods – and these remain the property of the owner. Hire-purchase, which purports to be a hiring with an option of purchase attached – an option, usually, of acquisition after a period, at a merely nominal price – serves many of the purposes of sale, yet preserves to the owner a remedy of retrieving his goods on the hirer's default. Also the criminal law operates here to prevent the hirer from disposing of the goods.

This technical device is not precisely a legal fiction, because, in the pure case, it involves in its description only averments of fact which are acceptable as true whether traversed (challenged) or in default of challenge. The description of the transaction as hiring can be true, with the reservation that this is an unusual hiring in which the right of termination is not precisely mutual. The hirer can terminate at will, the owner on the hirer's default.[28] Notwithstanding this imbalance, it may well be true to describe as hiring the pure case (as considered by the Law Lords in Helby v Matthews[29]) wherein at least a clear untrammelled right of return is available to the hire-purchaser. As it happens, commercial practice tends to trammel the right of return by a requirement of payment of some 'compensation for depreciation'. However, so long as the court regards any transaction as hire-purchase, it continues to carry important legal consequences; namely that the owner remains entitled to the property, and the hirer must not, without the owner's permission, part with the property. If the hirer purports to sell, or otherwise dispose of the chattel, against the owner's title, he is guilty of larceny as a bailee, and, in the ordinary case, the buyer, or receiver, acquires no title, because no one can give title to what is not his own.[30] So the owner is pro-

---

[28] A hire-purchaser with a fixed period (two years, e.g. with option of purchase at the end of two years or earlier) is also unbalanced as to the right of termination, because the owner may never have a right to regain his chattel.   [29] [1895] A.C. 471.

[30] There is some special law under the Factor's Act and Sale of Goods Act which creates apparent exceptions to this rule. Thus someone who has sold his vehicle to a hire-purchase company, and retained possession of it on hire-purchase terms, may be a 'seller in possession' and so able to give title to a third party. (Union Transport Finance Co. v Ballardie [1937] 1 All Eng. R. 420.)

tected, if only by the hirer's fear of prosecution. Indeed, it has come to pass that the prisons of England have housed many alleged, and convicted, 'larceners', whose larceny was the disposal of hire-purchase goods. It may well be the case that many of these were wrongly convicted; because the vast majority of modern hire-purchase agreements do so trammel the right of return that, in a proper analysis, it might emerge that the transaction was, indeed, a legal fiction, was substantially a credit-sale by the intention of the parties – was merely 'colourably' disguised as a hiring.

To this aspect the minds of judges and legislature have not been directed. Legal protections in this context have taken the form of interference by the courts on equitable lines when they have condemned certain clauses as penalty clauses.[31] If it appears that the hirer, on a default, loses not only his chattel, but some amount of money, not correspondng to any real loss suffered by the owner, such a clause will not be enforced. But, such is the technique of the law, if the hirer agrees to pay some large sum on his voluntary return of the chattel, that is not a penalty clause, because it is an undertaking characterised by a voluntary consent which is regarded as different from the consent to a penal clause. The logic of this, not uncriticised, is a strictly legal logic.[32]

The distinction here drawn shows that, in our law, the protection against harsh bargains is not an automatic process. The case-law of hire-purchase has not been productive of much, if any, new equity.

Something of novelty has, however, been seen in the judicial treatment of a situation which is of frequent occurrence in the motor trade. A dealer parts with a second-hand vehicle on hire-purchase terms, having praised its constitution and pronounced confidence in its performance. The dealer, however, is rarely the owner for the purposes of the transaction. The agreement prior to the passing of the chattel is usually made between the hire-

[31] The notion of a 'penalty' is of a term in a contract which sets fixed and disproportionate charges for delays, etc: 'Fixed suggests 'disproportionate'.

[32] The learning is reviewed in Bridge v Campbell Discount Co. Ltd. [1962] 1 All Eng. R. 385.

purchaser and a finance company, which has, one way or another, purchased the vehicle from the dealer, and now transfers to the hire-purchaser. The company usually exonerates itself expressly from all the conditions and warranties that are normally ancillary to sales of used chattels. When the vehicle breaks down the hire-purchaser is left, apparently, without a remedy. The dealer is not the owner. (If he were so, he would be responsible, at least on a footing of misrepresentation, or, in statutory cases, i.e. for goods within a certain price-range, he would be answerable as on a sale of goods.) Nor is the finance company attackable, because it has disclaimed liability in the contract, and has (usually) disclaimed responsibility for any promise, etc., made by agents. Nor is the dealer, at first sight, an agent of the finance company for the purpose of making promises and representations. Nevertheless, a court eventually decided – and, perhaps, in this way legislated – that dealers can, in general, be regarded as responsible for their warranties.[33]

The above instances of judicial protection are 'common law' cases, where statutes were not relevant. There is revealed a moral principle – a principle of fairness, which is difficult to formulate with exactitude, but which is recognisable by the 'reasonably feeling' person.

Parliamentary legislation in this field is clearer – and is also animated by a purpose that can be called ethical. The evil result of hire-purchase that engaged Parliament (becoming clear in the 1930s), is seen in the situation where a hire-purchaser has paid many instalments, and then defaults on payment. At common law the owner is now able to recover the chattel. Evidently the results can be a hardship disproportionate to the default. Therefore Parliament enacted, in 1938 (in Ellen Wilkinson's Act), that if a hire-purchaser has paid a third of the 'hire-purchase price' (the sum which would have changed hands if the transaction were continued and carried to completion) then the owner can only recover the chattel by order of the court. This will be recognised

---

[33] Andrews v Hopkinson [1956] 3 All Eng. R. 422. The statement in the text is general. The judge only decided that that dealer was liable on a warranty. Other judges have applied this in the light of the 'principle'. That is how case law develops.

by the reader as the technique of the Rent Act. Rights exist, but they are not enforceable unless the court deems it just for them to be enforced. Instead of return of the chattel, the court may make an order to allow the payment of arrears in a manageable way.

That statute protected goods of hire purchase price £100 or less (motor cars £50). Re-enactments and amendments have raised the limit considerably. (The present limit is £2000 and the latest statute (1965) expresses that the protection of the Act only applies to individual persons not, i.e. to limited companies.) For contracts within the range the statute insisted on a proper documentation. The hirer must be presented with a copy contract explaining clearly the terms. This is analogous to a clause in the Moneylenders' Act. Indeed Parliament has regarded the owner in hire-purchase as in the nature of a money lender. In fact he usually is so.

The statute also vests the hirer with rights as of a buyer in ordinary sale of goods. Warranties of reasonable fitness and of merchantable quality are implied: and this rightly, because, as pointed out above even though hire-purchase may be money-lending, probably it is also 'sale of goods'.[34] However until 1965 it was assumed that, for a seller to retain the property in the goods, he had to disguise himself as an owner giving goods on hire. (Notwithstanding some sale of goods law as to 'intention', this was considered to be the case as far back as 1893.[35])

But now the Act of 1965 gives a protection to a 'conditional sale'. This is a hybrid. There is an agreement to pay for the goods by instalments, and a transfer of possession, as in a credit sale. But the passing of the property depends on the discharge of conditions as to the payment of the instalments etc – stated in the agreements.

This, be it said, is of intellectual, rather than ethical, interest: because, if this creature be real, hire-purchase need never have been conceived.

[34] It is to be noted that a transaction of hire-purchase which is recognised as moneylending (as when goods are sold to a financier and resold on hire-purchase terms) the contract is invalid, as an unregistered bill of sale.

[35] Lee v Butler [1893] 2 Q.B. 318.

8

The Concept of Justice

The building at the mouth of the Strand is known as 'The Royal Courts of Justice' but every practising lawyer describes it as 'The Law Courts'. That the implied distinction is a well-known one is illustrated, in a legal chestnut, by the story of the experienced litigant who, when his solicitor wired triumphantly 'Justice has prevailed', replied 'Appeal at once'. But the difference between law and justice is not a music-hall joke; it is a fact well-known to and expressly recognised by the courts. Thus the Court of Appeal explicitly held that to say of a man that the law was on his side is to say something capable of a defamatory interpretation (Clark v Associated Newspapers [*Times*, May 1955]): and citation is unnecessary to confirm the experience of practical lawyers who so frequently hear from judges and magistrates words to the following effect; that the judgment given seems to reek of hardship and to operate unfairly, but that the language of the statute or of the binding cases is clear and it is not for the court to act against them. So, in Tulip v Tulip,[1] the Court of Appeal felt compelled to hold that a husband is bound by a deed which does not bind the benefiting wife. The court cannot alter such a position, for legislation is the function of Parliament and those bodies that Parliament appoints as delegates.[2]

[1] [1951] 2 All Eng. R. 91.
[2] See p. 159 for defeat of justice by formality. A recent example of a different type is Plant (Engineering) Co. Ltd. v Davis (unreported) in which a liquidator, who had, for technical reasons, taken assignment of an interest under seal, was held personally liable for damages that a

It is possible that a legal historian would find that justice was a more dominant notion in the courts in those early days (admittedly less civilised than ours) when the body of law was relatively unaffected by legislation. Every case was a new situation. Nowadays in any one year Parliament enacts more law than would have constituted the entire corpus of English law less than two centuries ago. The scope of the common law admittedly remains large. Within limits there is judicial legislation. The reader has already learned that in this century the House of Lords belatedly (in a case appropriately concerned with a snail) admitted that judges do change the law.[3] Within the narrow limits that beset judicial legislation one may seek an active concept of justice; but the bulk of the work of the courts is dominated by statute; and statutes can be unjust according to judicial standards. That, briefly, constitutes one reason why the expression 'Law Courts' is less misleading than the expression 'Courts of Justice'.

It must not, however, be inferred that the common law, the body of judge-made law, is necessarily characterised by what ordinary people call justice. We know of many anomalies. We have seen that for long it was much cheaper to kill a man than to injure him; and even after corrective legislation it cannot be said to be dearer. Modern legislation, which has been the fountain of much injustice (to the extent of retrospective enactment), has also been a corrective of common law injustice; for example, by the removal of unmeritorious technical defences derived from ancient statutes (e.g. in the repeal of the Statute of Frauds and the modification of the Statute of Limitations) and by the abolition or modification of common law doctrines, such as common employment and contributory negligence. On the one hand the common law is not perfect. On the other hand the legislature is constituted by men who possess some sense of justice, in so far as that is compatible with fixed party policy. One must also allow a

third-party recovered against the company. In contrast to occurrences like this, let there be quoted the well-known dictum of Scrutton L.J. 'It is justice, therefore probably the law.' (Gardner v Heading [1928] 2 K.B. 284.)

[3] I.e. not merely make new law where there is a lack of statute or precedents; but change the law by ignoring or overruling precedents. They can do nothing to statutes except 'interpret'.

margin of error for both, due to the fact that there need not be any common agreement as to what is 'just', whether for individuals, or for classes. Valuations change. Are individuals to be treated as equal units, or does one class require protection? Is protection just? or is it a mercy shown to one at the expense of another? In this field of inquiry, it is obvious that Parliament is more likely to be criticised as unjust than are the judges.[4] It cannot, however, be said that the judges can do no wrong and the legislature can do no right. That the judges can go wrong, and work injustice, is well illustrated by a line of cases in the Law of Agency. During forty years of this century it came to be believed that when a vendor engaged an agent on a commission basis to find a purchaser, the vendor involved himself in some kind of duty to the agent. If, for example, the agent found a purchaser and the vendor refused to enter into contract, or to complete, the vendor was held liable in damages to the agent for having prevented him from earning his commission. Perhaps the high-water mark of this learning was reached in the unreported case of Rowson v Alexander in the late 1930s, wherein it appeared that an actress, the well-known Frances Day, had agreed to pay to the agent who had procured the work a percentage of her earnings from quarter to quarter. When, through her alleged breach of agreement with the management, this work came to an end, the agent claimed damages against her because she had prevented him from earning commission. Though excellently defended by Mr Gerald Gardiner, as he then was, the defendant lost.

Then, in 1940, the House of Lords, in Luxor (Eastbourne) Ltd. v Cooper,[5] made it clear that estate agents and the like were not the beneficiaries of such warranties binding their clients. If an agent is employed on commission he only receives, and is only entitled to, commission on the money to which his principal becomes entitled. If the principal does not become entitled to any

---

[4] The judges are, incidentally, protected from accusations of injustice by their powers of committal for contempt. Let is be added that they use this power sparingly. Parliament has a rule preventing Parliamentary criticism of judges on specific matters.

[5] [1941] 1 All Eng. R. 33.

payment the agent is not entitled to any payment, and there is no warranty by which the principal undertakes that his agent shall earn anything. The law is otherwise, of course, if the principal asks the agent to do a specific job; then there is a contract of work and labour. But ordinary commission terms do not constitute such a contract. It follows from this that all the defendants of actions of that type in this century, before the Luxor case, lost them for the simple reason that the judges of the Court of Appeal and lower courts had misinterpreted the law; and there is no redress for this. That seems to amount to a considerable injustice.

The civil courts are rich in similar examples. Thus, early in the 1920s the Court of Appeal held that if a man does damage to another negligently, then he is liable to pay, not only for the harm that could reasonably be foreseen at the time-place in question, but for harm that followed causally, but which no-one could reasonably have anticipated. That is known as the rule in Polemis.[6] Pursuant to it, some very heavy damages were paid in the 1930s, 1940s and 1950s. But in 1961 a court of very high authority has (in the Morts Dock case)[7] expressed disapproval of Polemis. Anyone who has been negligent in the 1960s incurs a more limited liability. And examples could be multiplied to illustrate the truth that changes in the law cause changes in liability, so that one person suffers less (or more) than somebody else in *simili casu*.[8] On the criminal side, the differences are more striking. Once capital punishment is abolished, the blood of generations of executed murderers cries out from the lime-pits. Certainly when the law as to provocation was restated rationally, a large number of persons are demonstrated to have suffered a

[6] Re Polemis and Furness, Withy & Co. [1921] 3 K.B. 560. In that case a negligent act led to an unexpected fire which destroyed a ship. Until that time, according to the best opinion, damages in tort were limited to harm that the tortfeasor could reasonably have anticipated as a consequence of his conduct.

[7] Overseas Tankship (UK) Ltd. v Morts Dock & Engineering Co. [1961] 1 All Eng. R. 404.

[8] All the decisions overruled by Donoghue v Stevenson are in point. Also the cases on the liability of hospitals. Before National Health (as it is now), the hospital was not regarded as vicariously liable for its surgeons and its staff. Now a different view prevails (Cassidy v Minister of Health [1951] 1 All Eng. R. 574).

penalty which they did not deserve. But who has done wrong? Who has been unjust?

The Bible answers this. 'Justice, justice, shalt thou pursue.' That tells us that justice is not something static, something easily found. It is hard to find, and it changes. It changes in two aspects which, when they are considered, may appear to present rival criteria.

First, equality is hard to achieve; especially in time, for there is change of attitudes and of values and of laws. There is no equality of *Zeitgeist*. Therefore a person can be unjustly treated in the reaches of time, whereas, in the contemporary jurisdiction, there is little danger that difference of position in space will make a difference.[9]

Secondly, justice involves, in its equality, a certain rigidity, expressed in the rules. The rules can be just in many cases, but inequalities that could not always be anticipated emerge.

It is just that people be equally treated; it is just (as ancillary acquittal, from the rules of the criminal law, because his statement has been irregularly obtained, or because a judge has summed up badly, whereas another, not more guilty, fails to find any such technical paraclesis?

It is just that people be equally treated; it is just as ancillary to this) that rules should obtain. It can, nevertheless, happen, that the rules cause an inequality. Such a case was demonstrated when, of two murderers, one was hanged, and the other (the actual killer) was too young for the capital penalty.[10]

---

[9] But even this is not an exactitude. Thus a person whose land happens to be in an area where town planning action supervenes, is harshly treated in comparison with others.

In time, a recent change in the practice shows that plaintiffs could be unjustly treated as a result of Crown Privilege. The plaintiffs in the *Thetis* case were not allowed to see or refer to or call for government papers. (Duncan v Cammell Laird [1942] 1 All Eng. 587). Now, in consequence indirectly of legislation of 1947, and through the rethinking of the topic in re Grosvenor Hotel, London (No 2) [1964] 3 All Eng. R. 354 the court has power to consider whether a Crown claim of privilege is justified or not.

[10] R. v Craig and Bentley [1962] 3 All Eng. R. 961. In that case the older boy shouted to the younger one, urging him to shoot. Had he himself been the gunman, there could have been no reasonable plea for

Justice, then, is hard to define, and harder still to capture. That is why the Bible enjoins its 'pursuit'.

The above reflections confirm what has already become evident, that no distinction can be mechanically drawn (in the search for justice), between common law and statute; between judges and Parliament. But a rough useful distinction can be drawn on the following lines. The law claims justice as a legal morality. Justice is usually the ethical essence of a particular case. Laws can be so framed as to make justice more likely or less likely. But law in general, when it achieves any degree of universality (and universality is the essence of law), becomes in that process difficult to apply with justice in all particular cases. All general impositions and restrictions operate unjustly somewhere. One man's tax is another man's debt.

The word justice here is an ethical term. That is the proper interpretation. Yet it is not the only meaning. For example, at one stage in English legal history the distinction of ethical importance was between justice and equity. The judges of the Crown Courts were thought to be exponents of a severe justice unadaptable to unethical acts; and equity came to fulfil the law by the introduction of personal remedies that prevented at least the unethical abuse of justice. Later we know that equity itself hardened into a legal system. A maxim like 'equality is equity' expresses a doctrine of narrow application, which must be interpreted in a very sophisticated way.[11] Since the 1870s the common law and equity are integrated into one system; and justice, as a word, has lost in the popular mind the connotation of severity. It is still distinguished from mercy; nevertheless it is regarded as a moral value. Using the word, then, in an ethical sense, it is reasonable to suggest that, being ethical, justice turns its eyes to the merits of individual cases in the light of morality – like ethics, is prepared to regard every case as an exceptional case – whereas the law, aiming at wide generality, aiming at universality and certainty,

reprieve. The then Home Secretary can hardly be blamed for not reprieving one person on account of the age of another

[11] A typical application is the principle that a joint tenancy should be reduced, if possible, to a tenancy in common: against 'survivorship' (that there should not be a gain by one person on the death of another).

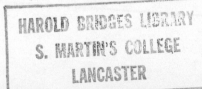

not incompatible with goodness, can be ethically unsatisfactory in particular cases. For this the compensation is certainty. In some branches of the law wide ethical doctrines have made themselves felt from time to time, and in so doing have created uncertainty in the legal system. In point are the doctrines of public policy, according to which some contracts could be defeated because their purposes were bad purposes from the standpoint of the period. Great restriction has, however, been put on these doctrines by English judges, one of whom said 'Public policy is an unruly horse; once you are astride it you cannot know where it will carry you'. Granting that it is unwise to argue from extreme developments, it may be pointed out that much totalitarian law takes the form of importing into a legal system extra-legal doctrines such as the welfare of the state. The English standpoint is well expressed by Lord Jessel: 'It is in the best interests of the state that contracts freely entered into shall be binding.'

In this connection it is important to remember that ethics varies with periods. In the early nineteenth century the otherwise harsh law was averse from harsh bargains, and there was a tendency to interfere with contracts. In the late nineteenth century there was judicial legislation, as well as parliamentary, creating complete freedom of contract. But even at that time a movement was beginning which has culminated in this century, one of the results of which is that unfortunate and stupid persons are protected against the consequences of improvident bargains, and classes of people are protected who stand in some disadvantageous relationship to society. The law having moved from status to contract, there has now been a reversion to status, not the least interesting features of which is the complex trade union law already discussed. At the same time – and in contrast – many aspects of commercial law have developed strictness greater than that of the nineteenth century. *Caveat mercator*: the merchant is still responsible for his own follies.

Given, then, a difficulty in the isolation of ethically valuable ends, given a change in the fashions of the 'moral taste', it may be said to be still undesirable for ethics to intrude into law to such a degree as to make the law uncertain, and legal acts and actions unpredictable.

Yet, within their context that, though narrow, is socially vital, it behoves judges and juries to behave according to a standard of justice which, paying proper regard to all rules, yet values the individual. Justice of this type is not blind, and is all the better for being wide-eyed. It may operate in ways which seem different from wisdom. A jury, and the judge who directs the jury, is expected to understand that the prisoner should have the benefit of doubts and the benefit of all the technical restrictions that hedge a prosecution. When a jury does justice it is applying itself, not to a wide question of guilt or innocence, but to the narrower question of guilt or innocence according to the evidence. Thus justice is the fairness which is the playing of a game according to the rules. The game is watched by the public: and they must be shown that the rules are being kept. Not only must justice be done, but it must appear to be done. (That is consistent with the openness of the courts to the public.) So the pedantry of 'off-side' preserves, in a way, the tradition of mercy which inspired old judges to be pedantic to absurdity about the language of indictments. It is something more than fair play, and something less, but is highly ethical. This type of justice was not a casualty of the war. Although some statutes were interpreted against the spirit of the law, 'because there was a war on', the 18b cases (and the D.O.R.A. cases of the first world war) demonstrate that justice is valued in Britain even when the state is in peril.

Cognate to the justice of juries, is the justice of the remnant of the civil jury, that is to say the judge finding facts. In the finding of facts there is a surprising scope for interpretation, which organises truth without actually distorting it. The judge working among ambiguous facts (because facts are inveterately ambiguous) may allow his eventual decision to be coloured by the ethical consequences. Then he finds the law which fits the found facts. On his finding of fact he is much less appealable than on his finding of legal consequences. On the latter he is quite likely to be theoretically exact. In point is a finding of that shrewd lawyer, the late Mr Justice Rigby Swift, who, presented with a man who admitted that he had lied on his proposal form, realised that, if this policy were repudiated, innocent persons would suffer.

Arguing therefore that one of this man's statements must be false and the other (being opposite) true, he decided to believe the proposal form, and not the admission! So the policy was enforceable.

Further, and here the direction of thought is different, there is a certain amount of common law tradition which allows every judge to prevent people from using the law too unethically. Outstanding is the common law doctrine that a man cannot benefit from the consequences of his own crime or his own fraud. Also there is the doctrine of estoppel, a rule, far from loose, against misleading one's opponent into detriment. But a case of the 1950s shows that it is not impossible for judges to allow injustice if their minds are convinced by purely legal argument. Thus there was a widow who was executrix of her husband's estate jointly with a clerk of a firm of solicitors that was acting for her. The widow and the clerk lodged the funds in a bank on joint account. By continuous forgeries the solicitor's clerk succeeded in emptying the account into his own pocket; for which operation he was in due course imprisoned. But when the widow sued the bank for the money, lost through their negligence or breach of duty, the bank pleaded that she had no right of action. The account was a joint account; the only possible plaintiff was, therefore, a combination of the two persons who were the creditors of the bank on the joint account. Not one of them alone, but both together or neither. And if, they argued, it was sought to join the forger, then how could he be heard to seek a profit from his own crime. In the court of first instance that argument, for all its barely masked effrontery, was accepted by the judge. In the Court of Appeal, later, the case was amicably settled; but it was clear, from the remarks of the Lord Justices, that the decision of their puisne brother would not have been sustained.[12] On a later occasion, it may be added, a Chancery judge expressed the view that a doctrine of estoppel might operate to prevent the success of such a defence. The widow's case (Brewis v Westminster Bank Ltd.) is cited here to show that the common law, for all its ethical limits, has its ethical resources. It also shows that the

[12] Brewis v Westminster Bank (unreported).

distinction between justice and law is a true one, notwithstanding that the two processes function together surprisingly well.

Let it be remembered that many of the provinces of the law are cold realms. On the authority of Lord Atkin, what the lawyers exercise is 'common-sense'. (Be it added, occasionally uncommon sense.) This need not have, though it may have, moral relevance. 'It all depends on the facts'.

Apart from the ethical irrelevance of their contents, the forms of law suggest an exclusion of the ethical, first, because laws are general, universal,[13] and ethical situations are frequently exceptional cases. Ethics offers the 'hard cases' that make bad law.

Secondly, laws, to be useful, must involve many technicalities.

Technique, in turn, may manifest itself in many circumstances as a cause of hardship, without apparent moral compensation. In point is Finnegan v Cementation Co., the case of the widow who presented her process for compensation for the death of her husband under technically wrong forms.[14] Comparable is the misfortune of every claimant who finds himself defeated by Statute of Limitation, or (until recently) the need for writing under Sale of Goods Act or Statute of Frauds.

Whenever 'time is of the essence', people can suffer loss, through delays not of their making. A strike (which is not a legal 'frustration') can cause a business man to lose his sale. In the legal process itself, long trials, and long appeal sequences, draw out while lives are spent in a miserable waiting. Dickens, a man of legal experience, has described these delays: e.g. Jarndyce's case in *Bleak House*. Not the least hardship is that of the prisoner

[13] This must not be taken definitively, because legal systems do include particular, *ad hoc,* legislation. The common law remembers Acts of Attainder, discriminatory laws, retroactive legislation calculated to deal with specific persons. These, however, are rarities in a mature, civilised, legal system.

[14] [1953] 1 All Eng. R. 1130. There took place in 1963 a modification of the Law of Limitation. In so far as Finnegan's case was controlled by a statute of limitation preventing an amendment, the case might be different now, because, for good reason, the courts allow process after the statutory period has elapsed. See Chatsworth Investments Ltd. v Cussins Ltd. [1969] 1 All Eng. R. 143. But the language of the statute creates difficulties for widows (Lucy v W. T. Henleys Ltd. [1969] 3 All Eng. R. 456).

who serves his sentence before he is acquitted.[15] Hamlet, who evidently knew much about the quillets of the law, counted 'the law's delays' as a valid reason for suicide.[16]

From the technicalities and technical purposes of the law flow consequences that people find to be hardships; and they call the law callous or stupid – 'an ass'. This is a constant criticism of some criminal laws.

Suffice it here to mention a few features. First, at a trivial level, they call the law an ass because of the frustrations of those who feel they have a right to park their vehicles, yet are not allowed to do so; or of those who cannot make sales and purchases except within specified hours. Here no moral issue is relevant.

More serious is the distress of those who find themselves liable for offences, or for torts, which, in a sense, they can truly say they did not commit. Is it just that a person be held liable for acts of which he knows nothing? On the civil side, any case of vicarious liability can operate as an injustice (a moral wrong) to a conscientious employer. Yet we have seen that there is good, and moral, justification for the rule. In civil affairs there are many statutory duties (e.g. fencing in factories) which are absolute, and which involve liability where an ordinary allegation of negligence might fail.[17] On the criminal side, many laws which are important

[15] Illustrative is R. v Whelan (unreported) in which a driver offending against the Road Safety Act 1967 had been sentenced by magistrates to three months of imprisonment, because he, being an occasional driver only, would not be severely punished by disqualification. The Court of Appeal held the sentence to be unjust after nine weeks of the sentence had been served. In cases of this type, be it added, bail is difficult, but not impossible, to obtain. Also unjust is the long detention in custody of an accused who is subsequently acquitted.

[16] It should not be thought that long litigation died with Dickens. In 1919 a case started from a claim made by Workington Harbour Board on a Contract of Indemnity for a contractor's failure. This reached the Lords in 1936 – who decided that the whole action was based on the misconstruction of the contract. A fresh action on lines suggested by this, commenced in 1937, reached the Lords in 1952 – who decided that the action was based on a misconstruction of the contract. One factor in the delays in these cases was the difficulty of finding masters and judges who had not, at some time, appeared in the case as counsel.

[17] Most, but not all, statutory duties are, these days, held to give rise

would be unenforceable unless the duty were absolute. (This may entail vicarious guilt, as e.g. for a servant's revenue fraud: Moussell Bros. v L.N.W.R. [1917] 2 K.B. 836).

In point are (in serious matters) the law against bigamy (R. v Lolley (1812) Russ & Ry. 237); against abduction of a female under 16 (R. v Prince (1875) L.R. 2 CC.R 154): against carnal knowledge of girls under sixteen. (Here a defence of ignorance is available to youths under twenty-four, and that has involved a technicality.)[18]

Less serious matters include revenue offences (e.g. against customs); adulteration of wines and spirits; offences relating to game; and public nuisances. (In tort the rule in Rylands v Fletcher can make a person responsible for a state of his land which he did not bring about or know about.) In these categories, laws would be ineffective if *mens rea* (guilty knowledge) required to be proved.

A much greater hardship, because of the odium reflected on a morally innocent person, is seen when a landlord, without guilty knowledge, is held liable for the tenant's possession of forbidden drugs. This, be it added, is an exceptional hardship, occurring among laws which can hardly be framed to do justice to exceptional cases. In the most recent case[19] the Law Lords reinterpreted some words which the Court of Appeal had (not without authority) held to constitute absolute liability. The words of the statute describe 'a person who (a) being the occupier permits premises to be used for the smoking of cannabis (hashish) or (b) is concerned in the management of any premises used for any such purpose'. The word 'knowingly' is, in the cliché, 'conspicuous by its absence'. Therefore, when hashish had been found in a flat, the defendant was accused; a school-teacher who did not live on the premises, but who collected the rent from tenants with whom she had no personal acquaintance. On those facts she was found guilty under sub-section (b). The Law Lords held (in effect) that the notion of guilty knowledge

to civil rights as well as to prosecutions. Of interest for the changing legal attitude are Phillips v Britannia Laundry Ltd. [1923] 2 K.B. 832, and Rudd v Elder Dempster Ltd. [1933] 1 K.B. 566.

[18] Twenty-three, the statutory age, lasts until the twenty-fourth birthday.　　　　　　[19] Sweet v Parsley [1969] 1 All Eng. R. 347.

must be read into the words: that their absence created an ambiguity (e.g. in the notion of management), which must be resolved in favour of the defence.

It remains to be added that there are laws against, for example, opium dens and brothels where the law would be unworkable unless it were presumed that owners and occupiers knew what was happening. Short of being absolute liabilities, these offences, being charged, throw a burden on to the defence.[20]

Finally, there will always be a sense of injustice when a person is found guilty of breach of laws which he did not know to exist. The principle that ignorance of law is not an excuse was valid when the laws were few and obvious. The aggregation of laws regulative of social relations, especially laws which say DO – rather than DO NOT – makes life difficult for the merchant, factory occupier, etc. The courts have held that knowledge of departmental regulations which have not been properly communicated cannot be attributed to the citizen, nor even to the judge. Nevertheless, the legal system is committed to the assumption that men know what they should know. Otherwise justice would be evaded by pleas of ignorance; and that result would be unjust.

JUSTICE: ADVERB LAW

In discussing justice we encounter a difficulty which will be called verbal, or philosophical, or real, according to taste. The difficulty is that whereas a simple uniformity of rule can operate unfairly, yet is equality of treatment greatly desired and esteemed as ethical.

The intellectual problems which arise from this regulative difficulty have, in the last thirty years been canvassed in the Supreme Court of the United States. Until the period of Franklin Delano Roovsevelt the Constitution and the Bill of Rights[21] and the XIVth Amendment[22] were interpreted by the court as

[20] Sherras v De Ruizen [1895] 1 Q.B. 918.
[21] The first ten amendments.
[22] (Passed after the Civil War) 'nor shall any state deprive any person of life, liberty or prosperity without *due process of law*, nor deny to any person within its jurisdiction the *equal protection of the laws*'.

protective of individual rights and of residual state rights. Only in New Deal legislation did the court encounter serious departures from this principle; and for long treated the new laws as constitutionally doubtful. The atmosphere of thought changed with the appointment of new justices, none of them of revolutionary spirit, but some less bound by precedent. Also there was an increasing awareness of a moral coefficient in the law: a coefficient that was only latent when the right of individuals (itself a moral claim) was taken for granted as a postulate of the system.

Since then there have been changes. An old judicial dictum that 'the Constitution is what we say it is' becomes ironically clear. There is still manifest a judicial conservatism. The court is 'restrained' and conscious of responsibility. Brandeis stated the attitude to precedent long ago. '*Stare decisis*' [Abide by the precedents] 'is usually the wise policy, because in most matters it is more important that the applicable rule be settled than that it be settled right.'[23] But after Brandies (himself a liberal) there supervened an awareness that a set of rules which had been adequate for an individualistic century, were privative of real equality. The concept of equality is richer in ethical overtones than is the concept of individual freedom; and, as was said above, makes a contribution to the notion of freedom. An increase in the claims of the coloured population has given new meaning to equality; and in Brown's case[24] the subtleties of equality were recognised.

In Britain the logic of justice has been less spectacularly presented. Here, the 'constitution' is lost among the ordinary municipal laws; and its preservation is an inherent function of the judge who does justice, whether or not, in so doing, he legislates a little.[25]

Here the problems have been made clear, to an extent, in the High Court, where the traditions are of justice; but most

---

[23] Burnet v Coronado Oil and Gas Co. (1932) 285 U.S., 393, 406.

[24] (1954) Brown v Board of Education. See p. 30 *supra*.

[25] In case this be misunderstood, let it be made clear that the British courts have no paramount power over the legislature as the U.S. Supreme Court has. Even if Parliament acted against the Act of Settlement etc., it is hard to see how the courts could express disapproval in any practical way.

clearly in relation to tribunals where quasi-judicial process [not a pejorative this] takes place. So, when a Watch Committee deprived a Chief Constable of office and pay because of his involvement in unsavoury affairs, their decision was upset by the High Court,[26] because the man had not been told the charges against him, and the 'trial' had taken place in his absence. On such occasions the courts teach the public something of the nature of justice.

Is it possible, then, to frame, in the English law, rules which achieve the just result, fair to individuals, rules which achieve ethical equality without ethical imbalance? The answer is that this can hardly be achieved in what we call substantive law – the aggregate of rights and duties – but can, in a measure, be realised in what I would prefer to call ADVERB law.[27]

'Adverb Law' is not an expression to be found in the books; but, in the author's submission, it is required in order to describe judicial practices, accepted by the profession, but not classifiable with formalities.

The practices in question are not peculiar to the criminal law. Thus in both civil and criminal jurisdictions there is an understanding that parties or accused persons should not be taken by surprise. Novelly, a recent amendment to the criminal law protects the prosecution against the surprises which are alibis.

---

[26] Ridge v Baldwin [1963] 2 All Eng. R. 66 (H.L.)

[27] Substantive law states legal relationships in terms of rights and duties, found to be the law. Adjective law is a term applied to the technical procedures which lead to, and determine the forms of, trials.

Adverb law is here submitted as a term to describe the judicial, rather than the formal, aspects of a trial. Adjective law describes the form. Adverb law describes how the substantial and formal rules are controlled in the judicial act.

It is not always easy to discriminate between the substantive and the adverb. In point is Nixon v Nixon ([1969] 3 All Eng. R. 1133) where a wife claimed a share in the business she had helped her husband to build. The claim was under S. 17(4) the Married Women's Property Act 1882, but, as litigation, unprecedented. The Court of Appeal held that the statute (which offers no definition of a married woman's interest) made possible this claim. Here we have either a statement that the substantive law protects the co-operative wife, or that the judges (in their judicial process) found it just to grant the claim.

The prisoner on indictment is protected from surprise by the rule that all the evidence against him must be passed, as it were, by a magistrate, and made available to the accused before the trial, and nothing can be added except by leave of the court. If novelty presents itself the inherent jurisdiction of the court is available to grant adjournment, if it does not exclude the new material.

In the civil law, before a case comes to court every allegation that matters is set out in pleadings; every document that may be used, or is relevant, is set out in lists and/or affidavits of documents, exchanged between the parties.

These technical provisions are set out in the 'rules of court', and for that reason can be called procedural, adjectival. But they are only the crystallisations into rule of a wide judicial scope – the right of the court to see that a trial is fairly conducted, with no traps being laid, no surprises sprung.

Pursuant to that principle the judges have discretion as to the admission or expulsion of evidence. Discretion is limited by principle, but not exhausted by any statable rules. There are rules of the legal game in plenty, but the courts act as umpires, or referees, whose function it is to ensure that the rules are observed not only in the letter but in the spirit.[28]

Compendiously, let the claims be what they will, whether between citizens, or between a citizen and the state, it should be made certain that the claim is made according to urbane decencies, and judged by objective standards. To elaborate a commonplace of British law (uncommonplace in the world), not only should justice be done (if it can) but justice should appear to be done. These appearances can hardly be other than genuine; and they are largely the effect of what is called the 'rule of law'.

The rule of law (concretized in our rules of law) amounts to much more than the proposition that the law applies to all of us. Universality, as such, is not necessarily an ethical good. A bad law, as well as a good law, applies to all of us. Rather, what is

---

[28] The danger implicit in the judicial function is that a judge can be tempted to interfere too much, to sound (in Bacon's phrase) as a 'tinkling cymbal', disturbing the forensic harmonies. Such conduct, of course, can constitute grounds of appeal.

meant by the rule, or rules, of law is that there are certain protections available to everybody in his claim for justice.

There is no exhaustive, or definitive, list of these rules. They include:

(1) The rule that trials should take place in the presence of the persons concerned; the parties to the dispute, that is, or the person accused, as the case may be. (If he is a foreigner, then an interpreter must be made available to him.) Moreover, when decisions come to be made, only the judge or judges may retire away from the public and the parties.

(2) That trials should be held in public. There are exceptions to this rule, as when secrets of national defence are before the court that tries treason, espionage, etc.; also, when details of sexual conduct are being investigated. In neither set of cases is the entire trial in camera.

(3) That no one shall be called to face trial, on claim or accusation, unless that claim or accusation be specified and detailed.

(4) That no one shall face claim or trial without adequate notice of the substance of the wrong that is alleged against him.

Consistently with 3 and 4.

(5) That no one shall be arrested except on charge disclosed to him at the time of arrest.

(6) That every facility should be provided to civil parties or accused persons, in their search for evidence. The right of persons to withhold evidence is limited to certain classes of privileged communications, as between solicitor and client, or between spouses. The right of the crown to claim privilege, a claim which has been seen to handicap claimants against police and departments of state, is now known not to be absolute. The court has the right to consider the evidence in question – and to decide whether or not a privilege should, in the interests of state, be recognised.[29]

(7) The right of accused persons not to be pressed for oral evi-

---

[29] Conway v Rimmer and another [1968] 1 All Eng. R. 874. In this the Law Lords did not follow the opinions of their predecessors in Duncan v Cammell Laird & Co. Ltd. [1942] 1 All Eng. R. 587, which had the effect of depriving the relatives of the victims of the *Thetis* disaster of information necessary for the pursuit of their claims.

dence, and their right not to give evidence unless they wish to do so. (Nor need witnesses say anything that might incriminate them.)

(8) On the other hand, their complete freedom of utterance.

(9) That what is said and presented in court shall be presented according to the rules of evidence. These rules include strict modalities, such as the need for oath, and the exclusion of hearsay. Also, there is a general exclusion of the irrelevant: and the legal notion of relevance is quite a narrow one. One instance is that, in a criminal trial, the history of a person is, in general, not admissible.[30]

(10) Rules protective of accused persons against too great a multiplicity of charges in any one trial.[31]

(11) The rule that, in the first instance (at least), the burden of evidence is not on the person accused.

The above eleven rules (the system is not exhaustively stated) can be reasonably described as a guarantee of objectivity in trials.

The law courts conform to these rules. What is not less important is that the courts insist that private persons, whenever they are called upon to exercise a responsibility in the nature of judging, shall be bound by some, if not all, of these rules. And the courts make the same demand of the departments of state.

[30] There are exceptions to this rule.

 a. When an accused person, by his defence, raises the issue of his good character, or attacks the character of a prosecution witness. By modern practice, the attack must be an unnecessary one. An implication that a prosecution witness must be guilty of some faults, or a simple accusation of lying, is not enough to justify the prosecution in leading the bad character.

 b. Certain evidence showing 'a system', when the accused says that the conduct proved against him is susceptible to an innocent explanation.

 c. Certain specific exceptions – as to convicted thieves found in possession of property suspected to be recently stolen; also some sexual cases in which identification is supported by evidence of previous deviation. (See R. v Straffen [1952] 1 All Eng. R. 1059.)

[31] Harris v D.P.P. [1952] 1 All Eng. R. 1044. The desirability of excluding counts because they may be prejudicial is a matter of judicial discretion, within the general principles. Much depends on whether the various charges arise from the same situation, or whether they are logically severable. In point is R. v Kray ([1969] 3 All Eng. R. 941) in which two murders were charged at the same trial.

To illustrate the principle, Britain is rich in a variety of social groups, having an identity recognised by the law, but not necessarily having clear legally-framed constitutions. Examples are churches, benevolent societies, trade unions and clubs. The concept of club is the key to the legal position.

A person who joins a club undertakes, implicitly or explicitly, to abide by the rules of that club. If these rules include discipline, he accepts that too.

To that agreement, provided it contemplates no clear illegality, the court is neutral. If someone be expelled, and complains to the court, the first problem of the court is to decide whether that club, and its rules, were ever intended by anybody to have legal significance. If agreement is involved it may be one of those agreements, known to the law, which are not intended to be legally enforceable. If that is the situation, then the court declines to interfere.

If, however, the association is of substantial size and significance the law tends to regard its agreements as contracts on which the courts can adjudicate. Here, too, the judges are reluctant. What will invoke them is the claim that some kind of trial should have been held and was not held, or, being held, was conducted otherwise than in accordance with basic rules of law. E.g. that a member was expelled without being told why, without his being called to an investigation, or given an opportunity to defend himself – or that there was a trial of sorts, but that it was unfairly conducted, with, e.g. the complainant doing at once the complaining and the judging.

If expulsion is a matter of procedure laid out in the rules of the club, the court can be invoked to hold that this member was not properly expelled; that he had not committed an offence warranting expulsion, or that the expulsion was carried out in a way inconsistent with the rules. Here the court is dealing with a contract, and will hold, if necessary, that a term of the contract is that any penalisation of members shall be subject to general proprieties on the lines of the rules of law. And always the court will interfere if someone proves that malice has been operative, even if formalities have been observed.

In this way the court acted so as to give damages to the estate of Bonsor.[32] In this way, at low levels, it may be said that the court has educated the people in certain principles which are moral principles. But not only have the organisers of clubs been so educated. The courts have also educated the government.

Nearly half a century has elapsed since a Chief Justice of England, the late Lord Hewart, denounced, in a book called *The New Despotism*, the lack of good judicial practice among officials to whom Parliament had delegated legislative, administrative, and judicial, or quasi-judicial, powers. Injustice seemed to be occurring where departments had power to make rules, with the force of law, as to town planning, for example, with all the consequent compulsory purchases, controls of building, etc. In public health, agriculture, etc. similar powers obtained.[33] In many cases the rules came into being unnoticed – 'lying on the table of the House' for a period, and then acquiring the force of law. After that decisions would be made at the administrative level, usually preceded by a departmental inquiry. Decisions, in many cases, would be simple affirmation or negation, with no reasons given.

Many attacks were conceivable, and made, on these legislative, administrative processes.

First, attack was possible by a plea that the rule complained of, or sought to be enforced, was *ultra vires* the enabling statute, doing harms that the legislators had not contemplated nor the letter of the law expressed. This is a difficult realm of law – the more so because the fact that the legislature has missed a point does not carry any consequence if the law is found to be unambiguous. Not always would ingenuity find 'latent ambiguity' that would enable a court to override a rule, or to give it the interpretation sought by the claimant.

Other lines of attack took the form of pleas that justice had not been done, or not been seen to be done; that inquiries, for

[32] See p. 41. Instructive are other trade union cases. See Byrne v Kinematographic Renters Society Ltd. [1958] 2 All Eng. R. 579.

[33] The problems are well discussed in the Report of the Committee on Ministers' Powers (1932). Cases of interest are Board of Education v Rice [1911] A.C. 179; L.G.B. v Arlidge [1915] A.C. 120; G.M.C. v Spackman [1943] A.C. 627; Ceylon University v Fernando [1960] 1 All Eng. R. 631.

example, had been unfairly conducted, that considerations had been entertained by the minister which were not within the contemplated purposes; that wrong reasons had been given, or no reasons, etc., etc.

To these attacks there were many defences. Some orders were absolute – unattackable, and their implementation unimpeachable because of the language of the enabling statute, which could be in the 'Henry VIII' form, to the effect that no appeal against these matters could be entertained by any court.[34]

A less violent, but equally effective, defence succeeded whenever the court found that the whole process was administrative, involving no need for judicial thinking on the part of the administration.[35] If, however, the court could find that the matter involved an inquiry of a quasi-judicial kind, then the rules of law became operative, and the arsenals of the prerogative writs provided *mandamus, prohibition* and *certiorari*, to command and to prevent any arbitrary conduct.[36]

[34] Henry VIII caused his Parliament to enact a Statute of Proclamations (31 Hy VIII c. 8) which gave to Royal Proclamations the force of statutes.

In the course of centuries the Royal Proclamations passed into the keeping of ministers responsible to parliament.

Public rights are endangered when the executive acts by proclamation (which is a rarity now): more probably when parliament itself delegates to other bodies the powers of making law and of administering it judicially without interference.

Valuable and valid delegation is quite old. The Mutiny Act 1717, followed in Army Acts, is an important source of laws approved by the courts. (There are modes of appeal.)

Suspect however, is any formula purporting to oust the jurisdiction. In point are the recent opinions of the Law Lords in Anisminic Ltd. v Foreign Compensation Commission ([1969] 1 All Eng. R. 208). That Commission was protected by statute in these terms: 'The Determination by the Commission of any application made to them under this Act shall not be called in question in any Court of Law'. It was argued in the House of Lords that a certain decision of the Commission was not a 'determination', good or bad, but a nullity. And the majority of the Law Lords so held. The ghost of Henry VIII failed to frighten them.

[35] A claim made by the Foreign Compensation Tribunal and not accepted by the House of Lords in the Anisminic case (*supra*).

[36] A good example of the limits to the court's jurisdiction is afforded in Dept. of Health & Social Security v Walker Dean Walker Ltd.

Since World War II, it is to be observed, the statutes seem to avoid the Henry VIII temptation, and there is provision for inquiries. To cope with 'administrative' conclusions, which, in the ordinary way, could only be attacked with (unprovable) allegations of malice, the courts have been reinforced by the Ombudsman.[37] The creation of this official, in order to consider complaints against the departments, is a tardy recognition that the delegation of powers by Parliament has created something like the continentally known *Droit Administratif*, which (in France, for example) is dealt with by special courts.[38]

In fine, it appears that judicial attack, along the lines of Lord Hewart's thinking, has done much to strengthen the claim of the British state to be a gentleman.

It remains to inquire whether in some fields the state may not have carried the standards of courtesy too far.

But, before the rules of law are criticised for their idealism, let a note of realism be sounded.

The law as stated in the books, including this, is well handled at a high level. The judges of the Supreme Court, the Red Judges, are highly qualified and are chosen for more qualities than the intellectual. But the majority of the criminal and civil processes that go on in this country are not in their hands. Their control of it is only indirect.

Thus ninety per cent of crime is dealt with summarily and by magistrates. Some magistrates are lawyers, but the majority are laymen, and the principles of choice that governs the award of the degree J.P. are far from clear.

It follows that the motorist charged with some offence not serious enough to warrant its treatment by the High Court, is involved in a game which admittedly has rules, but which at this level is a game of chance. Who can protect him against the magistrate who is determined to accept at full face value all prosecution evidence? If he is unfortunate enough to find himself

---

([1970] 1 All Eng. R. 757), in which certain findings of fact (whether cards had been stamped) were held (pursuant to the National Insurance Acts) to be the function of the Minister only.

[37] Parliamentary Commissioner for Administration.

[38] Adjectivally, not substantially, different.

faced with a serious charge which is yet not indictable, such as driving uninsured, he may have to present a quite complex legal argument (as to the validity of his policy) to men equipped for everything except the understanding of it.

Legally qualified magistrates, though chosen from lower levels than are judges, are evidently better; though they tend to be overworked, and consequently impatient. But any agitation for the legal education of lay magistrates is evidently justified.

In the civil law, especially since the jurisdiction of County Courts was raised to deal with claims up to £400, the majority of civil litigation falls into the hands of County Court judges and their registrars. These are, on the whole, well qualified men. Yet they are overworked, and forced to work in bad conditions, and cannot provide the time that is required for the proper treatment of serious issues. They live in a perpetual dilemma of enhancing the law's delays, or satisfying themselves with the superficial.

Over all these minor courts, and over others such as Traffic Courts, Rent Tribunals, etc., rises the aegis of the High Court. There are methods of appeal. Yet appeal is expensive. This brings us again to the basic criticism of the English legal system. 'Justice is open to all. So is the Ritz Hotel.'

In the last two decades some mitigation has been tendered in the shape of legal aid. The details of this are beyond the scope of anything but a specific treatise. At the time of writing many are benefiting from it – especially the really poor. In civil matters it is administered by professional committees, and their sittings add to the law's delays. In criminal matters the grant of legal aid is for the court; and the courts, even the lowest, will not easily deprive an accused person of some help.[39]

---

[39] It is not without interest that, whereas we in England have had the privilege of being ill at no cost for long before we enjoyed the privilege of cheap litigation, the position in the United States is that illness is strictly for the rich, but everyone is constitutionally entitled to free legal aid, however bad.

THE RULES OF THE GAME

In a period when crime has increased, is increasing and requires to be diminished, the criticism is freely expressed that British law favours the criminal. By this it is meant that the law, in its anxiety to ensure that no innocent man – even one in ten – be convicted, allows nine guilty ones to go free; and there is some reversion of opinion to the standpoint of Dickens' colonel (in *Barnaby Rudge*) who said: 'better hang the wrong man than no man at all'.

If it is true (and it seems to be true) that criminals are somewhat too 'sportingly' treated, one reason is, precisely, that Britain has, in one hundred and fifty years, made successive efforts to clear from itself the stigma of the immorality expressed by that colonel, and from the aggregate cruelties and injustices which constituted the criminal laws of the Regency and earlier years. Then 'sport' was to stone the unfortunate tenant of stocks or pillory; to applaud hangings and worse: to jeer at the dock. It is to be noted that only since 1836 have persons accused of felony been allowed legal defence.

Secondly, in a world largely composed of police states, Britain remembers that the 'police state' was anathema in Britain even before there were properly constituted police-forces.

This thought justifies a digression. In many states there are presented, to the tourist and journalist, law-courts which seem to be modelled on the patterns of the Anglo-Saxon judicatures. No one, however, introduces the spectator to the *agent provocateur* who may have been employed to encourage the accused person to commit the indiscretion with which he is charged. And nobody shows the visitor the apparatus of brain-washing, so brilliantly described by Koestler[40], or the machinery which produces the forced confession.

From the standpoint of democracy these are immoralities. Our 'rule of law' is much more than the bare statement that a person shall not be arrested or imprisoned except in accordance

[40] In *Darkness at Noon*.

with the law. The vital question to be asked is 'What law?'
Not, it can justly be claimed, a law which approves of the
agent provocateur. When the offences charged are relatively
venial deviations from the licensing system, it is accepted that
the policeman who joins in the 'drinking after hours' is an
acceptable witness: but he is not accepted if he was the person
who, in the first instance, invited the landlord to the contravention of statute. How much more important is it that police,
who are seeking to trap offenders by appearing to join with
them in real crime, should make clear to the courts what they
have done. If it appears that they were not only participants,
but instigators, the courts may even reject their evidence, and
take a different view from the ordinary of the charge laid.[41]

To state the matter another way, the law is moral to the
extent that it will not use means of which it disapproves, even for a
justified end. In this spirit, the Anglo-Saxon courts deplore any
coercion of confession, and show no enthusiasm even for unforced confessions. Hence an elaborate code of 'judges' rules',
elaborating the principle that before a confession be accepted,
the court must be sure that the confession was 'voluntary', not
induced by 'fear or favour'; and so little as the statement, by a
person in authority that 'it will be better for you to confess'
vitiates a confession as evidence.

Yet, be it repeated, no unction should be laid to the legal soul
for these protections. English law as we know it now is the end-
product of reaction from great severities and cruelties.

Two characteristics of the criminal law derive from our legal
history. First, to mitigate cruelties, it was the practice of judges
to insist on a pedantry of language in charges, and pedantries in
the mode of proof, in order to ensure that, if a conviction were
arrived at, the legal and civil consequences could not be said to
be made possible by looseness of thinking on the part of the
courts. Indictments were exact, and evidence was strictly limited,
as by Aristotelean unities, to the detail of the crime alleged.
No history was relevant.

Secondly, memories of Courts of Star Chamber and High
Commission, the preserves of the Crown's Commissioners, caused

[41] See R. v Birtles [1969] 2 All Eng. R. 1131.

the common lawyers to exorcise from their practice anything suggestive of forced confessions.

On this principle it was never a punishable offence at common law for the offender not to confess. The *peine forte et dure* applied by Inquisition and Star Chamber were never regarded by lawyers as tolerable by law. The common law allows the accused to refrain from statements at all stages.[42] The prosecution was never, in the modern practice, allowed to comment on a prisoner's silence, or failure to give evidence. The judge was allowed to comment to the jury on the absence of evidence that the prisoner could have provided had he wished. But even in that scope judges are careful. A striking instance, amounting almost to precedent, is the instruction by Devlin J. (as he then was) in R. v Adams[43] – a case arising from the fatal administration of drugs in a nursing home for old people – that the jury should attach no significance adverse to the prisoner in the fact that he had remained silent throughout and refrained from giving evidence.

Also judges are nowadays more careful than they were in the allowance made, positively or negatively, when they pass sentence on a prisoner who has stood trial rather than pleaded guilty. The Appellate judges have held it wrong to add to the proper sentence because the prisoner has (admittedly with the aid of perjury) denied his guilt.[44] A prisoner may be sentenced less severely if he has repented and/or 'helped the police'. But he should not be sentenced more heavily for not having been co-operative, or for putting the prosecution to expense. That distinction may appear metaphysical, but it is in the metaphysics of a theory of justice, which is (it is hoped) being described.[45]

The criminal law abounds with technicality: but its most important manifestation consists in the just and vigorous enforcement of the specific rules of law; that character is not

[42] He is expected to 'plead' – e.g. to say Not Guilty if he wishes to put the Crown to proof of the charge. If he does not accept the jurisdiction that constitutes a plea of Not Guilty.

[43] 1957. Unreported.

[44] R. v Harper (1967) 52 C.A.R. 21.

[45] The effect of English law is that we do not have here the American practice of plea bargaining – a 'tunnel of treachery'.

evidence, that hearsay is not evidence; that confessions are not to be extracted from accused persons; and that the accused never bears the burdens of proof. It follows from these rules that charges are only instituted when the police are equipped with more evidence than would justify a civil claimant in initiating his action.

The police have, be it added, difficulties that do not beset the lawyer who prepares a civil suit. They are limited as to their questioning of witnesses, because the witness may prove to be an accused person. By common law as restated in rule II of the judges' rules (1964) 'As soon as a police officer has evidence which would afford reasonable grounds for suspecting that a person has committed an offence, he shall caution that person or cause him to be cautioned before putting to him any questions, relating to that offence.' The caution tells the suspect as follows: 'You are not obliged to say anything unless you wish to do so, but what you say may be put into writing and used in evidence'.[46]

Because of irregularities in questioning, many confessions, or admissions, have been ruled inadmissible; many have been reduced in cogency; and many have made appeals possible.

The *modus operandi* of the judges who guard the doctrines of the law is well illustrated in the appeals against convictions on the grounds of wrongful admission of evidence, and/or judicial misdirection, that come before the Court of Criminal Appeal. (This court, incidentally, was only founded in 1907, after the Adolf Beck case; all previous appeals had been on strictly legal questions as to whether the jury's findings warranted the judge's verdict. This court is now part of the Court of Appeal.)

Appeals can be based on judicial pedantry – particularly that the judge or magistrate has not been pedantic enough. A judge must be exact. He has to explain to juries the fine distinctions between the degrees of recklessness and carelessness that make the difference between manslaughter and dangerous driving, between dangerous driving and driving without due care and

---

[46] The old formula added 'against you'. This has been omitted since the report in 1932 of the Royal Commission on Police Powers because, said the commissioners, the evidence is not only against him – it may help him!

attention. His to explain how wounding with intent to do grievous bodily harm differs from unlawful wounding. His to elaborate the grotesqueries that are so often involved in defences of consent to charges of rape.

Sometimes the law sets out a rigorous set of provisions. In point are the new rules as to the breath-test, the old rules as to searches.

In general, High Court judges do not go wrong in definition. What is usually the ground of appeal is the administrative, discretionary, admission or exclusion of evidence, and the evaluation of it in summing up.

Few appeals arise out of the Hearsay rule, but the rule is important. The rule amounts to one aspect of the basic principle that all evidence must be on oath in front of the prisoner or parties. (What a prisoner or a party said can be quoted.) What persons not before the court said is more properly classified with suspicion than with the circumstantial evidence which constitutes proof. A policeman is justified in arresting on the strength of hearsay, because he acts on 'reasonable suspicion' but 'proof' calls for the careful examination and cross-examination of witnesses. Quotations are not enough.[47]

The English courts recognise that the machinery of detection is different from the techniques of proof. They do not expect a puritanical restraint on the part of police. Evidence produced by execution of general warrants, and in illegal searches, will not be allowed. But evidence obtained through an improperly obtained statement is accepted.[48] Also the discoveries made by wire-

---

[47] Note that what is excluded is a statement quoted for its truth value. What another person said can, however, be a fact – a shout of warning e.g. or may constitute the occasion on which a prisoner or party said something.

A good example of the awkwardness of the Hearsay rule is presented in a quite recent case (Jones v Metcalfe [1967] 3 All Eng. R. 205). In a case of dangerous driving a witness had given the number of the badly driven vehicle to a policeman, who then traced it and obtained an admission from the accused that he was driving it at the material time. But in court the witness forgot the number. Held, therefore, that the principal evidence as to the vehicle was now hearsay; and a conviction (notwithstanding the admission) was quashed.

[48] R. v Gould (1849) C. & B. 364. Generally, see McArdle v Egan (1933) J.P. 103.

tappers can be utilised.[49] In this respect the English law differs from that of most of the American States, which have legislated wire-tapped evidence to be inadmissible. These laws are supported by the Federal Communications Act.[50] But in the context of the 4th Amendment, Supreme Court opinion has ebbed and flowed. Practices were tolerated in the days of Prohibition and Repeal which are not approved now. Nevertheless, there still broods over the Supreme Court the shadow of the great Holmes, autocrat of the constitutional law as his father was of the breakfast table. He declared (in Olmstead's case) that the state should not use 'dirty' methods. Implicit in this is the eighteenth-century theory that the law is designed to protect individuals and their property against the encroachment of the state. Their 'social contract' was to 'live and let live'.

The British attitude is not extreme, as the American exclusionary doctrine is. In turn, 'the continent' is more for the state. In this connection it may be appropriate to say that it is not true to say of the continental legal systems that men are guilty until proved innocent. Their practice is that once a *prima facie* case exists some burden is on the accused. That is not perverse. (In England the burden shifts psychologically, not formally.)

The French courts, be it mentioned, attach value to hearsay: but its absence from British courts would not be lamented were it not for the increasing intimidation of witnesses. The cross-examiner of a witness can ask: did you not say something else on another occasion? and can rebut the witness's denial by calling someone who heard. This is an exception to the hearsay rule. But the prosecution cannot so treat its own witness who, for understandable reasons, has 'forgotten', or 'did not see'.

As to character, there is a school of thought – and the continental jurists act in the belief – that character is a legitimate constituent of the circumstantial evidence tendered in proof of

---

[49] Fox v G.M.C. [1960] 3 All Eng. R. 225 and see vol. 16 of *Hansard*, No. 31, 1378–9. In R. v Stewart (unreported) evidence was accepted as to what a detective heard from a cell adjoining the prisoner's. In 1957, in a case before the Benchers of an Inn, wire-tapped evidence was not excluded.

[50] In Rathbone v U.S. (1957) 355 U.S. 107 listening in (on an extension) to threats was not regarded as wire-tapping.

guilt. Is it irrelevant, to a charge of burglary, that the prisoner has to his credit many convictions of burglary (especially if similar technique be involved)? In the 'system' cases, already mentioned, our courts have allowed some 'history' to be adduced, not to prove that because he sinned before he has probably sinned again, but to rebut such a defence as that the poison was accidentally administered, that the brides coincidentally were allergic to bathing, and so died in their baths. In the case of Straffen[51] a homicidal lunatic, the court allowed proof, 'in support of identification,' of the prisoner's previous record, and that is close to the continental thinking. But the courts still maintain the old doctrine. If evidence of this kind is inherent in other evidence (e.g. that the prisoner, at the time, was seeking to dispose of the proceeds of another crime) the court accepts it, but warns the jury carefully against the drawing of obvious conclusions from it. The trial judge has discretion, but this will always be exercised in the light of the rule that such evidence can be fatal to a fair trial (From the prisoner's point of view).

The judge has a discretion as to the admission of evidence. He may, in a proper case, hold that though some 'unfortunate' evidence has crept in, he will be able to persuade the jury to ignore it. The principle is difficult of application: but its obvious value is demonstrated by the recent R. v Sutton[52] in which one of two prisoners told in evidence that his colleague in the dock was a convict. If that had been allowed to cause the judge to cancel the trial and start again, an easy way would be open to accused persons to increase the difficulties of the prosecution unreasonably.

Confessions, if admitted, are voluntary ones. In many trials, there is to be seen a 'trial within a trial', wherein (usually in the absence of the jury) evidence is led to show how the confession was obtained. On its admissibility the judge then 'rules'. If it be admissible, the evidence goes forward to the jury, and, in a proper case, the judge can comment on its degree of cogency. Naturally, if there is doubt (and often when there is not) appeal is made against ensuing conviction.

But the subtle pedantry of the law is at its best, not when the confession is of doubtful admissibility, but when a prisoner's

[51] [1952] 2 All Eng. R. 257.   [52] [1969] 1 All Eng. R. 928.

statement is accepted, and the question of its effect is debated. Then the burden of proof is the burden of the controversy.

So, in Regina v Murtagh and Kennedy[53] the Judge of Assize said to the jury: 'If you do not think it safe to reject the explanation put forward by the Defendants ... acquit them both'. The layman may find it hard to understand why, on account of that direction, the Court of Criminal Appeal reversed the jury's verdict of guilty and acquitted the prisoners.

First, let it be observed what fine points the court will take in favour of the accused. The learned judge did not say: 'If you think it safe to accept the explanation put forward by the defendants' – that would suggest that some burden is on the defence. Instead, he said in effect: 'If you think it unsafe not to accept the explanation'. This does not suggest that the defence is under duty to explain. But the language used was so near to the improper form, to any untrained mind, that a juror might think that some burden of evidence was being thrown on the prisoners – that it was up to them to explain away or justify their conduct. The Court of Criminal Appeal felt that that danger was a great one. Certainly the niceties of logic are not to be expected from ordinary persons, especially those fatigued with long concentration through many hours and days of evidence and argument. If you say to a man in the street: 'All flesh is grass, therefore vegetarians are cannibals', he may have difficulty in not agreeing with you. It may not be much easier to distinguish the refinements of 'safe to accept' and 'unsafe to reject'. If in such a case the appellate court thinks that there could be confusion, or that confusion might be suspected in the verdict, then the only course is to quash the verdict, if only on the established principle that justice must not only be done, but must appear to be done.

The layman (assuming that he knows the facts of R. v Murtagh) might say in answer to this: Here were two men who were in control of a motorcar which was driven against a third person and killed him. That being proved, is it not reasonable to expect them to show why their conduct does not amount to murder? So reasonable is that view that we find the gist of it

[53] (1955) 39 C.A.R. 84.

stated in the last century by so great a jurist as James Fitzjames Stephen. In Stephen's view the act of killing is evidence of 'malicious' killing – the onus is on the prisoner to rebut the presumption or inference of malice. In this century that principle was adopted by so experienced a judge as Rigby Swift J. in R. v Woolmington,[54] when, after evidence that a man had shot his wife, the learned judge indicated to the jury that it was for the prisoner to show them that the homicide was not murder. The Law Lords, however, held differently; viz. that, from the beginning to end of a common law criminal trial, the burden of proof is on the prosecution and is never shifted. All that the prisoner contributes is in the form of his words – if he wishes to utter them – which becomes part of the evidence, and may create, or increase (or in some cases dissipate) a doubt in the minds of the jury. It is not for the prisoner to drive home his defence; it is for the prosecution to satisfy the jury that all the evidence – including that of the prisoner, if he gives any – establishes that the accused is guilty beyond reasonable doubt.

This statement of the law harmonizes many cases, including one that was for long regarded by many as exceptional: R. v Schama.[55] That arose out of a charge of receiving stolen goods; and the court said that if a man gives an explanation of his possession of stolen goods, and if that explanation *can* be true, then even if the jury falls short of believing it, their duty is to acquit. They can, it should be added, actively disbelieve and reject, and, in that event, convict. But the important point is that the prisoner is not called upon to convince his jurors. That same principle operates whenever an alibi is presented. The alibi becomes part of the total evidence, differing from what the prosecution has led in this way: that, being suggested by the defence, it does not require to be proved with the high degree of inductive certainty that must characterise convicting evidence.

The legislature has dealt recently[56] with alibis by enacting that accused persons should give notice of intention to adduce an alibi. That, however, does not affect the 'burden of evidence'.

Recently, Woolmington's case (which makes alibis stronger) has

[54] Woolmington v D.P.P. [1935] A.C. 462.
[55] (1914) 11 C.A.R. 45.   [56] Criminal Justice Act 1967.

come under adverse criticism from the Law Lords. It was pointed out in Sweet v Parsley[57] that, by reasons of the Woolmington rule, legislation has been discouraged in describing offences where an onus might reasonably be cast on the defence (e.g. possession of drugs), and, in consequence, language has been used which seemed to create 'absolute offences'. In Sweet v Parsley it was not necessary to overrule Woolmington v D.P.P. Therefore it continues to be law.

The consequence is that every prisoner giving evidence creates a situation of some subtlety, and in practice this subtlety imposes a psychological strain on the conscientious juror. Pedantry is made more difficult by reason of the fact that a large number of crimes consist in outward conduct in apparent breach of some prohibition – 'thou shalt not' – and when the facts are proved, for example the housebreaking, the assault, the conversion of money, the giving of false evidence, the resultant situation is one that seems to call for a very good explanation indeed on the part of the accused. (Few juries will believe – what one jury is reported to have accepted – that the man broke in merely to get a night's sleep, and took off his boots so as not to disturb anybody, and walked on the roof to enjoy the night air.)

Further, a good many modern crimes are offences against statutory commands, some prohibitory, but many positive of the type 'thou shalt'; and many of these statutes are so worded that when the failure to obey is proved the charge is proved, unless some matter of defence is proved by the accused. Here it does not pay the prisoner to be silent, for, although traditionally a penal statute is interpreted to the advantage of the prisoner and *contra proferentem* (the prosecutor), usually it is not sufficient to rely on ambiguities in the words. In practice accused persons find courts all too ready to see the purpose of the statute and not to allow too technical a defence to prevail. In point is the case of the motorist who pleaded guilty to driving an unlicensed vehicle. On the question whether the penalty should be assessed on the assumption that he was unlicensed for one quarter or for one year, the court held that the assumption must be one year unless he proved to the contrary. Lord Goddard there said, *obiter*, that it is possible in

[57] [1969] 1 All Eng. R. 347.

a criminal case, as in a civil one, for the onus to shift. That decision (Holland v Perry)[58] is, be it respectfully said, not high authority, but it indicates a *zeitgeist* moving in the law against the inviolacy of the individual, and his right to stand mute, allowing all the presumptions to go in his favour. This decision coheres with other dicta of Lord Goddard calculated to equate the logic of everyday life with the logic of law (R. v Sims),[59] and the logic of the civil court with that of the criminal jurisdiction (R. v Summers).[60] Both these equations (calculated to weaken the strong protection of prisoners) have been rejected by higher authority.[61] Meanwhile they have caused some defective directions to juries (as in Murtagh's case).

The tradition, in the highest courts, of reluctance to cast the onus upon the prisoner is praiseworthy in itself; but know its origin, and you are free to ask: is that justified in days of leniency, which was expedient in periods of severity?

Already there are situations where the defence takes on a burden. The clearest example is the plea of insanity, where the defence undertakes to exonerate itself (in a degree) by setting up proof of diseases of the mind etc. The standard of proof required here (and wherever an onus is on defence) does not equal the high standard required from the prosecution. The prosecution proves its case beyond reasonable doubt: the defence is only called upon to create a 'balance of probabilities' in its favour. Balance of probability is, be it explained, the standard of proof in civil claims. Although crime is said to be 'litigiously' treated in Britain (that distinguishes our system from inquisitorial systems where the state is arrayed against the accused) yet, in favour of the accused, the standard is higher than the normal of litigation.[62]

---

[58] [1952] 2 All Eng. R. 720.   [59] [1948] 1 All Eng. R. 697.
[60] [1952] 1 All Eng. R. 1059.
[61] R. v Sims is disapproved by the Privy Council in Noor Mohammed v R. [1949] A.C. 182.
[62] Incidentally it is worth observing that, while attempts are being made to de-formalise criminal procedure, formalities are as strongly preserved as ever in the civil courts; though some modifications have been reported. A recent development is in the Civil Evidence Act 1968 which allows the contents of other trials (*res inter alios acta*) to be used in evidence.

On the part of those who think that the criminal law is severe, it is complained that we rely on circumstantial evidence. Yet it is a platitude of logic and law that circumstantial evidence of guilt is more convincing than identification by witnesses.

What is in favour of prisoners is that judges are careful to state the criticism of circumstantial evidence more emphatically than they state its merits. The formulation is of the *doubt*.

In every summing up by a careful judge some such formula as the following is used: That the burden is on the prosecution, not on the prisoner; that taking the evidence as a whole, including the prisoner's evidence, the jury must ask themselves whether the prosecution has satisfied them beyond reasonable doubt, or, as some now put it, has made them sure. If the prosecution has left them in reasonable doubt they must acquit; and it would be explained that the doubt must be reasonable in the sense that such a doubt would influence them in the conduct of their own affairs; not a fantastic doubt – but a real doubt. Let them remember that it was not for the prisoner to prove his innocence, but for the prosecution to prove guilt beyond reasonable doubt. Courts have frequently referred to the principle so elaborated as the golden thread in English jurisprudence.

Golden thread, yes, but nevertheless an imponderable. The notion of reasonable doubt (like the notion of proof) is not hard to understand, but it is hard to define. How true are the words of Stephen: 'To attempt to give a specific meaning to the phrase "reasonable doubt" is trying to count what is not number and to measure what is not space'. That author explains that members of a jury are entitled to fill the gaps in the evidence with their inferences and their intelligent conjectures, but not beyond an ill-defined, indeed indefinable, limit. To give an example of the legitimate operation of a jury's inductions and of the principle of doubt, he says: 'If a man had the same reason for believing his wife to be unfaithful as the jury which tried Palmer had for believing that he murdered Cook ... he would, however fondly he might love her, believe her to be unfaithful and act on that belief, though the consequences would be destructive of his domestic happiness.'

The mention of Palmer's case reminds us that the whole question of doubt is a feature of that inductive process which is proof by circumstantial evidence. Before consideration of the wider issue it is important to stress the difficulty of judicial direction. It will be evident to all that few judges or recorders can explain the degree of doubt with the clarity of such a jurist as I have quoted. Consequently many summings up have been suspected of confusing juries. With this, among other things, in mind, Lord Goddard said in the case of Summers[63] that in general the classical direction on reasonable doubt was unnecessary; that it was better to tell a jury that they should not convict unless they were satisfied of the guilt of the prisoner.

That dictum has proved technically unfortunate for two reasons. First that judges, guided by it, have had to sum up without the traditional elaboration of the principle of doubt. But there are evidently cases where the old formula is indispensable. Thus in the case of Murtagh, we have a situation where the prisoner's story may or may not conjure a doubt. The jury needs to understand that the proof of malice must be made by the prosecution; that the prisoner is not expected to prove his case with the same degree of inductive certainty[64] that if his story creates a doubt, and the prosecution does not dispel it, then the jury must decide whether the doubt they are left with is a reasonable one – such as would guide them in their own affairs; or a fantastic one, which they can ignore.

In attempting to find a formula without using the word doubt the learned judge in Murtagh's case used apparently innocuous words that were held to amount to misdirection.

A second consequence of R. v Summers is that it gives the impression that a jury's function is similar in criminal matters to its function in civil matters. This (desirable or not) is a change because it is not consistent with established practice and authority. Unfortunately, it is difficult nowadays for a student of our laws to compare the workings of the jury system in the criminal and civil courts respectively. In the Old Bailey there are juries galore, but in the Strand jurors are rare birds; and old practitioners despair of hearing the beat of their returning wings. They still come to town to peck at libel, slander,

63 [1952] 1 All Eng. R. 1059.   64 NOT mathematical certainty.

wife-enticement or breach of promise; but they neglect personal injuries caused by negligence. Consequently it is not easy to demonstrate, what is theoretically possible; that, given the right summing up, a motorist at the Old Bailey can be acquitted of a motor killing, but can be mulcted in damages in the Strand for negligence in the same affair. And why? Because the civil jury has to be *satisfied*; but the criminal jury has to be *satisfied beyond reasonable doubt*. Because, further, the burden of proof in civil courts can be shifted by the proof of suggestive facts. In the criminal court that burden is always on the Crown.

The distinction is related to moral attitudes. Crime is shameful; conviction is disgrace; punishment. Therefore more protection is required for one accused of crime than for the civil defendant. The jury is given to the civil court as an assistant to an arbitrator; to the criminal court as a barrier between the law itself (embodied theoretically in the judge) and the naked accused. Theirs, in both jurisdictions, to find facts. Historically, their finding of facts against the directions of judges have saved many men from oppressive prosecutors and biassed judges; and in the old days, many a juror suffered gaol on account of his conscience (or party).[65] Now, when judges are not oppressive, juries remain to relieve the judge of the unacademic duty of believing or disbelieving witnesses. Their reward is an intellectual training with which many of them can (and do) dispense.

The law offers to the citizen two sets of examples of proof by circumstantial evidence. Both processes are logical, but neither is precisely governed by the logic of ordinary life; and one set of cases (the criminal) is further removed than the other from ordinary induction, because more logically relevant matters are held there to be legally irrelevant (for example, prisoner's character); because the prisoner is not forced to contribute his knowledge, or his personal behaviour under questioning, to the investigation of the whole issue; and because the contribution of the prisoner to the evidence is given greater effect in proportion to its inherent strength than would be warranted at the level of ordinary affairs.

[65] In our day a judge has been held wrong who merely bullied a jury into haste.

The logic of the civil court is also 'special' in, for example, the exclusion of hearsay evidence that could be helpful, and such as the French courts accept. But the civil court is, on the whole, less remote than the criminal from the logical processes of ordinary life. That is why it is so important that jurors who understand civil litigation should, when they come into criminal courts, be carefully directed. It must be hard for them to appreciate that a receiver's story has only to be credible without being true; or that the unsworn statement of one prisoner is evidence against him, but not against the man charged with him on the same indictment.

The juror also encounters the problems of evidence conjured by accomplices, whose evidence should be corroborated in a material particular; yet can be believed in the absence of corroboration, if the jury thinks that it is true. An added delicacy is that when one thinks of accomplices one is tentatively regarding the accused guilty.

To the layman these things are mysteries, and jurors enjoy themselves in learning them.

But one criticism of the legal process would not be made by an intelligent juror who had experienced the work of the courts; he would not join in any attack on proof by circumstantial evidence. For in its use of circumstantial evidence the law is operating no differently from the generality of the sciences: no differently from the reasoning that goes on in ordinary life.

In strict logic there is no evidence that is not circumstantial, for if one listens to an eye-witness one must decide, on circumstantial reasoning, whether or not to believe him. But accepting a distinction between the evidence of eye-witnesses and evidence made up of inferences and intelligent judgments, there is no certainty that preference should be given to the former. There are many examples of mistaken identifications – honest ones. In contrast, many important inquiries involve induction and produce truth. An engineer who locates a fault has intelligently guessed; certainly a doctor who diagnoses, and treats, has not calculated with mathematical certainty, nor has he seen the germ with the naked eye: but he has used circumstantial evidence.

Two inquiries held in the 1930s are illustrative of circumstantial evidence as used by lawyers in the investigation of affairs other than litigious. One was the inquiry into the typhoid epidemic at Croydon – where the outbreak of the disease was traced to a certain workman. The other was the Budget leakage inquiry that arose during the chancellorship of Mr J. H. Thomas. In both of these inquiries an interpretation was accepted which was not the only possible interpretation of the facts. But in each case the adoption of the alternative hypothesis was scientifically much more difficult. In the Budget case a large number of co-incidences – including two separate sets of apparent leakages – were explicable rationally on the hypothesis that they were linked by an indiscretion of a minister. Without that hypothesis they remained strange and only explicable with great elaboration. Occam's Razor therefore operated to cut the throat of the defence.

In a civil court the Thomas issues would certainly have been similarly resolved; in a criminal court probably so. Onus would be different – degree of doubt would be different. To exonerate Mr Thomas would have been unscientific perhaps, or unreasonable, not fantastic: just like a less scientific explanation of a typhoid epidemic. A jury should convict but could acquit.

In the case of Palmer on the other hand – the case referred to by Stephen – doubt would have been fantastic.

There a medical practitioner gave pills to a man; and whenever the man took them he became ill. The man became ill when the same medical man handled his food. The medical man had access to poisons. Moreover the same medical man was robbing the alleged victim on a large scale, and had much to gain from his death. Eventually that death took place in a way consistent with strychnine poisoning and hardly consistent with any other causation. For the rest Dr Palmer successfully concealed all traces of the medicaments and other phenomena.

Had a jury on those facts accepted the suggestion that the deceased had died of a rare kind of tetanus, they would have been acting on a fantastic speculation, giving the prisoner the benefit of a totally unreasonable doubt.

Admittedly, circumstantial evidence can be wrong. The evidence so skilfully marshalled against Mr Pickwick, by those superb solicitors Dodson & Fogg, happened to be misleading. But if there are miscarriages of justice it is probable that they take place not because of circumstantial evidence but in its absence. Such a case was that of Wallace,[66] where the whole prosecution rested on a logical confusion – the man was guilty because he had faked an alibi; but the only reason for thinking he had faked an alibi was the assumption that he was guilty. Some suspicion attached to him because he was a chess player. The impression of great cunning was conveyed to the jury; but no one told them that he was the worst chess player who had ever pushed a hesitant pawn.

If a conviction on circumstantial evidence be proved wrong it will be found that there was some great gap in it, or some great logical confusion in its presentation.

What surprises the critic of circumstantial evidence is that great miscarriages of justice have been due to what he trusts; namely the evidence of eye-witnesses. Eye-witnesses, in many cases, have been spectacularly wrong. Striking is the case of Adolf Beck who was convicted of frauds twice: on the identification of a dozen perfectly honest witnesses. They were proved mathematically to be wrong. Because of Beck's misfortunes the Court of Criminal Appeal was founded. Sixty years later it could still happen that honest witnesses, with a good view of a person, could be proved wrong, after his conviction and imprisonment, by the convincing confession of another prisoner (Chapman).[67]

(Apropos of which, and without reference to Chapman, it is also a fact that confessions are quite often false – responses to some exhibitionist impulse.)

Reasoning is more reliable than sight and hearing. Certainly, when subtle issues are decided involving states of mind, negligence for example, or malice in libel, then wrong decisions can be made, because sharp findings are required. But in the criminal court, as we have seen, the prisoner is protected when the issues are narrow. Then the principles of empiricism – i.e. benefit of doubt – operate in his favour. With that reservation one may say

[66] (1931)23 C.A.R. 32.
[67] R. v Chapman, an unreported case in which the Home Office (*ex gratia*) compensated the prisoner.

that criminal trials are scientific investigations cast in litigious form. That phrase is important. Litigation differs from a perfectly objective inquiry, because of rules about the burden of evidence. It has been claimed that inquisitorial methods are more scientific. If that be the case, it is hard to say why the French lay such emphasis on confession. The inquisitorial claim is, of course, arguable; but the difficulty is in being assured that there is no bias in the inquisitor.

Because of the fear of bias in the inquisitor, the modern critic can say, with, at least, plausibility, that criminals are protected by our law. Suggestions have been made to the effect that accused persons should be required to make statements: that, when the facts indicate it, an onus should be thrown on to the accused – in legal form, and not only psychologically. Some would dispense with jurors. Always their mentalities have been suspect.[68] To expect twelve persons to see a point that a clever man may miss is a policy untrue to any logic. More recently jurors have been intimidated.[69] For that reason the majority verdict has been introduced. It is arguable that, if these protections are required, it would be better to substitute a court of, say, three judges – and rely on that plurality as a safeguard against individual biasses and pedantries. For the task of justice is a hard one, calling for ability, not mediocrity. Mediocrity in government is a classical safeguard; in the court of justice not so. The jury system lends itself to the impression that a game is being played, not a search for truth conducted.

In our system the court is looking, not for abstract truth, but for a true verdict according to the evidence; according to rules of evidence which are not self-evident. The proof is not mathematical. Yet intellectually the process is scientific: to make diagnoses, to solve problems; exactly in the spirit of the Greek academicians who aimed at finding a formula within the rules, but so as to account for all the appearances.

[68] Indeed, the lowness of their brows is cited in their support. The theory is that the simple man is better at recognising the false than is the academic man who is expert at reconciling discrepancies.

[69] Yet in the past, juries have shown great courage. In the 1790's they took the edge off the laws against sedition. Theoretically, therefore, they present a dam or buckler against any trend to a police state.

By way of appendix let it be made clear that the rules of the game (the trial of the issue) do not all favour the person accused of crime. In no moral sense is he favoured. He is judged, in most cases, with a minimum of sentimentality. His position as an accused person creates a psychological disadvantage. He starts mistrusted. If a jury believes what it need not believe, and finds him guilty and he appeals, his case will be argued in front of judges whose principle it is not to interfere with the jury's findings. Unless some important error has characterised the conduct of the trial, including the summing-up, the jury's verdict will not be disturbed, however out of sympathy with it the Appellate Judges find themselves. Nor will the Court of Appeal consider what has happened in the jury-box.[70] Even if a convict got in there by mistake that fact is not fatal.[71] Nay more, if it transpires that some juror has shown bias, or been in possession of information as to the prisoner's past, even, indeed, if jurors later swear that they agreed to the verdict against their wills, no action will be taken on that account.[72]

The law is rigid; and the processes which vindicate the law are necessarily strict and unsentimental. Many sentiments operated in the making of the laws in order to create protections even for those who break it. Those protections are part of the rules. They cannot be added to, altered, or mitigated while the game is being played. And one of the rules that makes all losers unhappy is that a technically correct result must stand.

PROFESSIONAL ETHICS

If the law is a game, what of the players? That is to say: what of the professional players? The judges – advocates?

What is the moral position of a judge who finds himself dis-

[70] Ellis v Deheer [1922] 2 K.B. 113. Boston v Bagshaw (1966) 1 W.L.R. 1126.
[71] R. v Kelly [1953] 3 All Eng. R. 558.
[72] If an irregularity is revealed during the trial, even a triviality like juror speaking to counsel, the jury will be dismissed, and a fresh trial ordered.

charging a guilty man, because a jury has decided to acquit? or, harder, what of the judge entering a verdict of guilty which he himself would not have returned?

And what of the advocates, asks the layman, who act for clients whom they know to be villains; advocates who, if they do their work well, seem, as the Greek philosopher put it, to be making the worse cause appear the better?[73]

Let the two categories be separated, for practical reasons.

The judges, whether high or low in jurisdiction, are not, primarily, exponents of any cause. The judges of the High Court were called 'lions round the throne', in days when they were king's men. History is full of their roarings and their rapine. Also they left a literature, full of bloody morsels from the ovens of Coke, and redolent with the odours of Bacon.

Since the revolutions, however, and in consequence of the Act of Settlement, British judges have built a better, if not more learned, tradition; have established a reputation for objectivity and incorruptibility, and generally (if not in every particular) for firmness in the light of the law.

In their judicial capacity, these men have not been partisan. Only exceptionally does political panic appear in the records of their judgments. They are no longer the King's men, nor Parliament's men, though they administer – this is their task – the laws of the King in Parliament. The political generalist will explain their independence as a function of a well settled multi-party democracy, not to be compared with the situation of judges in one-party or totalitarian, regimes. This generalisation does not deprive them of merit.

That being said, they are limited as to their capacity; limited by their mental and individual moral capacities – all of which are variables; but mainly limited by their functional capacity, which is to administer the law. It is here that the question of judicial morality is raised, and answered. Allowing for all the interpretations of law and morality, it is law that they are charged to administer. Where morality and intellect become relevant, we see it manifested, in all the gradations from reaction to

[73] Shakespeare puts it more vividly, in the words of the Lord Chief Justice to Falstaff: 'Wrenching the true cause the wrong way.'

progress, from Eldon to Atkin. If, however, there is no scope for intellection or ethics, they cannot introduce it.

That is why the judge accepts the verdict of the jury, even though he scolds them.[74] (He no longer imprisons them, as did his elder brethren, even to the end of the eighteenth century.) Similar reasoning explains why Appellate judges keep severely to the established principle; that only a fault in the trial, or a verdict inconsistent with the evidence, justifies the quashing of a conviction. At this level, be it added, there is some latitude, over limited longitude.

For the rest, the standard they hold is the standard of the law and its traditions. There is, therefore, no pejorative in the expression 'puisne judge'. Unhappily, the same observation can not be made of the expression 'petty magistrate'.

To the legal profession, non-judicial, other considerations apply. Traditionally lawyers are suspect.

> '*In Craven Street, Strand, do the lawyers abound*
> *And down in the river the barges are found*
> *Fly, honesty, fly, to a safer retreat*
> *There is craft at the bottom and top of the street.*'[75]

In assessing 'the craft', let a distinction be made – a distinction between economic externals, and the legal immanent standards. When the old Chancery man, settling a case, bewailed an estate 'wasted on a lot of beneficiaries', he was telling the world two things; one, that he and his fellow lawyers can be greedy; secondly, that, nevertheless, they do what requires to be done in the discharge of their proper functions.

It is, therefore, irrelevant, or almost irrelevant, to the assessment of moral coefficients in legal practice, that many lawyers extract money from many people. Let the layman describe the solicitor as a saprophyte who consumes the substance of his clients, and let him regard (more charitably) the barrister as an economic parasite on that saprophyte (there are happier parasites!), he is still not considering the essential question, which is:

---

[74] This was done thirty-odd years ago by a judge who disapproved a verdict of manslaughter on facts that clearly constituted murder.

[75] Composed when the best courts were at Westminster Hall.

does the advocate behave morally in his work *quâ* advocate? Does he not behave unfairly, as his opponent behaves unfairly? Does he not say many things which he does not believe?

The answer is succinctly given, by one of the greatest American advocates. A hundred and fifty years ago, William Samson said to a New York jury: 'I am a poor tradesman labouring at my vocation'. What is that vocation? Briefly, it is not the search of an ideal; it is the pursuit of the best possible result for his client. Is he demonstrating truth? No, he is assessing evidence.

When these facts are realised, the glamour falls away from histrionics. Indeed, histrionics can lose cases. Equally irrelevant is the function of public entertainment beloved of American Attorneys General.[76] What emerges is the need for skill in the game of mixed chance and skill which is legal practice. If a cross-examiner puts a heavy emphasis on slight inconsistencies, if he draws the witness into exaggerations, he is not assisting the cause of truth; he is examining words, he is criticising evidence as given: for the verdict that is sought is not abstract truth, but the truth according to the evidence. Let it be added that the able advocate makes no attack which is likely to fail badly, or to antagonise the court. That would be, not immorality, but bad advocacy – which is unjust to his client. If he is unsubtle or ineffective, that is the client's fault. He should not have briefed him! Which leaves open the suggestion that one element of injustice in English law is the inequality of ability among advocates.

But, persists the critic, is it not worse than that? How can a man who knows his client to be guilty, or wrong in his claim or defence, co-operate with that man in a process of deception?

That question reveals an ignorance of legal practice – of the integrity which is the normal of legal practice. No barrister makes statements of fact which he knows to be untrue. Indeed, he does not make statements of fact at all – only submissions of interpretations of evidence. Further, he will not co-operate in perjury. If the client is indiscreet enough to tell him that he (the client) is guilty, then the barrister is precluded from putting him in the witness-box to swear to the contrary. So important is this

[76] E.g. The clowning of Mr Murphy in the tragic case of Alger Hiss.

that some barristers decline to see their clients, but insist that communication be mediated by the instructing solicitor. Others hold this to be a counsel of perfection, rather than perfection of counsel.

As to unfairness, this, too, is a variable, as are the forensic noses and whiskers on which Dickens commented.

There are counsel who think it right to take advantage of 'without prejudice' correspondence,[77] and who will say to the court: 'there was no answer to this letter.' (In a technical sense, this is true.) Others hold this to be wrong. But even the former will not think that he is deceiving the court. (He trusts the court to know the rules!)

To deceive the court, that is the cardinal sin. When the implications of that truth are examined, it becomes clear that advocacy is honest. Not to make the worse cause appear the better, but to make it appear as good as it can be made to appear. That is the work of the humble tradesman labouring at his vocation'.[78]

[77] A letter written 'without prejudice' is one that is never shown to the court. In correspondence of this type, people negotiate without being committed to any admission of liability etc. This is a very convenient legal technique.

[78] Compendiously, legal professional ethics are comparable to the ethics of other professions.

A medical man keeps a murderer alive. Some scientists have greater problems, which are beyond the scope of this essay. But, generally, a man has a duty to his craft, once he adopts it.

In the case of scientists, others are available to control the effect of the work: to decide whether H bombs should be made: to decide whether sonic booms should be risked, if only in the light of the law of nuisance. To few fall the task of Heisenberg, who is said to have retarded German work on atomic bombs during the war of 1939. Lawyers, happily, engage in work which calls for no such decisions.

An important logical similarity, and a difference between the professions is found in the duty of confidence. A doctor must not divulge the facts found in the consulting room. A priest must not divulge the secrets of the confessional. A lawyer must not divulge his clients communications to him.

From the legal point of view the rule is that a man must have an acceptable reason for refusing to answer questions in court: and there are few acceptable reasons. Loyalty is not an acceptable reason (re Fleming, unreported): and editors have been imprisoned for refusing to divulge their sources of information. These have no privilege, alternatively, those who confide in them have no privilege, comparable to that of a spouse who does not divulge communications made by the other during marriage.

In the courts the priestly and the medical 'privileges' are respected, in that order, but not completely accepted. A lawyer's privilege is always accepted. Certainly a lawyer must not conceal the planning of a crime (Bullivant v Att. Gen. for Victoria [1901] A.C. 196). Nor is it proper to conceal the name of a client from those who wish to do business with the latter. (Re Galinsky, July 1969.) But what is told to him by the client, he must not divulge. Otherwise few who are concerned with their legalities could safely seek legal advice.

But the lawyer's privilege does not put him in a position adverse to the court. On the other hand the court trusts the advocate implicitly.

It looks to him not to mislead, not to conceal, not to initiate, unscrupulous manoeuvres, Thus if counsel 'puts to' a witness (not merely 'suggests') some fact (including in this category the witness's bad character) the court assumes that he can and will prove what he says by evidence. If he has pleaded fraud, or the justification of a bad libel, the court assumes that he did so on instructions, and in the light of available evidence. Unfair he is allowed to be, in putting the worst construction on a witness's conduct. But as to allegations of fact he must be scrupulously fair. Even in the citation of law, he is expected to draw the attention of the court to authorities unfavourable as well as favourable.

For the rest, the court expects, on the part of the advocate, an aloofness from his client, and an almost total severance from his witnesses. These, he must not advise as to what they should say; and when he 'leads evidence', it must be with questions that are not 'leading', i.e. not suggestive of the answer.

Let it only be added that, within these narrow limits, the scope for good advocacy remains wide.

9

Ethical Neutrality

There are conflicts, in law and war, where right is not arrayed against wrong, but against another right. Studying such a position, a spectator or an arbitrator can be at a loss. But to call him, in that state of mind, ethically neutral is wrong. He is ethically undecided. What the scientists mean by 'ethical neutrality' is total indifference to ethics.

The claim of ethical neutrality, coming from men who generally classify themselves as Humanists, is usually made in error. Certainly the medical man, binding the wounds of the enemy of his country, or the enemy of society, is not determined by the ethics of his social group, only by his duties to Aesculapius. And since it has been said that among three medical men there are two atheists, one can expect a certain reserve in judgment on social issues where religious beliefs have so far prevailed. To describe this attitude as ethical neutrality is a great exaggeration. If scientists, whether inventive of weapons or therapeutics, think steadily of their moral position, they should realise that the reference to neutrality is meaningless. If they want indifference to all valuations, they are being anti-ethical, not neutral. Ethical neutrality (when analysed) is a meaningless phrase, descriptive only of the mind of the anonymous English magistrate who swore that he would be neither partial nor impartial.

An utter indifference to ethics is unethical – in the sense of bad. The materialist in conduct, the really practising atheist, is inseparable from the traditional wicked. He is totally different from the untheologically moral man with all his difficulties: from the courageous thinker who looks bravely on a cold world through the lenses of Spinoza.

The humanist may be hard put to it to find conviction to support his beliefs: yet he is moral. The 'real' atheist has nothing at all in which to believe. He will only follow his lusts. Scientists are unlikely to be in this category, whatever garbled account they may give of their spiritual equipment. One value at least the scientist will esteem, the value which is truth. Once he has entered into that order, he will appreciate other values as well. He will appreciate that a world of value is in being; and once he is aware of it, he is unlikely to be indifferent to it. These values will emerge for him as cogent forces if and when he is called upon to sacrifice truth. If a tyrant tells him that agriculture is determined by Lamarckian concepts which he is, accordingly, instructed to teach; and he believes that the proper concepts are those of Weissmann; then he is in the classical situation where a man must be wicked or be a martyr.

Happily, English lawyers have not, since our revolution, had martyrdom thrust upon them. Lawyers in other lands have been, and are, less fortunate. The English lawyer, the English law maker or practitioner, is heir to a moral tradition. He is not always expressing moral judgments, not because he is indifferent to ethical values but because the law is, in some measure, concerned with situations where ethics are irrelevant to the issues.

On the border of this class are international laws. No one is less 'ethically neutral' than the advisers of governments called upon to obey the laws of neutrality.[1] In point is the situation of the late President Delano Roosevelt, who, having allowed Congress to pass a Neutrality Act, officially adopting international orthodoxy, discovered that the U.S.A. was thereby compelled to favour aggressors, whose lines of communication were over land, at the expense of defenders, whose lines of communication were maritime. For the welfare of the world (including the U.S.A.) he organised the repeal of that measure.

---

[1] These are largely concerned with the legality, or otherwise, of supplies to belligerent nations. Material helpful in war is contraband. The laws of war restrict the freedom of the seas, by making it lawful for belligerent ships to intercept and search vessels suspected of carrying contraband. (There are differences of opinion as to the range of contraband.)

International law is law. That belief has been disputed, but the world has acted on it. Because, however, its sanctions, to be effective, must express themselves in war, the world lacks, and must continue to lack, a body of accepted doctrine imposing the decencies, according to our standards – for the moral person must always be his own judge – on societies unwilling or unable to be allegiant to them. Here pragmatism must prevail, with its doctrines of expediency and 'enlightened self-interest'. When quasi-morally positive action (short of war) has been initiated, in order to modify the practice and doctrines of international law, we experience such appalling phenomena as non-belligerency, cease-fire without armistice, and other devices for making war by preparing peace.

In international law we meet the word recognition. That describes the acceptance by a nation with or against its own moral approval, of a new political situation, of successful conquest, of successful rebellion. Moral issues feature vividly in the debate whether to recognise; but the ultimate test is the success, by physical force, of the power claiming recognition. Short of interference by force, governments find themselves on cordial terms with many regions that they hate.[2]

Nor is it easy for moral orders, such as the genuine democracies, to carry into international theory and practice the precepts of their own domestic ethics. Thus, for two centuries the doctrine 'one man one vote' has been the ideal of representative government, and representative government has been a keystone of the democratic structure. But when that great liberal President Wilson translated this theory into international language, in the doctrine of self-determination,[3] he succeeded in the creation of many entities which proved not to be viable. Any philosopher, analysing the notion of self, will learn that an entity based on geographical continuity or contiguity does not qualify, by those characteristics alone, for selfhood. In later days, this 'unruly steed' of self-determination has been fertilised (in the manner of Virgil's mare) by 'winds of change', and has deposited

[2] Sanctions short of war form a modern effort to express moral disapproval. But the sufferer is usually the British exporter.

[3] Perhaps with the ulterior motive, shared by all American presidents, of 'decolonizing' Britain.

on the map a polychrome aggregate of political nonentities. Subsequently, in the United Nations, the concept of 'one state one vote' has led to the regimentation of meaningless, but now legally significant, units into the cohorts of the log-rollers.

Nor is it self-evident that the morals of some democracies will be uniform among all democracies, unless the category of democracy be greatly restricted. Hence the difficulties of legal relationship between Britain and the ex-colonies where advanced white men, not without claims, stand in fear of backward black majorities. Currently, in this context, the advocates of universal suffrage have fought against acceptance of the expediencies of pragmatism, but without signal success.[4]

On other topics there are, between nations, differences of morality as expressed in law. Thus several states of the American union are characterised by matrimonial laws which are not acceptable in Britain. Also many civilised societies are polygamous, and that fact is relevant to the lives of immigrants to Great Britain.

No island is an island. The moralities of other parts of the world cannot be totally irrelevant here, if only because they are relevant to international political developments. But it would be impractical for international relations to be controlled by any one-sided desire for a raising of standards. Britain does not enforce the revenue laws of other lands:[5] but within the limits of treaties, she enforces such important criminal laws as are common to the jurisdictions. Murderers, thieves, and other criminals listed, can be extradited to and by those nations with whom extradition treaties are in being.[6]

---

[4] The contemporary issue of Rhodesian independence is complicated by the belief that Rhodesia is bound to obey, and is disobeying, British laws. It may reasonably be predicted that other nations will bring about a recognition. Britain has recognised worse regimes; and is currently exposed to the criticism *dat veniam corvis, vexat censura columbas*.

[5] Though it is not clear that a conspiracy to defeat foreign Customs and Excise would be unindictable here. (See Regazzioni's case [1957] All Eng. R. 286.)

[6] There can be difficulties. Thus attempted robbery, unlike attempted murder, seems not to be extraditable. (Re Atkinson, [1969] 2 All Eng. R. 1151.)

Here the courts must be wary of attempts by foreign states to capture escaped rebels etc, by accusing them of crimes in the nature of larceny. Many habeas corpus applications have been made in such circumstances, and in this decade the courts have found (in defence of persons in this class) certain technical difficulties in the Extradition and Fugitive Offenders Act, and have found themselves able to entertain appeals as to habeas corpus to higher courts, where many issues can be canvassed.

Below the level of major crime the court will not interfere with crimes, criminal abroad, and done abroad – even when planned here. So drug traffic over the Malay peninsular was held not to be in the category of serious crime or covered by the jurisdiction that derives from S.62 of the Civil Aviation Act[7] which allows municipal authorities to punish crimes done in aircraft. Similarly, patents and copyrights are, between groups of nations, respected and enforced. But no ordinary civil claim, whatever the moral merits, will be entertained here if the cause of action arises from events in a foreign country. By an extension of nationality, if the foreigner here, or Britisher abroad, who is protected by diplomatic immunity, commits a tort or even a crime, he may go unsued and unprosecuted.

That is typical of concessions that a legal system must make. The laws between nations, whether in the form of public international law, or private international law, being based on minima, necessarily fall short of high moral standards.

A series of efforts to raise the international standards took the form of Declarations of Human Rights. As far back as 1920 the powers that imposed or supported peace treaties caused the inclusion of undertakings to preserve the rights of minorities and of religious groups. These clauses were evidently not enforced.

In 1945 the Charter of the United Nations declared the need for promoting respect for human rights and fundamental freedom *without regard to race, sex, language or religion.*[8]

---

[7] R. v Martin [1956] 2 Q.B. 272.
[8] This probably refers to religions of a civilised type. No one seems to have asked what the attitude of the declarants should be to human sacrifices, or the Hindu practice of suttee – religious conduct made illegal by the British in their imperial days.

Many declarations have followed those introductory words; but, in the very place of the declaration (California), it was said by judicial authority that these pronouncements do not carry the force of law.[9]

The leading declaration (of 1948) was only accepted by a few nations, not including U.S.S.R. The principles are, briefly: that a human being should enjoy:

(1) The right to life, liberty and security of person.
(2) Justice administered at public hearings by independent tribunals.
(3) Freedom of thought, conscience and religion.
(4) Rights of peaceful assembly, and association.
(5) A right to work.[10]

Dealing with agreed minima, they are, for the most part, laws with a moral coefficient below the levels of aspiration.

In 1950 similar declarations were made by the newly-formed Council of Europe – and accepted by western European nations. A court was established to which petitions could be addressed: but no mode of enforcement was prescribed for the adjudications.

This is in the tradition of the International Court at The Hague, which was founded in 1920 in order to arbitrate between nations who expressed willingness (in treaties or otherwise) to accept the decisions. Courts of this type should not be described as ineffective. Law, we have seen, is not dependent for its definition on sanctions. Many laws, many judgments, get themselves obeyed, because there are obeyers.

This being said, it remains a sad paradox that the clearest laws of international law are laws of war – some of which have been described in documents produced at Hague conventions.

Laws such as those which proscribe the ill treatment of civilians were recognised as law at Nuremberg. Their strength consists, unfortunately, in the ability of fighters to inflict reprisal, on the

[9] Fuizzi v California (38 Cal.) – a case arising from the attempted restriction of the right of land purchase in the case of aliens.

[10] The fact that the trade unions have demonstrated the incompatibility of (4) and (5) has not been the reason for rejection on the part of the rejectors.

ability of victors to vindicate what is violated. These facts would be more comforting to the world if it were certain that the big battalions would always be on the side of God.

So far ethical relations between nations have been discussed. To describe the participants as ethically neutral is, be it repeated, wrong, because the phrase is meaningless. There is simply a failure to give moral teachings the force of municipal law.

In domestic law (municipal law is the technical term) the phrase is even more inept. Many laws are irrelevant morally because no mortal feeling, or sentiment, or principle, or judgment is challenging or under challenge, or it may be that ethical considerations are difficult to balance. So, when chemists are sued for damage done to Thalidomide babies, and the question arose whether a duty could be owed to a foetus of less than two months,[11] the lawyers were reduced to compromise, not necessarily a good (or bad) result.

NOTE ON INTERNATIONAL LAW AND MORALITY

It is too easy to distinguish two orders of international laws: viz. the public, in which nation disputes with nation, and the private, where individual persons are concerned as to possible conflicts of law in respect of their nationality, their domicile, their local property rights, and all the inter-relation between these.

Pursuant to that analysis, it is conventionally held, moral standards can be applied in the private sphere, where relevant, but never in the public, where always irrelevant.

Several changes in life and thought render this distinction obsolete. Nation trades with nation, and companies trade with nations – companies, quite often, larger than some small nations. They dispute (nation and nation or company and nation) in municipal courts, and find them more satisfactory than the International Court (the locus of nation v nation). So the distinction between private and public is one of degree: and the subject is open to thought.

[11] The common law has not treated as a person any foetus of less than six months development (for purposes of inheritance, or criminal law).

Vastly more important, however, is the emerging concept of international criminal law, which, if developed, would allow a nation to treat another nation, *or even an individual belonging to another nation*, as a criminal to be tried. That system would not have been derided in the days of early modern diplomacy, when princes alleged themselves bound by Christian principles, and vouched the same for their subjects.

In 1920, in certain German war trials, the issue was raised, with unconvincing results. At Nuremberg, and in other tribunals created therewith, men were tried for international crimes. If it be said that these were stated by statutes made by victors, and that the victors were judges in their own cause, the answer is that the statutes probably did nothing more than declare laws of international conduct that had long been known (applied e.g. to pirates) but in desuetude, because, unhappily, the only available sanction across the borders of nations is war. For the rest, there is a sense in which every criminal everywhere is tried by judges who are judges in their own cause: and it cannot be otherwise.

Had the precedent of Nuremberg been followed, principles of international criminal law could have been stated, and could have been applied. Had that been done, dangers of international interferences would undoubtedly have been conjured. On the other hand, many modes of interference, whether invasions by nations, or sabotage or hijacking by individuals, would have become dangerous trades.[12]

[12] Hijacking of aircraft is, notwithstanding certain pedantries, piracy at common law. The problem is: within whose jurisdiction.

10

Ethical Irrelevance

Several categories can be described among laws where no moral purpose animates the decision. The reader has already seen some examples of law which is law and nothing else.

Of non-moral rules – that is to say, rules which do not actually enjoy obedience because of the obeyer's conscience or moral awareness – our legal system contains a plethora. Much law is concerned with the economic planning of the legislators. Some social purpose is there, not necessarily to be described as ethically relevant. In town planning, etc, it is hard to detect opportunities for spiritual experience. Also there are groups of laws such as sale of goods, which are techniques and nothing more. A great deal of the 'technically significant only' is to be found in factory legislation, public health legislation, etc., where well-intended detail can appear remote from ultimate social purposes.

The whole of Revenue Law takes place in a non-moral atmosphere. The state does not claim that the tax payer's duty is a patriotic one. In 1932, a great Chancery judge[1] pronounced (in effect) that if a man so arranges his affairs that he is not affected by laws that would otherwise have been relevant, he cannot be accused of 'evading', or even 'avoiding'. About the same time it was said that in taxation law there is no ethics and no equity.[2] Consequently, for many decades, lawyers and accountants have sought means of preventing burdens of tax from falling on their clients. In some cases Parliament has assisted. But in most cases Parliament has been engaged in preventing 'evasions', if

[1] Romer L. J. in Re Inglefield [1933] Ch. 1.
[2] Kliman v Wentworth (1933) Tax Cases.

205

that term can (*pace* Lord Justice Romer) be applied to perfectly legal devices.

A Duke of Westminster set a precedent in the 1930s for the type of settlement which, on certain conditions, will save beneficiaries from death duties. A technique of what the American lawyers call estate management has developed lawfully from this.

In the case of Chapman[3] the court held it proper for trustees of a settlement to vary the terms of the settlement (a difficult operation always) in order to save infant beneficiaries from the incidence of heavy estate duties. Parliament has since enacted a measure facilitating such variations. But the Court of Appeal declined to approve a variation which would entail the transference of funds and family to those isles of the blessed, the Channel Islands, 'where falls not tax, nor rate, nor any charge, nor any claim sounds loudly'.[4]

As to the taxation of the living, great ingenuities have been achieved, with the aid of company law, to avoid or save taxes. But, since there is always a passing of money for some apparent consideration, Chancellors of the Exchequer have had little difficulty in closing these revenue gaps. One of the most spectacular devices has been dividend stripping. Essentially this is the purchase of an entire company before dividend is declared, then a payment of dividend, then a sale of the company at a loss. That loss corresponds to a bigger tax allowance than the dividend has been an increment. This device is countered by the language of a recent Finance Act.

In tax affairs there is frequently revealed the mental attitude of the one who says: if I swindle the tax man, who suffers? This is an irresponsibility; and serious, because that same attitude, of valuing the small and ignoring the large, is reflected in domestic attitudes to international affairs. So a philosopher can trace a relationship between the littering of the vernal wood (where the poet found lessons of 'moral evil and of good') to the proliferations of poisonous substances in the world at large, in the uncontrolled but now harvested sea, and in outer space.

In the smaller context of English law, perhaps there is more

[3] [1959] 2 All Eng. R. 48.
[4] Re Weston [1968] 3 All Eng. R. 338.

attention paid to the small controllable acts of the human body than to the human mind.

It is not that ethics looks to the heart and law to the hands. Though lawyers have said that the devil knoweth not the heart of man, they are sufficiently good judges of human purpose to justify the later utterance – that 'the state of a man's mind is as much a fact as the state of his digestion'.[5] The difference is between certain standards of obedience; those expressed when objective legal duties, not necessarily humane, are being considered, and those expressed when one uses words like CONSCIENTIOUS.

In general, away from equitable cases for which there are precedents, the law is not concerned with motives;[6] only with acts. Intentions only serve to distinguish a man's act from an accident. His purposes are irrelevant except in a few cases, like defamation and nuisance, where some kind of privilege is invoked. Otherwise, if a man is unreasonable in the exercise of his rights, is he therefore to be prevented from exercising those rights? The apparently reasonable answer, that would occur to 'the man on the Clapham omnibus', is: 'no: they are his rights'. Then what is the legal position when a person exercises his rights to the detriment of another, and does so out of spite, i.e. in the common sense, maliciously? He digs deep on his own land in order to deprive neighbouring land of the benefits of percolating water. Held, by the Law Lords, he has done no tort.[7] In the same decade the Law Lords considered the case of Allen v Flood.[8] Allen, the representative of

[5] Bowen L. J. in Edgington v FitzMaurice (1885) 28 Ch. D. 459. The metaphor is not of the most helpful, because digestion, too, is internal. The thought is valid, however, that diagnosis is not impossible, and involves little more than the resources of science.

[6] Exceptionally the word is used in trials of murder, but adds little to proof of intention.

[7] Mayor of Bradford v Pickles [1895] A.C. 587. To say that he has not acted on Ulpian's maxim *alienum non laedas,* is not acceptable argument, because the question of injury is precisely the question to be decided. On analogies from libel and nuisance one would expect a protection against the *prima facie* legal harm, by penalising it when malice is present.

[8] Allen v Flood [1899] A.C. 1.

a trade union, had coerced certain employers into dismissing certain workmen, because, for reasons which were not financial (and were therefore not reasonable), he wished to cause loss to his victims. If Allen was doing no wrong by pressing a union demand on employers (and, at that period at least, it appeared that he was not) then did his action become wrongful on account of his malice? Many judges deliberated on this: in three courts, and in a committee of judges convened by the Law Lords. Eventually, by a majority of Law Lords, and a minority of judicial opinions, it was held that the malice was irrelevant. In that way the same legal system that had made the world safe for the beneficiaries of trusts, also made Britain safe for shop-stewards. (More charitably, the decision may be viewed as part of the matrix of a new system in which the 'right to the job' is one of the doctrines, and a technique for defence of that right legally valid.)

Let it be added that the law does control irresponsibility in the proletarian field in a limited way. Gas workers, water workers, electrical workers, seamen, and persons in charge of installations important to human life, may not wilfully and maliciously break contract.

These may, conceivably, object that it is unfair for a sense of responsibility to be legislated into them, whilst countless others are allowed to be irresponsible.

This suggests the reflection that English law makes no demand for patriotism. (This is consistent with the lack of legal privilege in the Ministers of the Crown.) Yet no population has shown more patriotism in time of peril. Similarly, the law offers little, if any, reward to the volunteer, as we have seen. Indeed, volunteers in the last war were disadvantaged financially. Always, however, have volunteers abounded.

If a political party were to invoke patriotism as an appeal, it would inevitably be accused of fascism, or of recruiting a 'Labour Front', as did the totalitarians. The psychological fact is that patriotism, to be more than a mustering of escapists or conscripts, must be an altruism. Altruism, the reader is aware, is something which cannot be demanded, but is always forthcoming in a moral citizenry.

II

The Hedonistic Background: Political Morality

To the observer of modern trends, it may appear that the strong reaction of many fine lawyers against the analyses and recommendations of the Wolfenden Committee constitute a too heavy reply to some light special pleading calculated to defend male butterflies. In defence of the jurists (if any be needed!) let it be answered that the importance of the Wolfenden Report is only the importance of a symptom. The real attack is on the disease. Male homosexuality, it may be accepted, is not so prevalent as to endanger population. Nor need it be regarded with horror. If Israel abhorred it as an Egyptian abomination, if Rome ridiculed it as contemptible, yet the civilisation of Athens found in it an acceptable substitute for the training of women in conversation.[1]

The importance of the topic today is that it coheres with a hedonism which enjoys fuller and freer expression than hedonism ever enjoyed before. This is the age of the Pleasure Principle triumphant; the age of Eros, whose academic hierophants claim to have exorcised all sense of awareness of guilt, as unnecessary obsession with family phantoms, father figures, and mammary memories. Some modern psychologists, stating doctrine that was old when Bernard Shaw was young, describe the family as a

[1] In contrast, one of the only surviving inequalities between the English sexes is that lawyers well read in Wilde are ignorant of Sappho. Lesbianism is not a crime. Only in this century has it been held an unchastity (for the purposes of an action of slander). (Kern v Kennedy [1942] 1 All Eng. R. 412).

matrix of tawdry secrets and narrow privacies. But they have failed to describe any better system of education.

Worthy of consideration is the fact that, in the most success-ful of modern communes, the Israel Kibbutzim, close contact between parents and children is preserved, though the children sleep in communal dormitories. The important feature is that they learn from, and honour, their parents.

The danger of psychological restatements of obligation, it should here be interpolated, is not due to the falsity of the under-lying theories. Rather the danger arises from their truth. Today no one disputes the basic notions of suppressed forces in the personality, the censored id, and the latent possibilities of danger to the moral, law-abiding, super-ego. But from a theory which is helpful to the provision of therapeutics for the hysterical and deranged, it does not follow that no value should be given to normality. Let the normal be generalised, and with theoretical correctness, to one colour in the spectrum of all the abnorm-alities, yet it remains recognisable, and, more, it remains the basis of social organisation.

To confuse the legal and moral purposes of man by restating him as an aggregate of the ill-defined and uncontrollable is to make many mistakes. One mistake is the failure to recognise that the cause or origin of a phenomenon may well be irrelevant to the significance, utility, and adaptability of the object which is being considered. The second, and cognate, error, is the confusion of levels. To use a crude, useful, metaphor, not intended as a demonstration, the maker and seller of furni-ture is not influenced by the physical fact – the truth in physics – that the table he makes or sells is a congeries of atoms oscillating at all but random in the void. The furniture manufacturer is, to use what was once a philosophical obloquy, a pragmatist. Yet he is not so different from the medical man who prescribes a drug before the scientist has worked out what mysteries of molecular structure account for its efficacy. If they waited, no one would take an aspirin.

And so in politics, and in law and morals, which are factors in politics, the authority must operate on classes which are best organised from normal human beings, according to the common sense. No organisation is possible of human beings if the organiser is obsessed with generalisations which generalise away the substance. The subtleties of psychology are relevant to many deviations, but are not helpful as a principle of government. More important than this is the thought that to those who think of the human being as a potential of spiritual activity, in any of the orders of value, any chemistry which dissolves with its acids the concept of responsible personality is a destructive force.

If morality has any significance in the ordering of human affairs, that significance is clearest in a demand for a sense of responsibility. In order that responsibility be reinforced the moralist asks of the law: that if people are irresponsible, at least let them be effectively treated by the law. Let some concept of retribution be driven into their understandings. To this it is no reply that the criminal is maladjusted, and that prison accommodation is scarce. Meanwhile psychologism, a description of human conduct as sets and groups of reflexes, ignores the simple causations, the pragmatic successions of life as appreciated by common sense. Consequently, while active in the blaming of circumstances, the experts find it impossible to place responsibility on individuals. This is your priesthood, Heathendom! There follow, as sutlers in the psychological camp, some indoctrinated probation officers and welfare workers, many law-reformers under anti-Retributionist banners; and there is fanned a breeze of change which has already affected the climate of opinion and the atmosphere of law-making. This psychological materialism, or existentialism, coincides, in its efflorescence, with the full growth of the social-political varieties of materialism which have ideologically overgrown and possessed the hanging gardens, as well as the deserts, of the world. At such a time any questions of discipline, any question, therefore, as to the nature of a legal system, becomes at least as important as it has been in any recognised period of revolution. Especially is this true, in a mature state such as ours, when many developments, not all unmoral, have caused the enlargement of the scope of government and its direction into economic and physical, and away from spiritual, activity.

The most important variable of our time is the coefficient

of spiritual awareness in various sets of political institutions. Temporal government has not been the same as spiritual government, since the days when theocracy abounded. How much greater is the bifurcation, when it is possible to found an empire on the propositions that all the appearances of human conduct are describable in mechanical terms, that human conduct is the resultant of environmental forces, in which the only significant wave-movements are the ebb and flow of an inevitable redistribution of material supplies; and that all else is illusion. The legislators of such an empire, or body politic, are not likely to encourage in the subjects – or objects – of their laws any belief that man was created in order to enjoy life and freedom and the pursuit of happiness. Pleasure they will allow, as an opiate for their masses: even, as in the case of Nazi Germany, as a source of cannon-fodder. But their laws will not stimulate in the obeyers any sense of independent responsibility.[2] The overriding duties will be to obey all the sanctioned commands and to act for the purposes of the benefit of the state. What those purposes are will be, always arbitrarily, sometimes retrospectively, and seldom consistently, declared by those who from time to time are in a position to describe them. In such a system human conduct will be redeemed, perhaps, by being less entropic than it is in social orders where every minimum of effort tends to become a maximum, and every maximum of reward to be regarded as a minimum. On the other hand, there will be little scope for personal loyalties, and little tolerance. If the purposes of such a state require that a child is under persuasion and pressure to inform against his parents and siblings, no one will dare to cite the teachings of Deuteronomy in condemnation.

Here, however, there is danger of exaggeration.

It is popular belief in England that to 'inform' is not praiseworthy. There has, nevertheless, always been law that it is the

[2] It is not suggested here that a deterministic philosophy is incompatible with a doctrine of personal responsibility. Spinoza is authority to the contrary. From among the theologians there may be cited Chasdai Ibn Crescas, a fourteenth-century thinker, who held that it is part of a pre-determined order that human beings feel a sense of freedom, and behave, and should be treated, as responsible for their conduct.

duty of a citizen to tell what he knows about committed felonies. That law – as to misprision of felony – was thought to be extinct until the Law Lords, in Sykes v D.P.P., declared it to be extant.[3]

Here, apparently, is a duty to 'inform' which seems not to accord with the contempt with which the 'Common Informer' (now abolished) was always regarded.

Also it fits badly alongside our rules as to confessions. What is most strange about the law of misprison is that it puts the spectator of a crime, or the person aware without participation, in a worse position than the offender.

Is this attitude to prisoners, and is all the law about the need for cautioning those who could speak, consistent with a law which says to the person who knows about the crime: 'You *must* make a statement'? Yet a distinction may be usefully drawn in the moral field. The informer as to a crime, within the serious categories of crime, is not (it is submitted) in the same class as an informer for the government or the state. The citizen does not wish to be big brother, but he cannot escape the role of his brother's keeper.

In the days of absolute monarchy, when the crime that mattered most to the state was treason, the informer was as important to Britain as he is now to any totalitarian state. It is to the moral credit of Britain that he was always hated; and if it was argued that he was a patriot, the answer is summed up in a dictum of that greatest of Tories, Dr Johnson, who pronounced (notwithstanding his own devoted loyalty to the Crown) that 'patriotism is the last refuge of a scoundrel'.[4]

Dr Johnson's utterance was made in the century that followed the final destruction of absolute monarchy in Britain, and the abandonment of the dogma of the divine right of Kings. In that century, it was the privilege of the lawyers to demonstrate to the government that a ministerial claim to strong executive powers was as unjustified as any claim made by Charles I.[5]

[3] [1961] 3 All Eng. R. 33 The abolition, in 1967, of the distinction between felony and misdemeanour will not, it is thought, affect the principle, though restatement may well be called for.

[4] He was equally uncharitable to revenue men.

[5] Theoretically more unjustified, because until a revolution declared, or altered, the law, Charles I seemed in a position of unique privilege.

To that period, before the emergence of modern police, we owe legal statements restrictive of police powers – notably the laws against arrests and searches under general warrant.[6] Freedom from executive oppression was wrested from the Crown in protection of men, like Wilkes, whose main contribution to civilisation is in the literature of scurrility.

Bound up with that learning is the theory that 'Act of State' constitutes no defence in litigation.[7] Although the Crown in those days could not be liable in tort or crime, because the King could not be tried in his own courts, by the same principle (that the King can do no wrong), his ministers could not be held to do right, merely because they acted for the King.[8] That rejection of the concept of the state as a function of exoneration was further illustrated when governors of Crown Colonies were called to account in British courts on charges of felony.[9]

A further consequence of the legal tradition that the state is not legally dominant, except through laws which it makes (and which do not, actually, assert its dominance), is that never, since the revolutions, has martial law been proclaimed in Britain. Emergency Powers Acts have been passed which enable the use of troops; but never is the law superseded. Even the reading of the Riot Act is a legal operation, with limited consequences.[10]

These traditions (of the subordination of politics to law) gain importance as society regroups itself into large units, rather than large aggregates of individuals; for all the parts fail to equal in importance the whole, the state, that is, as to which it has been

[6] Entick v Carrington 19 State Trials. Eee also Wilkes v Wood *ib* 1153 and Leach v Money *ib* 129. On these cases the American Bill of Rights is founded.

[7] Restated in some modern cases of requisition for military purposes; *ex parte* De Keyser's Hotel [1920] A.C. 508 and Att. Gen. v Nissan [1969] 1 All Eng. R. 629.

[8] Lane v Cotton followed in Bainbridge v P.M.G. [1906] 1 K.B. 178.

[9] R. v Eyre (1868) L.R. 3 Q.B. 4 87.

[10] Martial law is often confused with the law of Courts Martial. Courts Martial are courts of soldiers on active service. They operate according to the criminal law of Britain, which includes some of the disciplinary rules of the Army Act. For long it was complained that soldiers had no appeal from Courts Martial, however fairly or unfairly conducted. That is, however, no longer the case.

claimed that the duties of its leaders and its organisers cannot in the nature of things be moral duties.

The theory of the non-moral state may or may not be acceptable to some states. Certainly it is not valid for England. Machiavelli, it was said above, does not speak to the Queen in Parliament who is Elizabeth II.[11]

In home affairs at least, the English state is a gentleman. Its affairs are not a justification for intrusion into the rights of individuals. That was settled, as we have seen, as long ago as the days of Wilkes. The theory, established then, that an act of state can be a tort, has been reinforced by a statute of 1947 which abolishes practically all of the protection afforded to the Crown against suit in its own courts. In those courts, instruments of the Crown though they still are (for, *pace* Montesquieu, the powers are not 'separate' in England), the judges pursue an ideal of justice which is a species of morality, and which is the morality of the state as well as of the citizen.

There is an element of paradox to be observed in the circumstance that while many persons are calling upon the state to abandon any claim it has to be the arbiter of private morality (if there is such a species), those protesters include many who demand from the state itself a high degree of morality. That morality is usually forthcoming, and is demanded by judges. This was seen in two world wars when persons dangerous to the state were not deprived of legal defences. In point is Liversidge v Anderson ([1941] 3 All Eng. R. 338), when Law Lords debated the right of a Home Secretary to act on his discretion under Rule 18B of the Defence Regulations, and did so even while the enemy was at the gate. Comparable is the trial of the dangerous William

---

11 Machiavelli, be it interpolated, is rather a maligned man, because many know his name and few his work. He was advising an Italian prince in the lawless days when the principalities of Italy were achieving national identity. The prince, in such environment, could not maintain a lawful power if he allowed himself to be scrupulous in his dealings with rival princes outside the realm, and potentials of conspiracy within it. He could not afford the sentimentalities of established urban civilisation. Let it be added that nothing in Machiavelli, or disciples such as Metternich, can be pleaded in extenuation of the complete immorality of twentieth-century tyrants.

Joyce, who, being charged (with treason) after the war, was consummately defended, and who, in the House of Lords, heard at least one Law Lord argue for his acquittal – because (as that Law Lord, the late Lord Porter held) the question of nationality should have been left to the jury (Joyce v D.P.P. [1946] 1 All Eng. 186). So is Britain fair to its enemies.[12]

There have been deviations (including some retrospective legislation in revenue matters). But a good case for the morality of England can be made out; and every one experienced in the criminal law can support the proposition that the law defends the accused even against itself.

The ideal of the state as gentleman is not one easily realised, and is subject to strain when the economic purposes of the state involve difficult decisions. The tradition, however, even in collectivist times, is that the unit of political importance is the individual. The individual, and his values, owe their recognition in Britain to the triumph of a protestant theology compelled to etsablish itself in the teeth of authoritianism. The opposition to it is stated, nowadays, by the exponents of a differently grounded, but not differently enforced, authoritarianism.

It is not suggested that the inhabitants of totalitarian states are without morality. Old traditions die hard. Also totalitarian life can engender a certain Puritanism in the *Parteigenossen*, not without resemblance to the dedication of some Puritans, even of some Victorian materialists in Britain. The lack of morality is in the state itself. This must, in the long run, affect the standards of the population, as, in the short run, it affects international standards.

That is the danger of law-making as a function of a state which is its own only purpose, its own ideal, its own idol. At the other extreme – and extremes tend to meet in the philosophies of society – a state which undervalues itself morally, which is obsessed with material purposes, and forms only a frame for the anarchic purposes of its citizens, will produce among its inhabitants a

---

[12] Worth mentioning is the Custodian of Enemy Property. That official does not expropriate the property of enemy aliens, whatever their degree of activity, but holds it with an intention of restoration at the end of hostilities. There are those who think that this is altruism.

reconciliation to the ethics of the 'accepted thing', which is not different from the helot mentality of the unfree. Responsibility will diminish to the acceptance of controls that cannot be avoided. A field for private morality is admittedly left open; but perhaps there is no great merit in a set of private moralities which fail to coalesce in that public morality which could alter the values and directions of government.

In totalitarian systems and their opposites (and the realities are not concealed by apparently democratic forms) the subject, or object, of the law is an abstract unit of no great importance. That type of organisation differs from democracy, by which is meant *not* the counting of heads, but the fact that heads count. It is integral to democratic theory that, when one writes about morals and the law, one is not implying the existence of two separate orders of obedience, of which the symbiosis is surprising or unnatural. The English law, at least, is self-conscious, and conscious that it is an open system, consequently morally self-conscious. When an English lawyer speaks of the rule of law, he is not referring to that moral negation which is an arid "legality'. (Bunyan stated the English distaste for that.) Granted that the rule of law includes the constancy and universality of the law as one of its principles. Yet it includes this function of certainty and justice among a number of traditions, clear in the midst of vagueness, of which one common factor is a valuation of the individual citizen as the subject of the law, not as its object.

In the light of the ethical indifference that prevails so widely, and in the increasing material context in which government is compelled to operate, it becomes important to ascertain whether or not our democracy is still 'on the side of the angels'.

There was a moment (at Nuremberg) when, by the assertion of law in international affairs, and a moral content in that law, Britain could be said to have redeemed the world by its precept. At Nuremberg the British prosecutors declared unwritten laws to be valid laws, and explained all international laws as functions of that fairness, that humanity, that religious awareness, which the Parliament and Judiciary of Britain have held always as the spirit of their deliberations. Let it be called natural law by those who like that phrase. It is submitted here that some such inspiration is a *sine qua non* of democracy.

Is this an element of religion? It has been said in this century that England is no longer a christian country. This is a précis of opinions in Bowman v Secular Society.[13] The finding is that freedom of the press includes the legal rightness and respectability of criticisms directed against religious belief. But religion and morals are standards of behaviour independently of their incorporation in theological doctrine. Nor must it be forgotten that those old campaigners, the Benthamites and Mill, who fought for the abolition of religiously grounded restrictions, were emphasising a moral coefficient in the law – namely the value of the independent human mind. It was a religious and highly moral man, Milton, who wrote the best indictment ever penned of the censorship. After him, a list of the English reformers includes some 'God-intoxicated' men.

NOTE ON THE PRESS AND THE STATE

Our state has been described as a gentleman. In return, it seems to receive a modicum of courtesy from the press, and even from less disciplined agitators. This becomes clear when one compares, with our press, on the one hand the scurrilities of America and France (which differ from each other only in elegance), and on the other, the servilities of the press in that section of the world where the horrors that are uttered against the enemies of the regime inform us of what would be said against the government if that press were free (and if *Pravda* really meant truth).

In the eighteenth century the kind of criticism that is now hurled against ministers in France and U.S.A. was prosecuted in England as sedition or seditious libel. From the General Warrants that were hurled about there developed much common law, which is enshrined now in the American Bill of Rights. Since the governments of those days were highly personal, as were the attacks, the prosecutions were of a form calculated to charge a sort of treason as well as what we now call criminal libel. By the

[13] [1917] A.C. 406.

laws of those days, once the judge had ruled on the nature of the scurrility, all that was left to the jury was the question of publication. A great liberal, Charles James Fox, steered through Parliament a law giving the jury the right to find the 'general issue'. Thereafter juries seem to have rendered prosecutions for sedition unproductive.

Other factors of change are clear. One hundred and fifty years of highly respected monarchy have given to Parliamentary government a formality and an impersonality which protect the temporary holders of ministerial office from personalities' expressive of the bitterness that bad government can evoke. Perhaps the increase of electronic familiarity is diminishing this protection. Meanwhile the legal apparatus has rearranged itself. Sedition is now a charge usually proferred against those who purposively undermine the allegiance of the armed forces, or scheme to upset the state. (One of the statutes involved is the Aliens Act.) Newspapers have not, in the last one hundred and fifty years been charged with these offences. Thus criticisms of the Boer War and of the Suez campaign were not regarded by the law officers of the crown as seditious.

In respect of personal attacks, the simple charge of criminal libel (defamation calculated to cause breach of the peace) has protected the reputations of leading politicians, as when Lord Alfred Douglas was imprisoned for his lucubrations against Winston Churchill at the end of the 1914 war.

In later war-time, law was enacted to prevent the spread of alarm and despondency; and the crown found itself able, with the aid of defence regulations, to prevent the appearance of some Communist periodicals.

From the foregoing it appears that Milton and Charles James Fox did their work well. Was it too well?

This question is suggested by the power of newspapers and other publications, of press or of spoken word, to inflame sections of the population against other sections. In civil law there is no group libel. But common law, it is submitted, knows an indictment against this. Yet in the 1930s very scurrilous anti-Jewish diatribes went unprosecuted, even while *Der Stuermer* was mobilising Germany for a massive campaign of genocide.

After the war (1946), at a northern Assize, a man named Caunt was prosecuted for such publications: but an indifferent prosecution, presided over by a probably too liberal judge (Birkett J., as he then was), allowed that accused to be acquitted.

The 1960s have seen the addition of a new colour (if one may say so unfrivolously) to this situation. Such statutes as Race Relations Acts and the Theatres Act 1968 declare it criminal to generate hatred against any section of the community. In 1967 a Jew-baiter, named Jordan, was prosecuted to conviction and imprisonment. (That the accused was a schoolmaster is a disturbing feature of the event.)

At the time of writing, newspapers and other organs of communication are becoming stronger than ever before. To ask whether they need control is to ask the question latent in this essay: what can be left to morality if it be not absorbed in law? In this context the word also connotes the urbane decencies. It may be the case that a 'levelling down' of society, a pollution of values, is weakening these restraints.

Table of Cases

Index